# Sustainable Rural Livelihoods

## What contribution can we make?

*edited by Diana Carney*

# Sustainable Rural Livelihoods

## What contribution can we make?

*edited by Diana Carney*

Papers presented at the Department for International Development's Natural Resources Advisers' Conference, July 1998

Department for International Development 1998

A catalogue record for this book is available from the British Library, London, UK

ISBN 1 86192 082 2

Department for International Development
94 Victoria Street
London SW1E 5JL

Typeset by the Overseas Development Institute, London.
Printed by Russell Press Ltd., Nottingham.
Cover photo: © Chris Stowers/Panos Pictures

# Contents

# Foreword

In November last year I presented to Parliament a White Paper on International Development setting out the Government's policies for achieving the sustainable development of this planet. These policies aim to address the single greatest challenge which the world faces – eliminating poverty.

An estimated 1.3 billion people live in extreme poverty. Although increasing numbers of people live in towns and cities, the majority of people in developing countries still live in rural areas. Poverty remains disproportionately a rural phenomenon. The livelihoods of the rural poor must be improved if the International Development Goal of reducing by one half the proportion of people living in absolute poverty by 2015 is to be achieved.

In July, DFID's Natural Resources Division hosted a Conference to produce guidance on how best to promote improved and sustainable livelihoods for rural communities. The Conference followed a process of consultation. This book contains papers presented to the Conference and highlights the main conclusions reached. The Conference concluded that the sustainable rural livelihoods approach has the potential to play an important part in the challenge of eliminating poverty.

The outcome of the Conference will help DFID when working with all partners and, crucially, with communities themselves to reduce rural poverty. We will continue to share our experiences and work with others.

Secretary of State for International Development

# INTRODUCTION

# 1 Implementing the Sustainable Rural Livelihoods Approach

## Diana Carney

## Introduction

The 1997 UK Government White Paper on International Development commits the Department for International Development (DFID) to promoting 'sustainable livelihoods' and to protecting and improving the management of 'the natural and physical environment'. These objectives are both expected to contribute to the overall poverty eradication goal. The Natural Resources Policy and Advisory Department (NRPAD) of DFID is working with other DFID departments to try to establish what exactly is meant by the livelihoods approach and how DFID personnel and others can work to promote this in their day-to-day operations.

This book, which contains the main papers presented at the 1998 DFID Natural Resources Advisers' Conference (NRAC '98) on Sustainable Rural Livelihoods, represents one step in the process of opening up the dialogue. The **Key Issues** papers address issues of policy consistency by expanding upon the relationships between sector wide approaches and decentralisation and sustainable rural livelihoods (Chapters 2 and 3). They also seek to expand the traditional concept of 'rural' by examining both livelihood diversification and rural/urban linkages (Chapters 4 and 5). The **Entry Point** papers go into some detail about the contributions to the sustainability of rural livelihoods that can be made by involvement in any particular area. Possible 'entry points' range from the more traditional natural resource sub-sectors (forests, livestock) to emerging priorities such as ethical trade, but in all cases the emphasis is on people, not resources *per se*.

The final chapter of the book summarises the key points made in the less formal, but no less important, sessions at NRAC '98. The SRL approach, as this chapter argues, is about working together to build on people's strengths. The contribution of all sections of DFID is vital; papers presented by colleagues from outside the Natural Resources area stress this and suggest the need for more active collaboration. Contributions from UNDP and the Institute of Development Studies (IDS) offer some important guidelines about how we might proceed with both analysis and action to promote sustainable rural livelihoods.

This introductory chapter summarises current thinking on sustainable rural livelihoods (SRL) within the group that has come together at the behest of NRPAD to tease out the issues.[1] Members of the group – which met four times during the first six months of 1998 – are drawn from within DFID (NRPAD, Social Development, Economics, Engineering and Enterprise Development) and from outside organisations (research institutes and NGOs). The chapter is also informed by an extensive process of consultation and review of literature.

At the core of this chapter lies a framework for analysing livelihoods. The framework is holistic and dynamic and recognises the many complex interactions in rural livelihoods. It also explicitly emphasises the importance of institutions and organisations to livelihoods. This framework is intended as a means for understanding livelihoods and DFID's contribution to them, rather than as a programme of action. The second part of the chapter moves to this question of action and suggests ways in which DFID activities, skills and partnerships will need to change in order to promote sustainable rural livelihoods and eventual poverty eradication.

## Defining sustainable rural livelihoods

The starting point for the SRL committee was to agree on a definition for a sustainable rural livelihood. A slightly modified version of the definition originally developed by Robert Chambers and Gordon Conway was accepted by all:

> *A livelihood comprises the capabilities, assets (including both material and social resources) and activities required for a means of living. A livelihood is sustainable when it can cope with and recover from stresses and shocks and maintain or enhance its capabilities and assets both now and in the future, while not undermining the natural resource base.*

It is important to note that the concept of SRLs is a normative one. DFID aims to improve the lives of poor people and to strengthen the **sustainability** of their livelihoods; this it believes to be in everyone's long-term interest. The approach is inherently responsive to people's own interpretations of and priorities for their livelihoods. However, while it starts with people, it does not compromise on the environment. Indeed, one of the potential strengths of the livelihoods approach is that it 'mainstreams' the environment within an holistic framework. What this means is that DFID may not always be in complete harmony with its clients, although, over time, it would hope to become so (as clients themselves recognise the importance of sustainability – something which poverty often

# Figure 1: Sustainable rural livelihoods: Framework

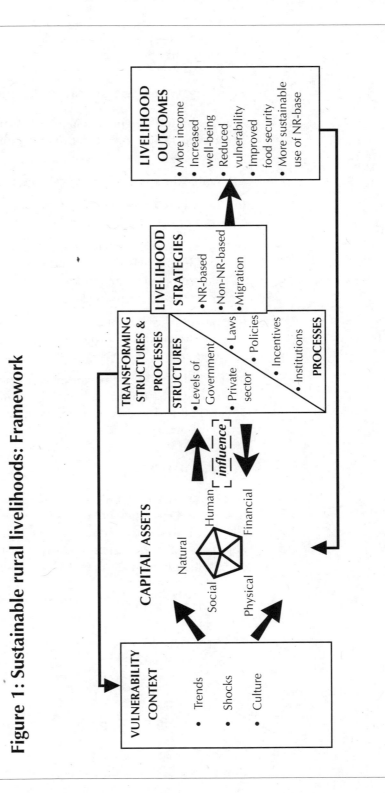

forces them to neglect). This is a possible source of tension and is an area which requires further investigation.

# A framework for sustainable rural livelihoods

Much effort has been put into refining a framework for analysis of livelihoods (see Figure 1). It is expected that the framework will serve the following purposes:

(i) define the scope of and provide the analytic basis for livelihood analysis

(ii) help those concerned with supporting SRL to understand and manage the complexity of rural livelihoods

(iii) become a shared point of reference for all concerned with supporting livelihoods (whether in DFID or in partner organisations), enabling the complementarity of contributions and the trade-offs between outcomes to be assessed, and

(iv) provide the basis for the development of a set of concrete intermediate objectives which DFID should pursue with its partners as a means to supporting the development of SRL.

The value of the framework is as a practical tool upon which much of the SRL approach is based. For this reason it is vital that it is both widely understood and widely accepted and that guidelines and methodologies for its use are developed.

## *Capital assets*

The framework currently in use draws heavily on work conducted at the Institute of Development Studies (see for example, Scoones, 1998), though it has been adapted to accommodate DFID's particular concerns and practical objectives. At its heart lies an analysis of the five different types of assets upon which individuals draw to build their livelihoods. These are:

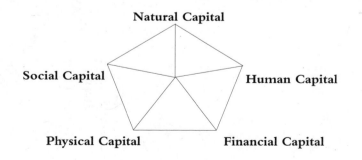

Box 1 describes these different types of capital assets in more detail.

---

**Box 1: Capital assets**

**Natural capital**
The natural resource stocks from which resource flows useful for livelihoods are derived (e.g. land, water, wildlife, biodiversity, environmental resources)

**Social capital**
The social resources (networks, membership of groups, relationships of trust, access to wider institutions of society) upon which people draw in pursuit of livelihoods

**Human capital**
The skills, knowledge, ability to labour and good health important to the ability to pursue different livelihood strategies

**Physical capital**
The basic infrastructure (transport, shelter, water, energy and communications) and the production equipment and means which enable people to pursue their livelihoods

**Financial capital**
The financial resources which are available to people (whether savings, supplies of credit or regular remittances or pensions) and which provide them with different livelihood options

Adapted from Scoones, 1998.

---

The different types of assets are presented in the shape of a pentagon. This is a schematic picture akin to a five-axis graph on which access by different groups or households to each different type of asset can be plotted. Access can imply anything from individual ownership of private goods to customary use rights for groups.

While this 'plotting' of assets is necessarily subjective – the axes are not calibrated and there is no need for common denomination of all assets in a money metric or similar – it is hoped that the analysis will provide a useful starting point for thinking about how and in what combinations assets do translate into sustainable livelihoods.[2]

The major challenge of the pentagon is that it forces users to think holistically rather than sectorally about the basis of livelihoods. It also ensures that in our support to livelihoods we build on the positives which people already have in their grasp. Though many people in rural areas of developing countries are desperately poor, they do have strengths upon which we can, and should, build. There is a subtle, but important, difference between starting with an analysis of strengths as opposed to an analysis of needs.

The framework does not suggest that there is a one-to-one link between people's asset status and the sustainability of their livelihoods. Nor is there an easily definable minimum or 'cut off point' on any single axis, below which people can be considered to be 'poor' or 'vulnerable'.[3] Nevertheless, it is intuitive that there is a close correlation between people's overall asset status, the resources upon which people can draw in the face of hardship (inclusive of non-physical assets such as education and access to social networks), and their robustness. This robustness can be displayed both by rising out of poverty (including reducing one's vulnerability to shocks and

**In our support to livelihoods we build on the positives which people already have in their grasp**

stresses) and by increasing one's ability to influence the policies and institutions which define one's livelihood options (and, indeed, one's access to those assets which are the basis of robustness). Building up assets is thus a core component of empowerment.

The overall analysis of capital assets is most likely to be conducted for different social groups. Before undertaking the analysis of capital assets, there may therefore be a prior step of social analysis to distinguish particular groups (though this would be subsequently enriched and possibly even modified according to the analysis of group members' capital assets). As a rule of thumb, when plotting asset status, the further a group lies from the central intersection of the pentagon the more robust its members are likely to be. Generally speaking it is the overall area of a pentagon (the shape created when asset status is plotted on each axis) that is important, rather than the absolute magnitude of access to any particular type of capital.[4] This fact underpins the SRL approach's multi-dimensional notion of poverty and well-being.

Drawing pentagons is a first step. The next step captures the dynamic elements entailed in the notion of sustainability. How has asset status (pentagon shape and size) been changing over time? Are people on an upwards or a downwards trajectory? Is the trajectory consistent across all axes? What changes are projected to take place over the next 10–15 years or so (as the population density and the state of resources change)? What are the root causes of changes and how do they vary between different wealth or social groups?

Among other things, this type of analysis of change might reveal the characteristics of those who have 'escaped' from poverty in a particular area and tell us much about the combination and sequencing of assets and livelihood strategies which has enabled them to do so.

## Transforming Structures and Processes

The SRL framework is built around capital assets but also requires analysis and understanding in many other areas. First, there is a need to understand the **vulnerability context** in which assets exist (the trends, shocks and local cultural practices which affect livelihoods). Second, it is vital to understand the structures (organisations, from layers of government through to the private sector in all its guises) and processes (policies, laws, rules of the game and incentives) which define people's livelihood options. There are two main (and related) ways in which these structures and processes impact upon livelihoods.

- They are critical in determining both who gains access to which type of asset and what the effective value of that asset is (think, for example, of the additional value of land to livelihoods in the European Union as a result of EU agriculture policies).

- In conjunction with people's asset status, they help define which livelihood strategies or activities – natural resource-based or otherwise – are open and attractive (for example, policies which outlaw private trade severely limit the likelihood of people becoming traders; if the state institutions which purchase agricultural produce are very corrupt, it is less likely that people will invest in surplus agricultural production).

Furthermore, markets and legal restrictions have a profound influence on the extent to which one asset can be converted into another type of asset (e.g. natural capital into financial capital or human capital into physical capital). All things being equal, convertibility is a positive aspect which should be nurtured, as it increases the options available to people who are striving to improve their livelihoods and to withstand shocks and stresses.[5]

**The livelihoods framework explicitly links the micro with the macro**

Thus, the livelihoods framework explicitly links the micro with the macro and emphasises that policy and institutional analysis must take place at all levels.

## *Livelihood outcomes and indicators*

People aspire to a range of outcomes. The livelihoods approach builds on the findings of participatory poverty assessments (Booth *et al.*, 1998; Hanmer *et al.*, 1997). These have taught us that we should listen to those with whom we are working and learn from them about their own objectives, their own understanding of what it means to be in and to escape from poverty (as well as their own beliefs about the root causes of that poverty). If we genuinely believe in the livelihoods approach, then we should be prepared to negotiate the indicators of our success with those whom we are trying to support.

The main caveat relates to environmental sustainability. Short-term survival rather than the sustainable management of natural capital (soil, water, genetic diversity) is often the priority of people living in absolute poverty. Yet DFID believes in sustainability. It must therefore work with rural people to help them understand the contribution (positive or negative) that their livelihoods are making to the environment and to promote sustainability as a long-term objective. Indicators of sustainability will therefore be required.

## Understanding rural livelihoods

The first objective of the framework is to provide the analytic basis for livelihood analysis. The holistic nature of the framework is both attractive and alarming in that it suggests the need for a very full (lengthy, costly, complex) process of analysis before plans for support of livelihoods can be drawn up.

While there is no doubt that the approach does call for a broader analysis, the news is not all bad.

- A single (though dynamic and iterative) analysis of livelihoods may well provide the basis for numerous contributions from the various different departments of DFID or from other donors or NGOs. Costs can therefore be spread/shared.

- DFID recognises that poverty eradication will not take place overnight. The livelihoods approach suggests the need for longer-term commitments to particular areas/groups. Again, this should reduce the overall ratio of costs to operational expenditure.

- DFID is not working alone. Partnerships are key to the picture. DFID will thus find itself working with organisations with ample accrued wisdom of relevance to livelihood analysis. The framework should provide a means by which to structure existing information and identify gaps. It will seldom be a question of starting from scratch.

- The approach does not suggest that a 'complete picture' must be painted before any activities can get underway. It invites those involved to take a broad view of people's needs and to cast aside preconceptions about what types of donor activity are likely to be the most beneficial. However, once a suitable 'entry point' has been identified, activities can often begin.[6] Further analysis may well be required but this will be undertaken as an integral part of the project or programme itself.

Much work is currently underway to refine and make more effective methods of poverty analysis.[7] This is an area in which we are still learning and it would be wrong to pre-empt the findings of ongoing research. Rather, we should ensure that we are both poised to assimilate others' findings and also ready to contribute to this burgeoning body of knowledge ourselves. The lessons of livelihoods analysis should be learnt collectively and built upon. It will be appropriate: to incorporate existing lessons and methodologies from participatory work and stakeholder analysis; to elevate the learning process within projects; to work with other donors and governments in the area of methodology development; and to be far more systematic in our experimentation with new approaches or combinations of approaches.

Table 1 gives an idea of the range of methods which might be used to assess the vulnerability context of livelihoods. Similar tables can be drawn up for other sections of the livelihoods framework (see also the comments on tools for analysis in various of the chapters in this volume). It will be particularly important to develop and refine robust systems for analysing assets and policies and to use these to understand the basis for DFID involvement in any area (see endnote 2). This is a task to which all the various DFID departments can contribute.

**Table 1: Analysis of livelihood vulnerability context**

| Component | Key issue | Examples to look for | Data Collection | | |
|---|---|---|---|---|---|
| | | | Part. | Stats | Other |
| **TRENDS** | | | | | |
| *Resource stocks* | What is happening to natural resource stocks and quality? | Degradation/renewal trends | X | | GIS |
| | | Loss of resources to urban use | | x | |
| *Population density* | What is current density and how is this changing? | Density figures | Maps | x | |
| | | Population growth figures | | x | |
| | | Information on out-migration | X | | |
| *Technology* | What technologies exist which are of likely benefit to people in the area? | Technology database | | | |
| | | Local knowledge/varieties | X | | |
| | | Technologies in use in this (and similar) areas | X | | Observation Literature |
| *Politics* | How are people in the area placed in terms of political representation? | Voting figures | | x | |
| | | Local support for party in power | X | | |
| *Economics* | How do economic trends affect livelihoods? | Ethnic origins | X | x | |
| | | Distance to nearest seat of government | | | Observation |
| | | Price trends of locally produced goods | | x | Monitoring |
| | | Percentage of local goods which are traded | X | x | |
| **SHOCKS** | | | | | |
| *Climate* | How does the climate affect people's livelihoods/well-being? | Annual rainfall | | x | |
| | | Rainfall variability | | x | |
| | | Climatic disasters | X | x | |
| *Conflict* | Is there any civil or resource conflict (or likelihood of such conflict) in the area? | Accounts of conflict | X | | |
| | | Legal cases pending | | | Court files |
| **CULTURE** | | | | | |
| *Culture* | What effect, if any, does culture have on the way people manage their assets and the livelihood choices they make? | Unexplained differences between this and other areas | X | | Observation |
| | | Accounts of the way things are done (and constraints) | X | | |

Part. = Participatory methodologies; Stats = Statistics

## From analysis to action

Livelihood analysis is not an end in itself. It is valuable for DFID only if it informs action in support of poverty eradication.

### *Where to intervene?*

The framework groups particular components of complex livelihoods together (vulnerability context, capital assets, transforming structures and processes, strategies and livelihood outcomes; see Figure 1). From this list two areas can be identified in which DFID can make a particularly positive contribution. DFID can:

- contribute to the robustness of and increase the opportunities available to individuals/groups/communities by building up their asset base (expanding the area of their pentagons); and

- help ensure that the structures and processes which define people's options are working in favour of the poor.

Other areas are less suitable for DFID intervention.[8] The vulnerability context of livelihoods is relatively fixed in the short to medium term. Structures, processes and assets are all far more amenable to externally promoted change (and themselves feed back into determining the vulnerability context in the longer term). At times DFID might feel it appropriate to intervene directly in support of certain outcomes. Thus emergency food aid or food for work programmes represents a short-term means of promoting food security. However, in the longer-term developmental context, it is people's inherent capacity to withstand shocks (without resorting to fickle emergency supplies) that should be built up.

When it comes to livelihood strategies, DFID can certainly make a contribution. However it is proposed that it should do this by expanding people's options and choices rather than supporting them in a way that assumes that they have chosen a particular livelihood strategy and they will stick with this in perpetuity and to the exclusion of other strategies. This is a change from the past when the tendency was to assume that rural people were farmers/forest dwellers/fisherfolk and to assist them as such. The suggestion now is that DFID should understand that people are (or are not) farmers and help them to get the best out of farming if relevant. At the same time, though, DFID should recognise inter- and intra-household diversity and the fact that core capabilities can be capitalised upon in a number of ways. There are, therefore, multiplier effects to be gained from building up core assets and helping to develop policies and institutions which provide people with choices.

Based on this argument, the list of provisional objectives for DFID which appears in Box 2 has been drawn up. These objectives relate directly

**There are multiplier effects to be gained from building up core assets and helping to develop policies and institutions which provide people with choices**

---

**Box 2: DFID objectives for SRL**

To promote sustainable livelihoods through the provision of:

- more secure access and better management of natural resources
- a more supportive and cohesive social environment
- more secure access to financial resources
- improved access to high-quality education, information, technologies and training and better nutrition and health
- better access to facilitating infrastructure
- a policy and institutional environment which supports multiple livelihood strategies and promotes equitable access to competitive markets for all.

---

## Table 2: Existing NRD-led contributions to proposed DFID objectives

| Objective | Example by types of intervention | Examples from existing projects |
|---|---|---|
| Access to and better management of natural resources | ○ Soil and water conservation<br>○ Land tenure<br>○ Applied NRM research<br>○ Systems research<br>○ Management of common property resources, e.g. forests, freshwater lakes, grazing land,capture fishery<br>○ Community wells<br>○ Agricultural services | ○ Land tenure - Uganda<br>○ Zambezia ADP, Mozambique<br>○ ABLH, Kenya<br>○ Kavango Farming Systems, Namibia<br>○ Western Ghats Forestry, India<br>○ Fisheries III, Bangladesh<br>○ Amboro, Bolivia<br>○ Range Inventory and Management Project, Botswana |
| More supportive social environment | ○ Support to self help groups<br>○ Local NGO capacity development | ○ Wajir - Kenya<br>○ Rainfed Farming, India<br>○ AKRSP, Pakistan<br>○ Wenchi Farming Systems, Ghana<br>○ BRAC, Bangladesh |
| Access to financial resources | ○ Group savings and credit | ○ Zambezia ADP, Mozambique<br>○ AKRSP, Pakistan<br>○ Rainfed Farming, India |
| Education, information, training, technologies, health and nutrition | ○ Agricultural education<br>○ Agricultural research<br>○ Agricultural extension<br>○ Health indices | ○ Wenchi Farming Systems, Ghana<br>○ Rural Strategy Units, South Africa<br>○ KARI, Kenya<br>○ ASSP, Bangladesh<br>○ Zambezia ADP, Mozambique<br>○ Rainfed Farming, India |
| Access to facilitating infrastructure | ○ Drinking water supply<br>○ Bioengineering<br>○ Improved access to markets | ○ ActionAid, Nepal<br>○ Bioengineering, Nepal<br>○ Rural roads, Zambezia, Mozambique |
| Policy and institutional environment | ○ Sector programmes<br>○ Institutional support<br>○ Policy support units | ○ Agriculture sector approach, Ghana<br>○ Forestry policy and institutional change, South Africa<br>○ Western Ghats/Himachal Pradesh Forestry Programmes, India<br>○ Veterinary services, Uganda, Zimbabwe, Tanzania<br>○ Rural strategy units, South Africa<br>○ Land tenure, Uganda |

to the five capital assets and the transforming structures and processes of the framework.

A number of points should be made about these objectives:

(i)   They cut across and subsume all three DFID objectives which appear in the White Paper.[9]

(ii)  They strongly suggest the need for all DFID departments to work together to promote sustainable (rural) livelihoods.

(iii) There is no suggestion that all six objectives should be pursued simultaneously, rather they define the scope of the types of activities in which DFID might engage.

(iv) Already the objectives are not comprehensive. For example, the one relating to physical capital focuses on infrastructure rather than other forms of physical capital (such as the direct external provision of machinery or livestock as a means of production). The feeling is that DFID can make more of a difference here.

(v) It might be both possible and desirable to narrow the objectives down still further, based upon DFID's own understanding of its comparative advantage (though this would be a controversial process).

Natural Resources Division (NRD)-led projects currently play a role in meeting all six objectives. Examples of this are shown in Table 2 and in Box 3.[10] However, NRD (as currently constituted) clearly does not take the lead in any but the first objective area.

---

**Box 3: Project examples**

**Rainfed farming projects – India**

The isolated tribal communities comprise some of the poorest and most vulnerable groups in India. Their livelihood options are limited. Most families have limited access to land for cultivation, but common property resources (e.g. trees, grazing, water) play a vital role. Environmental degradation can be severe.

The projects are working with communities better to manage common property resources to the benefit of all. Environmental degradation is being reversed. Participatory approaches to technology development and transfer have led to large increases in productivity on family land holdings. The food gap has been sharply reduced and surplus produce is marketed. Community groups are, for the first time, demanding Government services.

The programme is now working with communities to explore other livelihood options, both NR and non-NR based. Communities have established savings schemes and the project is exploring options for providing credit.

**Land tenure – Uganda**

Poverty assessments show that lack of secure access to land (natural capital) is a major determinant of rural poverty across large parts of Uganda.

DFID is working with the Government of Uganda to redraft land legislation. Crucially, it is also financing a major process of research, awareness raising (including drawing on experiences from neighbouring countries) and consultation with communities, NGOs and Members of Parliaments.

DFID support demonstrates the characteristics of the livelihoods approach. The starting point is the rural poor and an holistic understanding of their livelihoods. The consultative process has led to changes in proposed legislation, a much more informed and open debate, and is helping to develop social capital with communities and NGOs.

Secure access to land by the rural poor requires changes in policies, legislation and institutional arrangements (the rules of the game). These rules will only help to address poverty if they are based on a full understanding of the needs of the poor. DFID is also willing, in principle, to work with civil society and Government in implementing the revised land legislation. This should enable the rural poor to manage sustainably land resources (natural capital) to generate positive livelihood outcomes and increased financial and human capital in the longer term.

---

## What to do?

**The SRL agenda ...
embraces the fact that
rural people's livelihoods
are very diversified, that
they are intimately
connected ... with the
livelihoods of urban
dwellers and that the
prospects for
advancement and for
increased robustness of
rural people may not
always lie in the sectors
with which they have
traditionally been
associated**

It may be possible to limit DFID contributions to these six objectives. That does not, however, solve the problem of how to ascertain in any particular circumstance which objective, or set of objectives, should be pursued. Indeed, the SRL agenda has a tendency to expand rather than to contract the options for DFID contributions. It embraces the fact that rural people's livelihoods are very diversified, that they are intimately connected (in both positive and negative ways) with the livelihoods of urban dwellers and that the prospects for advancement and for increased robustness of rural people may not always lie in the sectors with which they have traditionally been associated (forestry, agriculture and fisheries) (see Chapters 3 and 4 on these topics). It recognises the value of working directly with rural people to increase the extent to which they achieve positive livelihood outcomes. However, it also places a strong emphasis on working at the policy and institutional level to ensure that assets are effectively transformed into positive livelihood outcomes.

Unsurprisingly, there is no scientific means of deciding exactly what DFID should do in any circumstance. There are, nonetheless, more and less robust ways of making decisions. The more robust ways (for which principles and guidelines will be developed in time) will entail several types of analysis, particularly of the local context, circumstances and partnership options (Rennie and Singh, 1996). However, like the less robust ways, they will remain heavily dependent upon personal judgement. It is important, though, that the processes of decision-making are carefully documented both for reasons of accountability and for the sake of institutional learning.

The following types of analysis are proposed. Type one (livelihoods analysis) and type two (partnership analysis) are likely to take place simultaneously and iteratively; the emphasis is on a dynamic process of analysis which goes well beyond a 'snap shot' view put together after a short participatory exercise.

### Livelihood analysis

The analysis of capital assets should have revealed much information about the asset status of particular groups and how this is changing over time. Participatory assessment of people's livelihood objectives should yield a picture not only of what people are aspiring to but also of what they feel are the major constraining forces or factors (including how structures and processes affect their livelihood options). If people appear to be particularly lacking in any one of the five capital assets, it will be necessary to probe with them the extent to which they feel that this is a factor which prevents them from moving forward (or whether it is relatively unimportant given their choice of livelihood strategy).[11] Likewise, if people are particularly well-endowed in one area (e.g. natural capital) but are still unable to achieve positive livelihood outcomes (improved incomes, reduced vulnerability, etc.), it will be important to understand what the critical missing assets or undermining structures and processes are. There will therefore be a strong emphasis on institutional analysis; it will invariably be good practice to draw up an inventory of existing structures and processes (both informal and formal) which impact upon people's livelihoods.

### Partnership analysis and formation

DFID is not working in isolation. Livelihood analyses should be conducted in conjunction with partners. It is hoped that the organising principles behind the SRL framework will provide a powerful tool for explaining to partners and potential partners the way in which DFID understands rural livelihoods and the role it can play in supporting them. DFID's own activities will, as suggested in the White Paper, be guided by the partnerships which it forms (whether with the public or private sectors in developing countries). They will also be moulded by commitments under international agreements and DFID's objective to support countries in the development and implementation of National Strategies for Sustainable Development (see Chapter 14). This type of analysis entails a 'matching' of perceived needs with the range of partners which is available in any given area. Partnership opportunities in the remote rural areas in which DFID works may be very thin on the ground. Since DFID does not work alone, its range of options for contribution is likely to be narrowed considerably at this stage.[12]

> **DFID's own activities will be guided by the partnerships which it forms. They will also be moulded by commitments under international agreements**

### Effectiveness analysis

The third type of analysis is, if anything, even more qualitative than the previous ones. It entails developing an understanding of where DFID can make a difference. This has two dimensions to it:

- In which kinds of activities at which levels is DFID likely to be effective in contributing to poverty eradication (given what is already known about the policy process and the scope for changing this, about social relations, institutional competence and the rule of law in the country in question)? Which constraints to livelihoods can actually be addressed by a donor and its partners in the context in question?

- Of the range of possible effective interventions, which is likely to yield the greatest returns in terms of positive outcomes and eventual poverty alleviation?[13]

### Indicators for rural livelihoods

As has been mentioned above, it is expected that indicators for SRL activities will be negotiated with those who stand to benefit from DFID's activities. Negotiation goes beyond cursory consultation and participation – it is an active and ongoing process of dialogue between the various parties, all of which are expected to share information with the others. (It has been noted, for example, that were DFID to be more open about the cost of its activities, quite different priorities might emerge from the people with which it is working.) Indeed indicators, and the processes around their negotiation, can form a valuable tool for communication between outsiders and potential beneficiaries of DFID contributions.

There are a range of different types of indicators at both project and programme level. Those which are of the greatest concern for the staff of NRPAD are objective verifiable indicators (OVIs) within the logframe context. In order to be useful, these OVIs must display certain key characteristics, namely they must be: specific, measurable, usable, sensitive, available and cost-effective (Ticehurst and Cameron, 1998). They must also clearly relate to outcomes; we are concerned with impact (or output analysis) rather than the level and timeliness of inputs which may have little to do with outcomes.

It may be quite difficult to ensure that negotiated outcome indicators display all these characteristics. In particular there is a concern that widening the scope of indicators (e.g. going beyond indices of production to thinking about the impact of change on people's livelihoods) will increase the cost of indicator monitoring and will also introduce renewed elements of doubt about causality and attribution. One answer to this concern is that status monitoring will be far more integral to projects themselves. Baseline data collection – which has been notoriously poor – will be a core task within the initial livelihood assessment. Verification of progress will be directly written into project activities.

**Status monitoring will be integral to projects themselves**

Even if this is the case for projects working directly with poor people, there are inherent problems associated with measuring impact when the target is organisational or institutional reform. It is insufficient to measure the number of people sent on training courses or similar. However, it is extremely hard to identify indicators of key behavioural changes, let alone of how these changes have impacted on sustainable livelihoods over the long term. This is an area in which further work is certainly required for, in the absence of such work, it is likely that DFID activities with less tangible outcomes will lose out to those with more concrete and readily attributable achievements. Work is also likely to be needed to develop robust indicators of sustainability and other more 'external' concerns.

## What are we doing that is new?

There are many important ideas wrapped up under the heading of SRL. Not all are new. Indeed, the holistic conception of poverty upon which the approach is based is similar to that of the Integrated Rural Development Programmes of the 1970s. Many other elements of the approach, such as the participatory paradigm on which it is built, have developed over time and already lie at the heart of a number of donor projects. Other aspects of the approach are more incidental – that is they are not inherent to the approach but are the product of complementary lines of thinking (though they cohere well with the approach). Under this category would fall the emphasis on multi-institutional approaches, on liberalisation and decentralisation (see Chapter 3 for discussion of the impact of decentralisation on rural livelihoods).

Table 3 summarises what the new approach is aiming to produce. It juxtaposes these ideas with a portrait (something of a caricature, it is true)[14] of the IRDP approach and what is loosely termed 'pre-White Paper DFID'. Nevertheless, the table does stress some important differences.

## Issues arising

Needless to say, consultations undertaken over the past six months have identified a number of valid concerns about the new approach. At the outset there was some confusion about exactly what the approach might entail. The White Paper uses the term 'livelihoods' in a rather economic sense, essentially referring to people's incomes and employment opportunities. Others understood this to be a far richer concept, one which unites economic development, reduced vulnerability and environmental sustainability, while building on the existing strengths of poor people. The SRL committee has clearly adopted the latter inter-pretation, as summarised in this paper.

However, definitions have not been the only difficult issues. Beyond worries about the complexity of livelihoods analysis (addressed above), the following points have been frequently raised and will continue to be debated.

**DFID staff should have better access to continual professional development ... and they should operate in a learning environment**

- The changes implied in the SRL approach demand not only new skills, but also the identification of specific competencies for DFID staff (particularly in management and policy analysis but also in analysing non NR-based livelihoods in rural areas). Technical skills remain critically important when it comes to identifying opportunities, developing dialogues with partners and implementation. However, the planning and analysis process should not, at the outset, be technically led. DFID staff, particularly country advisers, should have better access to continual professional development if they are to spearhead this approach and they should operate in a learning environment. There will also be implications for future recruitment.

- DFID's current structure, resource allocation procedure and incentive system are not conducive to sectoral coordination, planning based on shared objectives and responsiveness to needs which are identified within projects rather than at the outset (and which fall beyond the initial sectoral scope of activity). This problem is compounded by the

## Table 3: How does the SRL approach differ from previous donor efforts?

| | IRDP | Pre-White Paper DFID | SRL |
|---|---|---|---|
| **Starting point** | Structures, areas | Resources, needs | People and their existing strengths and constraints |
| **Conceptions of poverty** | Holistic, multi-dimensional Recommendation domains suggest uniformity (an operational simplification) | Income-based, simple, measurable Risk associated with resources not people | Multi-dimensional, complex, local Embraces the concepts of risk and variability |
| **Problem analysis** | Undertaken by planning unit in short period of time, viewed as conclusive | One-off project identification with some participation | Inclusive process, iterative and incomplete, based on holistic livelihood assessment. Dynamic |
| **Sectoral scope** | Multi-sectoral, single plan, sector involvement established at outset | Single sector, single plan (log-frame), sectors admitted to country programme in advance | Small number of entry points, multi-sectoral, many plans (nested logframes?), sectoral involvement evolves with project |
| **Level of operation** | Local, area-based | Either policy or field level | Both policy and field level with clear links between the two |
| **Time taken to prepare projects** | Initial identification rapid; detailed planning time-consuming | Protracted. Detailed design the norm. Shift from 'blueprint' to 'process' projects has failed to reduce preparation time | Understanding of livelihood options time-consuming. However, projects start as discrete interventions and build on these. Preparation time therefore 'spread' over longer overall project time |
| **Time frame** | 5–10 years | 3–5 years | Longer commitment |
| **Partner organisation** | National/local governments | National governments, local NGOs | Local and national govt., NGOs, rural organisations, private sector |
| **Project management structure** | Dedicated project management unit created | Project within host organisation | Project within partner organisation |
| **Co-ordination** | Integrated execution (donor-driven) | Donor-driven when required (seldom) | Driven by shared objectives and needs identified by those involved |
| **Spatial focus** | Rural, area-based | Rural areas exclusively | Rural areas as part of larger systems |
| **Project size** | Large, sometimes with preceding pilot | Medium | Start small (limited areas of activity) and grow |
| **Indicators** | Production changes, uptake | Specified at outset | Production/conservation oriented People and outcome-oriented, negotiated. Develop over time |
| **Sustainability** | Not explicitly considered | Increasing concern | Key aspect of livelihoods. Also at political/fiscal levels |
| **Environment** | Treated as add-on (if at all) | Treated as add-on (if at all) | Opportunity to mainstream environment as part of livelihood development |
| **Capacity building** | Minor concern. Relied on idealised conception of capacity | Major concern | Major concern |
| **Supporting research** | Adaptive technical, socio-economic | Production system-based | Livelihood strategy-based Action research |
| **DFID core country staff** | Project co-ordinators. | Sectorally defined professional advisers and field managers | SRL facilitators |
| **Skills needed for core staff** | Administrative, technical | Technical, policy | Managerial, policy |
| **Relationships between DFID professional advisers** | Despite integrated projects, often limited direct contact between sectoral advisers | Variable. Systems do not promote working together except in final project screening | Shared framework promotes joint approach and promotes quest for complementarity |

independent dynamic of sector programmes and planning in partner countries. This issue was raised in all the Breakout groups at NRAC '98 and formed the starting point for the presentations from representatives of other disciplines within DFID which are summarised in the final chapter of the book. On the positive side, everyone recognised the opportunities inherent in collaborative activities. On the negative side there are significant costs associated with cross-sectoral work. It must be ensured that the benefits exceed the costs and that undue emphasis is not placed on structures for coordination rather than the substance of and underlying rationale for working together.

**DFID's project cycle is perceived by many as being too time-consuming.**

- DFID's project cycle is perceived by many as being too time-consuming. It is not conducive to risk-taking, to process projects or to systematic learning. The recently announced increase in the aid framework may make matters worse by pushing the Department towards larger, more capital-intensive projects which may well be at odds with the SRL approach (though in the longer term one could envisage extensive commitments being borne out of this holistic approach).

- There is a feeling that sector programmes are in reality even if not in theory at odds with the livelihoods approach, especially in sectors such as natural resources which are not exclusively public sector-led. Sector programmes are usually designed in support of single, production-oriented Ministries and have not been very effective in responding to needs identified by users of services (this issue is addressed in Chapter 2, which argues that there is no inherent conflict between the two approaches, especially when the need for policy-level interventions is informed by effective livelihood analysis).

- The SRL framework appears to argue for what has traditionally been called an area-based approach. At a decentralised government level, one might be able to deal with the complexity entailed by the approach. Furthermore, expressly focusing on certain geographical areas would facilitate coordination between DFID departments. While these are persuasive arguments, due weight must also be given to important policy-level interventions. The SRL approach explicitly links the micro with the macro, the local with the national. The area-based approach may be effective in generating credibility with partner governments and may cohere with governments' own policy processes (support would thus be important in the context of partnerships). However, it should not result in the creation of islands of excellence. In addition, focusing on particular areas should not obscure the people-centred ethos of the SRL approach.

# Final word

This introductory chapter has attempted to summarise the core elements of the proposed SRL framework. This framework is holistic and dynamic. It suggests that DFID must develop and maintain a broad understanding of livelihoods and their context and sustainability. It does not suggest that DFID should attempt to intervene at all levels and in all aspects of rural livelihoods, nor that it should revert to excessively complex integrated programmes. However, it does imply that the wider livelihood impacts of all potential DFID activities should be actively considered before deciding whether and where to intervene.

The main 'value added' of the approach lies in:

- the dynamism of the underlying analysis
- the realism of the cross-sectoral analysis (rural people do not live their lives in 'sectors') and the resulting ability to identify genuine constraints;
- the fact that it builds on people's strengths
- its emphasis on understanding the full implications of all types of (externally driven) changes, so that a realistic assessment of costs and benefits can be made
- the explicit links it makes between the micro and the macro, between individuals' access to assets and the policies and institutions at all levels which determine these
- its emphasis upon sustainability – of both resources and livelihoods.

The chapter has also presented an overview of some of the debates and concerns which have been occupying the SRL Advisory Committee over the past six months. It is by no means comprehensive. Indeed it stands as an introduction to the other chapters in this volume which provide considerably more detail, linking this to the framework in order to enrich and develop it.

But the scope of the livelihoods debate and approach certainly goes well beyond the subject matter of this book. NRAC '98 and the papers presented there represented a starting point for thinking about the nature of the new approach and the contribution that those present might make to operationalising it. Our hope is that this volume will widen the debate, intensify the process of learning and prompt others to think how they might contribute. In the final instance the approach must be judged on its practical applicability and the contribution that it makes to DFID's poverty eradication goal and its commitment to the International Development Targets.

# Key references

Booth, D., Holland, J., Hentschel, J., Lanjouw, P. and Herbert, A. (1998) *Participative and Combined Methods in African Poverty Assessment: Renewing the Agenda.* London: Department for International Development.

Hanmer, L., Pyatt, G. and White, H. (1997) *Poverty in Sub-Saharan Africa. What Can we Learn from the World Bank's Poverty Assessments?* The Hague: ISS.

Rennie, J.K. and Singh, N.C. (1996) *Participatory Research for Sustainable Livelihoods: A Guidebook for Field Projects.* Winnipeg: International Institute for Sustainable Development, World Bank.

Scoones, I. (1998) *Sustainable Rural Livelihoods: A Framework for Analysis.* Working Paper No. 72. Brighton: Institute of Development Studies.

Ticehurst, D. and Cameron, C. (1998) *Review of Current Status of Impact Monitoring Systems for Rural Development and Rural Livelihood Programmes.* Chatham: NRI, World Bank.

# Endnotes

1   Although there is a considerable degree of consensus among those involved in the process thus far, some areas are inevitably more problematic than others. This paper highlights some of those issues in brief. However, it should not be assumed that all the views presented are shared by all SRL group members.

2   Follow-on work will be needed to develop and refine methods for and modes of analysing capital assets. Although there is no suggestion at this point that capital asset analysis conducted in different locations by different people should be directly comparable, it will be important to come to a general agreement on a framework for a participatory process of negotiation with partners during the analysis.

3   This would be tantamount to introducing 'poverty lines' on each axis and would suffer the same criticism of reductionism and arbitrariness as have such lines in the past. Nevertheless participatory analysis in a particular area might show there to be a very close correlation between, for example, access to land (one component of natural capital) and poverty (subjectively assessed). In such a case it might be feasible to work with the notion of a cut-off point for poverty on the 'natural capital' axis.

4   There are, though, no hard and fast 'rules' on this. The framework does not intend to suggest that all five types of capital are equally important to all people and at a generic level it says nothing about trade offs and substitutability between assets (see Chapter 14 on this).

5 Convertibility might not be so positive if it increases the vulnerability of certain groups. This can happen when land becomes saleable, for example, and is annexed by more powerful groups or household members.

6 The eight 'Entry Point' chapters which follow attempt to provide criteria for choosing any particular entry point.

7 This is, for example, a key theme of DFID's new ESCOR (Economic and Social Committee on Overseas Research) strategy. A number of groups within DFID are also working on ways to assess the extent to which policies can be considered 'pro poor'.

8 The framework is not, though, intended to be a straitjacket. Responsiveness to local circumstances and domestic policies/ partners is also critical to success in poverty eradication. This will require flexibility.

9 These are: (i) policies and actions which promote sustainable livelihoods; (ii) better education, health and opportunities for poor people; and (iii) protection and better management of the natural environment.

10 Project examples are drawn from those which have been suggested during consultation as having a particular livelihoods focus. The list is far from comprehensive and is not intended to suggest that other projects are not meeting DFID objectives.

11 For example, my own lack of natural capital does not constrain me from achieving positive outcomes.

12 This type of analysis is complicated by the fact that some potential DFID activities will be 'internal' to partner organisations (as is the case with programmes which support institutional reform within Ministries).

13 This raises questions about poverty lines and the cost of working with the very poorest. The current attitude to this concern appears to be opportunistic; no firm guidelines are in place. It should be noted that initial post White Paper suggestions that we should work only with the poorest groups or only in lower potential areas now appear to have given way to a less prescriptive poverty eradication agenda. The SRL approach recognises that there are a multitude of ways in which beneficial outcomes can be achieved. If the poor purchase large amounts of their basic foodstuffs it may be just as appropriate to work to lower the price of these goods as it is to increase their own production.

14 Many DFID programmes and projects are already increasingly in tune with the SRL approach and all approaches evolve over time.

# KEY ISSUE PAPERS

# 2 The Sector Approach and Sustainable Rural Livelihoods

*Stephen Akroyd and Alex Duncan*[1]

## Introduction

The sector approach and sector investment programmes (SIPs) have been widely promoted in the past three to four years in response to perceived shortcomings of project-led approaches to development aid. However, concerns have been expressed about both the concepts and their practical application. This chapter discusses the extent to which they provide an appropriate framework for improving the sustainability of rural livelihoods, as a means of achieving DFID's poverty eradication goals.

The following concerns about sector programmes and SIPs have been raised:

- that they may not be compatible with the poverty objectives identified in the recent UK Government White Paper on International Development
- that they are by nature top-down and neither participative nor demand-led
- that they create a presumption that aid should be disbursed through government channels
- that they are by definition sectoral, whereas the promotion of sustainable rural livelihoods requires cross-sectoral measures
- that they may not be appropriate in the complex NR sector
- that there is a marked absence of poverty objectives in some SIPs
- that it is not clear how much importance should be attached to SIP preconditions nor what should be done when they are not met.

The central message of this chapter is that while the promotion of sustainable rural livelihoods (SRLs) must be based on an holistic analysis which recognises the complex set of objectives, resources and constraints which determine households' strategies, actions by governments to promote SRLs must be based on best-practice lessons learned in recent years in policy-making and public administration.

The latter requires a clear understanding of the role of the state in relation to the private and non-profit sectors. If livelihood analysis suggests that SRLs are best promoted in a given case by support to the non-state sectors, appropriate entry points may be defined which do not involve government. Where it is determined that the state does have a role, it is important to ensure that capacities for policy-making, budgeting and managing this role are adequate; there is a good case for donors to support these functions. Donors should also strive to minimise the extent to which their own priorities and practices add to the problems facing recipient governments in terms of management and resource prioritisation. The sector approach offers one means of doing this.

It would be a mistake to conclude (as occurred fatally with integrated rural development projects) that, because the nature of SRLs is cross-sectoral, special cross-sectoral instruments must be devised as the main means of promoting them. Adopting new forms of SRL-specific instruments runs the risk of: (i) undermining necessary policy and institutional reforms; and (ii) causing SRL-promoting measures to become marginalised in terms of mainstream development.

The role of government in promoting SRLs should be to: create an enabling framework for broad-based growth; deal with market failure problems to enhance productivity; and develop targeted policies and programmes to benefit defined socio-economic groups, such as the poor or those in isolated areas. In several respects, sector approaches can be effective as a means of strengthening governments' abilities to perform these roles.

This chapter is structured in two main parts. The first summarises lessons from the early years of applying the sector approach and SIPs. The second discusses the extent to which the sector approach contributes to sustainable rural livelihoods and the achievement of DFID's poverty objectives.

## The sector approach and experience of SIPs

### *What is the sector approach?*

The sector approach (also known as the sector-wide approach) is a means of managing: (i) government's role in a sector; and (ii) aid provided to it.

The **sector approach** is based on having in place:

- a strategy for the sector (coordinated where necessary with strategies for other sectors) which *inter alia* spells out the role of the state in relation to the private sector (commercial and non-commercial)

- an expenditure programme which integrates government and donor contributions

- a common management framework, and
- funding commitments from both donors and government.

A **sector investment programme (SIP)** is a particular lending instrument which, among others, can be used to implement the sector approach. Non-SIP instruments which under different circumstances may be used to achieve the objectives of the sector approach include: stabilisation and structural adjustment; public expenditure reviews; and civil service reforms. Adaptable Programme Loans[2] (APLs) are increasingly being used by the World Bank as short-term flexible mechanisms to assist capacity-building and strategy development. Private sector or NGO support, and multi-donor subsector programmes can also be used to support service delivery and capacity-building.

## *Why the sector approach?*

There are good reasons to develop the sector approach as an alternative to fragmented projects. Indeed, there is a great deal of experience of the shortcomings of development assistance provided through projects alone. Some of the more persistent problems have been that:

- Even where individual projects are well designed and implemented, the multiplicity of donors, objectives and management procedures has made it difficult for developing country governments to manage sector development and aid flows effectively and to prioritise spending. In 1992, for example, Zambia had 200 projects underway in the agricultural sector alone (Okidegbe, 1998).

- Money is fungible, which means that donors may well end up funding activities which they regard as low priority.

- Benefits from projects may not be sustainable where fundamental problems persist within government and the broad policy environment. Problems are typically associated with an inability to prioritise expenditure between sectors and to provide for recurrent costs, inadequate incentive structures for an effective civil service, and poor capacity to undertake management roles.

A principal justification for the sector approach is to highlight these problems and provide a framework for government and donors to address them. Overall, the sector approach offers much of value to increasing the effectiveness of development aid through clarifying aims and strategies, and linking investment programmes with necessary policy, institutional and budgetary reforms. Central to the sector approach is a recognition of the time dimension and the need for recipients and donors to work progressively towards an improved framework for the sector and not to develop unrealistic expectations as to the rapidity with which this can be done.

**Overall, the sector approach offers much of value to increasing the effectiveness of development aid through clarifying aims and strategies, and linking investment programmes with necessary policy, institutional and budgetary reforms**

A challenge is to determine which instruments are appropriate to achieve the goals of sector programmes under which circumstances. Four scenarios have been developed:

### Scenario 1
Under ideal conditions, where donors are confident that policy is responsive to the articulated needs of the poor, that the civil service functions effectively, and that a central budgetary system exists in which forward budgeting matches actual disbursements, the appropriate form of most development assistance (other than that channelled through NGOs and the private sector) would be through the Ministry of Finance (with associated conditionality as necessary). However, this represents an unrealistic scenario in most developing countries.

### Scenario 2
More commonly, donors do not have confidence in central budgetary processes. However, they may have some degree of confidence at the sector level. Under such conditions the appropriate approach would be a SIP, often complemented by public expenditure reviews (PERs), civil service reforms and conditionality.

### Scenario 3
Where donors have insufficient confidence at sector level for a SIP to be considered appropriate, the objectives of the sector approach may still be partially pursued by disaggregating to the level of sub-sectors, or individual services. To assist the delivery of aid at this level, a range of more flexible instruments are available – for example, multi-donor supported national programmes, PERs, adaptable programme lending, institutional strengthening, and private sector support. There may be scope for providing support to individual projects which are not clearly linked to a sector framework, but these will have limitations, and may even hinder progress towards resolving more fundamental public management problems.

### Scenario 4
Where donors perceive a failure of government so extensive that aid cannot effectively be delivered through public institutions, NGOs and the private sector may provide the only feasible alternative other than complete withdrawal.

## *Experience with SIPs*

There are conditions under which SIPs can represent a genuine advance on previous fragmented project-by-project approaches. Frequently these conditions obtain in the transport and social sectors, but less often – so far at least – in the natural resources sector. Reasons for this relate to the inherent diversity and institutional complexity of this sector, as well as to continuing technical disagreements on issues such as extension.

SIPs have, however, often been over-ambitious. In many of the countries in which SIPs have been put in place, the necessary features exist only partially.[3] Donors and governments have failed to recognise the scope and limitations of the instrument and to use it appropriately. However, SIPs are changing as lessons derived from early programmes are fed into the design of current sector approaches. These tend now to be more realistically defined, with more attention being paid to the budget framework, and less ambitious time-scales.

## Ownership and consultation

**Local commitment and ownership of the strategy process, as well as identification of beneficiary priorities, are critical to the objectives of a sector approach**

Local commitment and ownership of the strategy process, as well as identification of beneficiary priorities, are critical to the objectives of a sector approach and to measures which protect the interests of vulnerable groups and promote rural livelihoods. Two issues are important here. The first is the need for stakeholder consultation, to ensure that publicly provided services are responsive to user needs. Stakeholder consultation may be especially weak where the beneficiaries of government programmes are poor or politically marginalised. Second, political sustainability of the programme will depend upon the degree to which influential interest groups stand to gain or lose from the proposed reforms.

In designing stakeholder consultations, experience shows the importance of clear parameters which avoid arousing unrealistic expectations. The design must distinguish between 'importance attached to' and 'influence over' the reforms and must avoid confusion between consultative and management responsibilities among stakeholders. For example, while reform of extension will be of importance to farmers – and they should be consulted in formulating the sector strategy – farmers should not be responsible for managing the implementation of the reforms. In the case of the Zambia ASIP, stakeholder consultation mechanisms were put in place at national and district levels, under private sector chairmanship, but ultimately broke down because of a confusion over roles. Much has been learned about participatory techniques which can be integrated with livelihood analysis to feed into strategy design and monitoring.

## Decentralisation

There is a risk that a focus on a particular sector may conflict with decentralisation as sector budgets continue to be determined centrally, rather than as a result of local priorities. However, in practice, sector approaches have, through focusing attention on financial management, also been a vehicle for encouraging innovative district funding arrangements. Sector approaches may also complement support programmes for local government, although perhaps surprisingly there appear to be few such initiatives at present.

## Common funding

Common funding arrangements for sectors continue to cause difficulties for donors. Although donors generally accept common funding as a desirable long-term objective, there are legal and administrative difficulties which prevent them from putting the goal into practice. Particular problems occur in certain recipient countries where the record on corruption is poor. However, there are interesting innovations in this area. In Zambian health sector reforms, a 'district basket' to which donors and the government contribute was established (an arrangement that is currently under stress, however). Jointly supported Agricultural Research Funds are also increasingly popular (though their effectiveness has yet to be adequately assessed).

# Compatibility of the sector approach with sustainable rural livelihoods

## Introduction

Having discussed experiences with the sector approach, this section examines the extent to which the approach can contribute to the achievement of sustainable rural livelihoods as a means for promoting the poverty objectives outlined in the White Paper on International Development.

In brief, we suggest that the sector approach is one among a set of possible means for promoting SRLs. It is not, however, the only one. Its particular value is as a means of improving the focus and functioning of governments in addressing the policy and institutional questions which have such a profound impact on people's livelihood options and strategies. However, while the sector approach has considerable strengths, it does not provide for actions at all the levels needed, and there are circumstances in which it is not relevant. There is a good case therefore for DFID to support the sector approach, but to recognise its limitations.

**Support the sector approach, but recognise its limitations**

As a starting point, it is important to reiterate that the sector approach is policy-neutral (it is neither inherently pro-poor nor anti-poor) and, while biases may arise in its implementation (as with any policy or programme), these can be largely guarded against. However, the approach does have the merit of focusing attention on the importance of clear objectives and of government and donors agreeing on these. It therefore provides a means by which DFID and recipient governments can discuss substantively the extent to which their aims coincide or differ. It is one way of giving expression at the policy level to the notion of partnership between DFID, recipient governments and (to the extent that inclusive consultations are undertaken) other players from civil society and the private sector. It is therefore a means of providing DFID staff with experience and information that will help to determine the degree to which visions are shared and governments are committed. These factors are not easy to judge (and change over time) and will necessarily influence the nature and extent of DFID's involvement in particular countries and sectors.

Where a pro-poor agenda is agreed, the sector approach provides a management and financial framework which, under the right conditions, enables important parts of the SRL agenda, though not all of it, to be addressed.[4] This will only happen, though, when particular sector programmes are linked with a broader, cross-sectoral vision.

A first feature of the approach is that, as with most official aid mechanisms, it assumes that the aid donor will engage with the recipient government, and not channel all its support directly to NGOs or the private sector. Our own view is that the importance of policy reforms to successful development and poverty alleviation means that donors such as DFID have no serious alternative but to engage with governments if they are to achieve their objectives. This issue is not therefore a significant limitation on the value of the sector approach.

Second, the approach does not deal with problems at the wider levels of the macroeconomy, governance and civil service reforms. There are circumstances in which these must be addressed prior to, or at least in parallel with, actions at the sectoral or local levels, as they will otherwise act as binding constraints on progress at lower levels.

The remainder of this section considers the question: 'How far, and under what circumstances, is the sector approach an effective means of strengthening the policies and institutions referred to in the SRL framework?'

## The SRL framework and the sector approach

We examine this question in the context of the roles for government which we classify in terms of:

- strengthening the enabling environment
- addressing market failures
- addressing social objectives through specific policies and programmes.[5]

In promoting SRLs, these categories are mutually reinforcing and mutually dependent. For example, policies to promote enterprise development among the poor are likely to achieve the greatest impact in an environment which provides access to other supporting services (e.g. rural finance or basic infrastructure) and where market incentives are not reduced or distorted by macro-economic policy.

### Enabling environment
The objective is to promote an enabling environment for broad-based sustainable growth, through measures to promote effective governance and macroeconomic stability and to ensure confidence in the wider environment

and operation of markets. Such measures are intended to facilitate broad-based growth of incomes, but they are not specifically focused on the poor.

There is a good deal of evidence that shortcomings in the wider environment go a long way towards explaining Africa's halting economic performance. Against a hostile economic background, little can be done on a sustained basis to reduce poverty and improve SRLs: income growth cannot be kept up, and the funding base for social services will stagnate or contract. Further, there is evidence that profitability is a necessary condition for sustainable NR management.

Arguably, over the past 15–20 years, progress, albeit uneven, has been made in improving the wider economic environment in sub-Saharan Africa and this is now beginning to be reflected in improved growth performance and prospects.

There is a good case for DFID to continue to provide support to: stabilisation, structural adjustment programmes, electoral and judicial reforms, civil service reform, and actions to protect and conserve the environment. Some measures relevant to SRLs may also be needed at the international level where DFID may use what room for manoeuvre it has to promote the interests of developing countries through, for instance, trade reform or international environmental conventions.

Sector approaches do not directly address many of the wider constraints; they do, however, provide a discipline for ensuring that the question is at least asked of whether these constraints hinder sector performance and whether adequate steps are being taken to address them.

### Market failure: ensuring efficient, high–quality services

These are measures to provide public goods and services, address externalities, ensure markets are contestable, and improve information flows. They will promote productivity-enhancing growth through strengthening social, environmental and economic services from which the poor, but not only the poor, benefit. Public/private partnerships will feature prominently at this level in many countries.

Arguably, the sector approach has most to contribute to SRLs by addressing instances of market failure which hinder efficient economic growth. While there is a good deal of variation as to priorities between countries, the most important agenda commonly relates to efficient and equitable rural services as a means for promoting small enterprise development and employment growth in the NR and non–NR sectors. There are also other issues which require government action, such as ensuring the appropriate regulatory regime for safety, health and environmental protection purposes. What is important, though, is that government (and donor) priorities in such areas are informed by analysis of livelihoods and the types of services and regulations which are supportive of them.

The sector approach has the merit of focusing analysis on the role of government in relation to the roles of the private sector and NGOs. It

**The sector approach has the merit of focusing analysis on the role of government in relation to the roles of the private sector and NGOs**

provides a framework through which resources can be allocated according to agreed priorities, services made responsive to user needs, and service delivery provided through an appropriate mix of public and private sector bodies. The concept of market failure is now used in many developing countries in the NR and other sectors to determine where public funding is best spent from the perspective of promoting efficient growth; the sector approach provides a mechanism by which such analysis can be conducted and applied in practice. This has helped to sharpen the debate on prioritising spending.

### Social objectives

These measures include redistributive policies and programmes which favour particular groups (notably the poor, women or those in isolated areas). Such measures are not primarily directed towards maximum growth. They may be intended to establish new economic activities, or to provide services or relief. Interventions of most relevance to SRLs would typically include targeted actions to: promote equitable access to resources, markets and economic services; remove barriers to participation; reform basic services such as health, education, water supply and extension; and improve rural infrastructure. Making choices among these competing demands requires means whereby rural groups can articulate their needs, as well as analysis of how cost-effective alternative programmes are in reaching the poor.

For these social objectives to be met, it is likely that some of the resources allocated through a sector approach will need to be explicitly targeted towards poor and disadvantaged groups, as it cannot be assumed that the latter will necessarily benefit directly from measures to address market failures. Support for people involved in smallholder farming, livestock husbandry and artisanal fishing is rightly often seen as one means of promoting both growth and the interests of the poor, if not the poorest.

However, with limited resources, there is likely to be a trade-off between aggregate economic growth and targeted pro-poor interventions. Difficult choices will have to be made, especially if there is a wish to meet the needs of the ultra-poor.[6] One argument favours promoting broad-based economic growth over targeted interventions, on the assumption that the benefits will eventually trickle down to the poorest groups, primarily through the mechanism of the labour market. In agriculture, for example, governments may be unwilling to allocate resources towards low-potential areas where they see returns as being lower or more risky than in better-endowed areas. An alternative approach tends to favour direct pro-poor interventions as a more effective means of tackling poverty, on the grounds that, in the absence of such measures, unacceptable levels of poverty and inequality would result. An improved empirical base for assessing the real trade-offs would go a long way to resolving the differences between these two approaches, although there will always be room for debate. The sector approach provides a mechanism for DFID and the government, together with other stakeholders and external donors, to undertake the necessary analysis and strategy development.

Although government and donors may agree on the need for targeted actions as an element of a sector strategy, effective implementation requires reliable and timely information on the characteristics and needs of the intended beneficiaries. Such information may be difficult to obtain in many countries in which sector programmes are being pursued. To target the poor effectively, a poverty and/or livelihoods assessment, which may be based on PRA, may be needed during the preparation of sector programmes. This should provide a basis for discussion between government and donors on how poor groups are to be targeted and by which means.

Critical to the success of targeted interventions is empowerment and the participation of poor stakeholders in consultation processes. Experience shows that, even where decentralisation is pursued and the need for stakeholder consultation accepted, the actual involvement of local government and community-level organisations has been limited (Jones, 1997). This raises questions as to how the poor can best be reached and who can legitimately claim to represent their interests.

**Difficulties arise where domestic government priorities differ from those promoted by donors**

In reaching consensus on the allocation of resources between services and the inclusion of a pro-poor agenda, difficulties arise where domestic government priorities differ from those promoted by donors. This is particularly likely for agriculture, where there is considerable disagreement over the appropriate approach to be taken with certain key services (e.g. extension). Where the recipient government and the donors cannot agree on a poverty agenda, donors may in some instances be reduced to seeking alternative mechanisms for achieving their poverty objectives, for example, working through NGOs and the private sector (scenario 4, above). This may also be a suitable approach where government institutions and planning processes are particularly weak and ineffective, though it must be recognised that, from a perspective of promoting development, this solution is far from ideal. Parallel measures should, therefore, continue to be taken where possible to engage with the government with a view to securing agreement on wider strategy, and strengthening capacities in the future.

### Cross-sector policies and programmes

One issue frequently raised is the extent to which sector approaches are compatible with resolving problems which are essentially cross-sectoral.

At a minimum, in cases where it is determined that government has a role, there is a need for the relevant departments to develop a common view of the problem, and to coordinate their approaches. At local level, district governments may provide a cross-sector linking mechanism.

The difficulties with interdepartmental coordination have often in the past led to over-complex multi-sector implementing mechanisms. However, the record with these is such that they should only be established with the greatest caution, not least because of the risk that their cross-cutting nature

nature means that they may hinder the activities of other parts of government. Ultimately the question of whether inter-departmental coordination is more effective than establishing a special-purpose agency is an empirical question. The sector approach will facilitate much, though not all, of the necessary analysis and actions.

## Conclusions and recommendations

For the sector approach to be successful, donors and partner governments must recognise its scope and limitations. They must also be willing to consider a broad range of instruments through which the approach can be implemented. In general, the sector approach, and SIPs as a particular instrument, are most successful under conditions of macroeconomic stability and where the sector can be narrowly defined in terms of the ministries and institutions involved.

Where a SIP is not appropriate owing to the stringency of the preconditions, the underlying sector approach still has much to offer in terms of highlighting the need for prioritising resource allocations between sectors, establishing an expenditure programme and promoting more effective and efficient public management and administration. This may require disaggregating the approach to sub-sectors, particular services, or individual institutions.

Most importantly, for the sector approach to be effective against poverty, anti-poverty aims must be incorporated into a shared sector strategy, with interdepartmental coordination and commitment from both government and donors. In order to achieve this, care must be taken to ensure that the needs of the poor are well articulated and that the process is not hijacked by influential groups. Where the needs of the poor are not fully understood, it is unlikely that they will adequately be addressed, whatever policy instrument is used.

## Key references

DANIDA (1996) *Guidelines for Sector Programme Support (Including Project Support)*. Copenhagen: Ministry of Foreign Affairs.

DFID (1995) *Guidance Note on How to do Stakeholder Analysis of Aid Projects and Programmes*. Social Development Department, July 1995. London: DFID

Harrold, P. and associates (1995) *The Broad Sector Approach to Investment Lending: Sector Investment Programs*. World Bank Discussion Paper No. 302,. Washington D.C.: World Bank.

Human Development Network (1998) *Sector Wide Approaches: From Mythology to Reality*. Learning and Leadership Centre – course notes, February 1998.

Jones, S. (1997) *Sector Investment Programs in Africa – Issues and Experience.* World Bank Technical Paper No. 374,. Washington D.C.: World Bank.

Okidegbe, N. (1998 draft) *Agricultural Sector Investment Program – Sourcebook.* Washington D.C.: World Bank.

Stickings, J. (1998 draft) *Papers on Poverty and the RNR Sector: Issues and Experience – No. 1 Agriculture Sector Investment.* Chatham: NRI.

World Bank (1997) *Sector Investment Programs in Sub-Saharan Africa: Issues and Recommendations.* Findings No. 94 (September 1997).

## Endnotes

1 The authors of this paper acknowledge the assistance of Stephen Jones and James Gilling.

2 An APL is an instrument for serial loans under an approved overall programme with variable loan sizes and simplified approval processes. The loan is disbursed in phases which are designed to build on previous performance.

3 The essential features as defined by the World Bank (Harrold, 1995) are: (i) sector-wide scope; (ii) a coherent sector policy framework; (iii) local stakeholders in charge; (iv) all donors sign on; (v) common implementation arrangements; (vi) minimal expatriate technical assistance.

4 This is reflected in the White Paper: 'Where we have confidence in the policies and budgetary allocation process and in the capacity for effective implementation in the partner government, we will consider moving away from supporting specific projects to providing resources more strategically in support of sector-wide programmes or the economy as a whole. In this way the government concerned can develop the capacity to deliver services on a permanent basis' (para.2.22).

5 This classification is very close to the categories (enabling, inclusive and targeted) used in DFID's new Poverty Aim Marker System.

6 In Bangladesh, for instance, there is a range of programmes which can directly improve the income opportunities for middle-income groups and the rural poor. It is much more difficult to reach those who are so poor as to be nearly destitute.

# 3 Decentralisation and Sustainable Rural Livelihoods

*Ian Goldman*

## Introduction

During the 1980s, many developing country governments became interested in decentralisation as a means of regaining political legitimacy, to give people more of a voice in local affairs, or sometimes to gain partisan advantage. Later, donors came to consider decentralisation as a way of overcoming some of the difficulties of integrated rural development (IRD). These included IRD's neglect of local institutions and its centralised and complex approaches which led to bypass and the weakening of local institutions (e.g. through the creation of project management units). Decentralisation appeared to offer a locus for integrated rural development, an institution to deal with it (local government), and the potential for downsizing central government and promoting 'good governance'.

This chapter addresses the institutional issues relating to sustainable rural livelihoods, focusing in particular on decentralisation. In its analysis it considers people not just as clients (involved in a two-way service relationship) but as citizens who have fundamental rights to democratic accountability and to a role in decision-making about the services they receive. Adopting a 'citizen' approach is therefore participatory and empowering; it should make a significant contribution to the development of human and social capital.

The chapter is divided into two main sections. The first briefly reviews the arguments for and against decentralisation. The second considers the effects of decentralisation on the sustainability of rural livelihoods. A short conclusion follows.

# Decentralisation: A brief review

## *What is decentralisation?*

Decentralisation is essentially the transfer of the locus of power and decision-making, either downwards (sometimes referred to as vertical decentralisation) or to other units or organisations (sometimes referred to as horizontal decentralisation). The power that is transferred can be political, administrative or fiscal. Four types of decentralisation are commonly recognised, though in reality most situations entail a mixture of all four institutional types:

- *deconcentration*: vertical decentralisation within an organisation e.g. to local administrative offices of government
- *delegation*: vertically or horizontally to sub-national governments or parastatals
- *devolution*: whereby power is transferred to sub-national political entities such as states or local government
- *privatisation:* whereby power is delegated outside to the private sector (commercial or non-profit).

Privatisation will be treated as a separate debate and is not considered further.

## *What have been the results of decentralisation?*

While there is no conclusive evidence as to the impact of decentralisation on livelihoods, decentralisation does seem to have a positive effect on the performance and responsiveness of service delivery organisations.[1]
The main recorded **benefits** have been:

### Administrative – deconcentration

- a reduction in bureaucracy and improved responsiveness as government is brought closer to its clients/citizens
- institutional capacity-building at local level
- better scope for partnership development with organisations outside government
- the promotion of innovation (which is important if we are looking for new institutional responses to poverty).

### Political – devolution

- increased transparency and decreased corruption
- increased participation in decision-making (which tends to unlock the latent capacity of rural communities)
- increased job satisfaction and improved motivation as staff cohere in 'client-centric problem solving approaches to service delivery,

giving rise to trusting and respectful relationships between clients and public servants' (Tendler, quoted in Manor, 1997b:18)

- improved targeting of the poor
- better identification and implementation of micro-projects (e.g. through demand-driven rural investment funds (DDRIFs)).

### Fiscal

Decentralisation has proved to be a cost-effective way of administering government. Local government structures have usually increased the local resource base, both by collecting their own taxes and by lobbying for allocations from the centre.

The main **problems** reported with decentralisation are as follows:

### Administrative – deconcentration

- Accountability usually remains to the centre. This can increase central power, which now permeates much lower down, unless provision is made to develop a system of local accountability
- Traditional patron–client relations between administrators and villagers may prevent villagers from pressing their demands.

### Political – devolution

- The legal framework specifying the powers and responsibilities of local government is often unclear, which reduces accountability. This can be a particular problem where decentralisation is legislated quickly, often for political reasons, without thought as to how it will be implemented (as in Lesotho)
- Sometimes apparent devolution can also increase central political power (as happened in Zambia in the 1980s when District Governors were appointed by the ruling party and the right to vote was restricted to party members)
- Accountability in a devolved system often remains weak and more strongly oriented to the centre than to local voters. This can be a critical flaw
- Elites may capture new local government positions and then ignore the poor
- Local governments are often hamstrung by a lack of funds and so lose credibility
- What corruption remains tends to become more obvious. This can create the impression that corruption has in fact increased (this happened, for example, in Karnataka, India)
- Greater inequalities develop between communities and regions with different levels of organisational capacity
- There can be an expansion of unnecessary bureaucracy

- Decentralised authorities have a foreshortened time perspective, which can have a negative impact on issues such as the environment.

### Fiscal

- The raising of local taxes tends to be unpopular and difficult (as Crook (1994) found in Ghana), meaning that larger central contributions may be needed at the outset. Later, as local governments gain credibility, local contributions can rise.

(See Manor (1997a and b) for good review of issues, and the various Aiyar papers for short summaries)

## Sector–specific impacts

**There appears to be much scope for the deconcentration or decentralisation of many agricultural services**

The situation is more complex when one tries to differentiate the impact of decentralisation on various sectors. Once again it is difficult to isolate the impact of decentralisation on livelihoods. However, there is some evidence that decentralising health and education yields benefits for both livelihoods and organisational performance (Piriou-Sall, 1998; Smith, 1997; Parry, 1997). For example, Smith (1997) reports on results from Papua New Guinea which demonstrated substantial improvements in health (notably a lowering of infant, childhood and maternal mortality and increased life expectancy) as a result of devolution.

In the case of natural resource management there is also evidence that decentralisation of service provision is beneficial. Decentralised services are better able: to use locally adapted technologies; to support coordinated action by communities; to promote partnerships (Esmail, 1997; Goldman and Holdsworth, 1988); and to enable people to benefit from resources (such as

---

**Box 1: An example of devolution – Colombia**

Colombia instituted wide-ranging local government reforms in the 1980s. Municipalities were made responsible for local roads, water supply, sanitation, agricultural extension, primary education, health clinics and hospitals, and natural resource management. Each municipality has an extension office (UMATA), responsible for technical assistance to small farmers on agricultural, livestock, fishery, environmental, social and gender issues.[2] The UMATAs are funded by the municipal government, which receives budgetary transfers from central government and has access to matching grants from the national co-financing system (Fondo DRI). The UMATAs provide free extension services to some 450,000 small farmers out of an estimated total of 1,600,000 farmers. The UMATAs receive technical support and training from a programme of the Ministry of Agriculture which is largely responsible for monitoring and quality control.

Fiszbein (1997) undertook a study of the success of this overall devolution. Around three-quarters of municipalities surveyed had improved water supply, and expanded the road network. Road maintenance had also improved. The public had participated in choosing projects and had contributed free labour and materials. The greatest improvements occurred in more remote rural areas. In general 60–90% of people sampled said they trusted local government more than central government.

*Source:* Garfield *et al.* (n.d.); Aiyar *et al.*, 1995c.

parks) that would otherwise be under threat (Caldecott and Lutz, 1996). There appears to be much scope for the deconcentration or decentralisation of many agricultural services (except where conflict within the community and danger of capture by local elites is a serious risk). Box 1 gives some details of a very interesting decentralisation programme for agricultural services in Colombia.

Water supply and roads also show benefits from decentralisation (Garn *et al.* 1997; Humplink, 1997). The evidence suggests that technically more complex construction is best handled at higher levels, while maintenance and administration are best handled locally.

The following factors affect the relevance of decentralisation: economies of scale; complexity; diversity of clients; stability of the environment; size of units; whether activities will cross administrative boundaries; and what process to adopt if it is decided to go forward. These factors also impact on the type of coordination mechanisms which are appropriate, and the relevant type of organisation or network of organisations (Mintzberg, 1993).

Table 1 summarises the issues for various sectors. Table 2 draws implications for the provision of support to sustainable agriculture. Most factors favour decentralisation in this area.

## *Summary*

Decentralisation has considerable promise in:

- reversing the neglect of local institutional development
- improving development projects and making them more flexible and more sustainable
- enhancing government responsiveness
- increasing information flows between governments and citizens
- promoting greater participation and associational activity
- enhancing transparency and accountability
- achieving political renewal and integrating society with the state
- reinforcing and invigorating democracy at the national level
- promoting early warning of potential disasters
- carrying out small-scale regulatory functions.

It has at least modest promise in:

- reinforcing central government commitment to rural development
- broadening the project focus beyond agriculture
- reducing absenteeism among government employees
- promoting cooperation between NGOs and the government
- reducing regional disparities

## Table 1: Factors affecting decentralisation for different sectors

| | Sustainable agriculture | Water supply | Wildlife | Education | Health |
|---|---|---|---|---|---|
| **Economies of scale** | Only for large agro-processing and very large businesses | For large urban supplies | For large parks/major tourism ventures | For secondary schools/further education | For large specialist hospitals |
| **Technical system** | Small farmers – simple | Simple for basic systems, not major pump scheme | Complex knowledge of wildlife required | Simple | Complex for hospitals |
| **Complexity of environment** | Complex – local knowledge needed for appropriate solutions | Simple | Wide range of issues – attitudes of community/tourists/demand for land | Standardised | Standardised |
| **Diversity of clients, livelihood systems, etc.** | Depends on area – often very diverse | Not a major issue – some tension between household, industrial and agricultural use | Diverse – community, employees, tourists, 'guardians of biodiversity' with multiple uses | Standardised product little adapted to clients | Standardised product but depends on disease pattern |
| **Unit size/span of control** | Dealing with many small farmers | Many villages/wells/pumps. Few large schemes | Whole area can be dealt with in conservancy approach. Parks few/large | Dealing with large numbers of institutions | Dealing with large numbers of clinics and relatively few hospitals |
| **Cross area boundaries** | Large projects | Catchment management and major dams | Parks may well cross. Also conservancies | Further education and possibly secondary schools | For specialist hospitals/major campaigns, e.g. immunisation |
| **Stability** | Depends on rate of change, but can change year to year with agricultural cycle. Also effects of drought etc. | Depends on variability of rainfall | Depends on issues such as invasions, poaching, etc. | Stable as standardised and takes many years to feed through the system | Generally stable, but punctuated by epidemics when need for a crisis response |
| **Political issues** | Land – e.g. land reform. Subsidies | Availability. Location of schemes. Charging structure | Highly political as users often not local – if benefits do not accrue locally. Develop stakeholder forums | | |
| **Fiscal issues** | Payment for extension? Subsidies on inputs/crops. Tax on land/crops. Free-rider issues | Payment for water – differential payments for types of users | How does revenue accrue locally? | What payments system for infrastructure/maintenance/operation/inputs, e.g. books? | What payments system for infrastructure/maintenance/operation/inputs, e.g. medicines? |
| **Institutional issues** | Best handled locally – can be decentralised with specialised services provided centrally/regionally | Village water best locally, also municipal schemes. Bulk distribution perhaps regional. Catchment schemes regional | Must be local benefit and so link to decentralised structures, local government or community. Parks handled regionally/centrally | Primary schools can be handled locally; secondary locally or regionally. Further education handled regionally/centrally | Clinics/primary health care can be local, local hospitals – local/regional. Specialist hospitals – regional |

## Table 2: Implications for support to sustainable agriculture

| | Implications for sustainable agriculture |
|---|---|
| **Economies of scale** | Favours decentralisation |
| **Technical system** | Favours decentralisation |
| **Complexity of environment** | Favours decentralisation |
| **Diversity of clients, livelihood systems, etc.** | Favours decentralisation |
| **Unit size/span of control** | Varies – can mean efficacy of central mass media campaigns, also need for support to groups |
| **Cross area boundaries** | Only major projects<br>Favours decentralisation |
| **Stability** | Need for very flexible and organic system to respond to dynamic nature<br>Favours decentralisation |
| **Political issues** | Favours decentralisation<br>Issues such as land reform best driven centrally |
| **Fiscal issues** | Favours decentralisation, although if tax is to be raised, local politicians may have difficulties<br>Probably more difficult to raise fees than for education/health |
| **Institutional issues** | Extension services can be handled locally, specialist services (such as adaptive research, regional and basic research) should be national |

- tackling the problems of complexity and coordination
- paying greater attention to socio-cultural factors
- empowering women
- tailoring development to local conditions
- facilitating scaling up from successful pilot projects
- reducing corruption.

However, it has little to contribute to meeting the objectives of:

- alleviating poverty within an area (decentralisation should not be adopted to tackle poverty *per se*. It should be part of a package of other measures, including rules to guide spending and ensure that poverty is targeted)
- accelerating economic growth
- reducing overall government spending
- enhancing macro-economic coordination and stabilisation
- easing the problem of excessive agricultural taxation
- mobilising local taxes

- promoting planning from below (lower levels often lack skills and just produce wish lists)
- promoting mass community participation in projects (as many local governments are constituted well above village/community level).

## Decentralisation and sustainable rural livelihoods

The introductory chapter of this book highlights the need to build an understanding of rural livelihoods to inform any programmes of intervention. In deconcentration and devolution programmes, as with all institutional reform initiatives, a proper client/citizen needs analysis should form the basis for action (see Box 2). This should include analysis of local strengths and vulnerabilities and should lead to the development of appropriate strategies to eliminate poverty. Once these have been drawn up, consideration can be given to the most appropriate structures for implementation.

**In deconcentration and devolution programmes, a proper client/citizen needs analysis should form the basis for action**

The introductory chapter also proposes six intermediate objectives for DFID as it seeks to promote SRL. The first five of these objectives relate to building up the different capital assets in the SRL framework. Decentralisation can have a profound effect on people's access to particular assets, as follows.

### Natural capital

There is evidence that under decentralised systems, local people's ownership and role in the development of communal assets (such as nature reserves and parks) increase. Indeed, unless there is a community stake in such ventures, they are often at considerable risk. However, the short time horizons of many politicians can mean that it is unwise to hand complete responsibility for such resources to local government; there may well be a need for regional/national oversight to ensure sustainability. There is also danger in land reform being handled locally as the process can become derailed by local elites.

### Human capital

There is evidence of increased capacity building in decentralised systems. Such systems can help to overcome people's alienation from the state, increase women's participation and contribute to addressing the needs of the poor.

---

**Box 2: Lesotho – analysing client needs**

In Lesotho, the Agriculture Sector Investment Programme process has been deferred, and an Agricultural Policy and Capacity-building Project has been defined to support a devolution process. The Ministry of Agriculture will initially deconcentrate, then subsequently devolve some of its services to local government (a process which will run in parallel with reforms in other Ministries). As part of the ongoing reform process, the Ministry of Agriculture is undertaking district surveys using participatory methodologies to assess who is doing what with agriculture and to define and describe a set of client categories, resources and needs. These are used to develop an understanding of appropriate services as a basis for reform of the Department. For this to become a more 'citizen-oriented' approach, mechanisms for ongoing farmer involvement will also be required.

---

### Financial capital

Decentralisation may have a mixed effect on people's access to financial capital. At a community level, the amount of capital available may increase as more revenue is raised through local taxation. One of the success stories of local governments has been in the management of demand-driven rural investment funds (DDRIFs) which typically fund construction of small-scale infrastructure (either social or productive). There are successful examples of such funds in the Free State in South Africa, in Zimbabwe, Colombia and Brazil. However, increased taxation means that individuals may have fewer resources to invest in their own productive activities. Particular challenges can arise when communities are called upon to contribute in cash or kind to self-help projects but at the same time are asked to pay local taxes, sometimes apparently for similar things (e.g. roads). These problems are less apparent when decentralisation is accompanied by increased transfers from the centre.

### Social capital

Decentralised systems seem to be more effective at building partnerships than centralised systems. Where direct community involvement is required (e.g. for primary health care), decentralisation to local government is not sufficient: it is important to build direct community involvement (e.g. in health committees).

### Physical capital

Decentralised systems seem to be better at planning and funding the construction and maintenance of small-scale infrastructure than their centralised counterparts. Sometimes local people are directly contracted to maintain local infrastructure which builds the positive links between use, maintenance and – potentially – user charges. However, it may be more appropriate for construction and maintenance of larger-scale infrastructure to be contracted out or handled by a regional or national body.

The sixth proposed DFID objective ('policy and institutional environment which supports multiple livelihood strategies and promotes equitable access to competitive markets for all') is a directly institutional one. Its various components, and the effect of decentralisation on them, can be considered as follows:

### Policies and institutional environment

Experience with change management suggests that it is important to tackle the strategic apex of the policy environment as well as the bottom (i.e. decentralised levels of government). This means that the strategic planning, coordination, control and policy capacity of the organisation/sector should be developed simultaneously with work to improve the client interface.

### Supporting multiple livelihood strategies

From an implementation point of view, this is most easily addressed through

**One of the success stories of local governments has been in the management of demand-driven rural investment funds**

a devolved (i.e. non-sectoral) system in which activities are prioritised according to a needs analysis and expressed demand. This suggests the need to look at interventions with local government. Deconcentrated systems inevitably take a sectoral approach which is less appropriate.

**Promoting equitable access to competitive markets for all**

Ensuring equitable access within an area is not a strength of decentralised systems if local elites capture power. There are, though, examples of systems to ensure representation of the poor, or women, through seat quotas in decentralised bodies. It is also possible to steer the direction of services or funding by imposing criteria for the use of central government funds.

In short, then, this institutional objective seems most likely to be met through devolved systems in which there is some degree of local accountability and integration (although there are intervention strategies that can be applied in deconcentrated situations which should improve responsiveness to the needs of the poor).

## Conclusions

The sustainable rural livelihoods framework puts people at the centre of its analysis and programme for action. However, it explicitly recognises the importance of 'transforming structures', especially the various levels of governments and the non-government organisations which have such a profound effect upon people's livelihoods. Although there is some contrary evidence, decentralisation does seem to have a positive impact upon livelihoods. It is therefore important that DFID both supports existing programmes that involve decentralisation and learns lessons from these programmes so that experience gained can feed back into the design of future programmes.

Within **existing** projects DFID should:

- ensure that effective livelihood analysis has been conducted for current and potential clients and revise service concepts accordingly (this is just as vital in sectoral programmes as in more broad decentralisation programmes)
- consider whether actual service delivery (as opposed to strategic issues) could be handled by local government, privatised or deconcentrated
- in sectoral projects, work at strengthening the strategic apex as well as the lower-level units.

In its **future** work on decentralisation it should:

- ensure that there is high-level political support for decentralisation and that a weak Ministry of Local Government is not left to struggle with strong sectoral departments

- ensure that the political dimension is adequately covered (for example, support capacity-building with councillors and ministers and not just bureaucrats) – this should help limit accountability problems
- consider rule-based systems for decision-making (e.g. for DDRIFs) to help ensure that poverty is adequately targeted
- support increased transfers to promote devolution/deconcentration.

## Area-based projects

One way to integrate support to different sectors and to decentralisation is to place a significant emphasis on area-based projects, supporting local governments, such as DDSP Mpika in Zambia or the Pilot District Support Project in Zimbabwe. Support could be provided at either regional or local levels, but the units which are supported should have significant power over local development. Alternatively, DFID might work with the equivalent of the Ministry of Local Government to review potential or to experiment at local level. However, local government can be far from the village, and additional mechanisms may well be required to build in local responsiveness and involvement. This is a very important area for further work. There are, as yet, few models for integrating community-based planning and decision-making with a local government system.

**There are, as yet, few models for integrating community-based planning and decision-making with a local government system**

## Sector Investment Programmes

There is also the question of the relationships between decentralisation, SRLs and Sector Investment Programmes (SIPs). SIPs are inherently sectoral and usually centrally driven, which can put them in conflict with (the objectives of) decentralisation programmes. If they are not linked to a decentralisation or area-programme, they may be very negative in SRL terms. However, the Lesotho example of Box 2 shows how a SIP design process can result in a very different approach, focusing on capacity-building for deconcentration and later decentralisation. Indeed, McLean *et al.* (1997) suggest that SIPs can in fact foster decentralisation (effectively deconcentration), for example, through the creation of sectoral committees at district level.

## Types of programmes and projects

One of the major arguments for decentralisation is that it can provide a responsive, learning environment for development. Interventions in support of decentralisation should themselves be 'process projects', responsive and flexible, though with an appropriate orientation, milestones and support process agreed in advance. DFID should support projects with partners who are committed to a similar direction/objectives. It should also support project design that encourages learning and reflection (such as the Pilot District Support Project in Zimbabwe and the Rural Strategy Unit in Free State, South Africa) and gives adequate emphasis to monitoring and evaluation, a common weakness.

Overall, then, DFID has some good experience in supporting devolution and deconcentration which can and should be applied in developing institutional approaches to support sustainable rural livelihoods in the future.

## Key references

Aiyar, S., Parker, A. and Van Zyl, J. (1995a) 'Decentralisation: A New Strategy for Rural Development', World Bank Agriculture and Natural Resources Department, *Dissemination Note* No. 1. Washington D.C.: World Bank.

Aiyar, S., Parker, A. and Van Zyl, J. (1995b) 'How Well has Decentralisation Worked for Rural Development?', World Bank Agriculture and Natural Resources Department, *Dissemination Note* No. 2. Washington D.C.: World Bank.

Aiyar, S., Piriou-Sall, S., McLean, K. and Williams, M. (1996) 'The Political Economy of Democratic Decentralisation', World Bank Agriculture and Natural Resources Department, *Dissemination Note* No. 9. Washington D.C.: World Bank.

Carney, D. (1995) 'Management and Supply in Agriculture and Natural Resources: Is Decentralisation the Answer?', ODI *Natural Resource Perspectives* 4. London: Overseas Development Institute.

Mintzberg, H. (1993) *Structure in Fives: Developing Effective Organisations*. London: Prentice Hall.

Piriou-Sall, S. (1998) *Decentralisation and Rural Development: A review of evidence*. Washington D.C.: World Bank.

Silverman, J. (1992) 'Public Sector Decentralisation: Economic Policy and Sector Investment Programme', World Bank *Technical Paper* 188, Washington D.C.: World Bank.

## Other references

Aiyar, S., Parker, A. and Van Zyl, J. (1995c) 'Decentralisation Can Work: Experiences from Colombia', Agriculture and Natural Resources Department, *Dissemination Note* No. 3. Washington D.C.: World Bank.

Caldecott, J. and Ernst, L. (eds) (1996) *Decentralisation and Biodiversity Conservation: Issues and Experiences*. Washington, D.C.: World Bank.

Crook, R.C. (1994) 'Four Years of the Ghana District Assemblies in Operation: Decentralisation, Democratisation and Administrative Performance', *Public Administration and Development* 14, pp 339–64.

Esmail, T. (1997) *Designing and Scaling up Productive Natural Resource Management Programmes: Decentralisation and Institutions for Collective Action.* Washington D.C.: World Bank.

Fiszbein, A. (1997) *Decentralisation and Local Capacity: Some Thoughts on a Controversial Relationship.* Washington, D.C.: World Bank.

Garfield, E., Guadagni, M. and Moreau, D. (undated) *Colombia: Decentralisation of Agricultural Extension Services.* Washington D.C.: World Bank.

Garn, H.A., Katz, T. and Sara, J. (1997) *Lessons from Large-scale Rural Water and Sanitation Projects: transition and innovation.* Washington D.C.: World Bank.

Goldman, I. and Holdsworth, I. (1990) 'Agricultural Policies and the Small-Scale Producer', in Wood, A.P., Kean, S.A., Milimo, J.T. and Warren, D.M. (eds) *The Dynamics of Agricultural Policy and Reform in Zambia.* Des Moines: Iowa State University Press.

Humplick, F. and Moini-Araghi, A. (1996) 'Decentralised Structures for Providing Roads: A Cross Country Comparison', *Policy Research Working Paper* 1658, Washington D.C.: World Bank.

Manor, J. (1997a) *Explaining the Popularity of Decentralisation.* Washington D.C.: World Bank.

Manor, J. (1997b) *The Promise and Limitations of Decentralisation.* Washington D.C.: World Bank.

McLean, K. and Okidegbe, N. (1997) 'Sector Investment Programs can Foster Decentralisation: Emerging Lessons from Zambia', World Bank Agricultural and Natural Resources Department, *Dissemination Note* No. 14. Washington D.C.: World Bank.

Parry, T.R. (1997) 'Achieving Balance in Decentralisation: A Case Study of Education Decentralisation in Chile', *World Development* 25, pp 211–25.

Smith, B.C (1997) 'The Decentralisation of Health Care in Developing Countries: Organisational Options', *Public Administration and Development* 17, pp 399–412.

## Endnotes

1   Manor (1997b) suggests that it is too early to draw lessons. However, some programmes have been underway for many years, which suggests that there is a deficiency in monitoring and evaluation of decentralisation programmes.

2   A 'small farmer' is defined as one with less than two Family Agricultural Units. The definition of this unit is based on the requirement for extra-family labour and on the share of family income from agricultural activities (this should be at least 70% of total family income).

# 4 Livelihood Diversification and Sustainable Rural Livelihoods

*Frank Ellis*

---

*'Rural families increasingly come to resemble miniature highly diversified*
*conglomerates'*
*(Cain and McNicoll, 1988)*

## Introduction

The key point of departure for this chapter is that nowadays farming on its own rarely provides a sufficient means of survival in rural areas of low income countries. For this reason most rural households are found to depend on a diverse portfolio of activities and income sources, among which crop and livestock production feature alongside many other contributions to family wellbeing.

This diversification of sources of survival is not just a transient phenomenon, reflecting the uneven transition between full-time agriculture and full-time industry and services, which is how it conventionally tends to be interpreted. On the contrary, it appears to be enduring and pervasive in many low income countries, especially in sub-Saharan Africa (Bryceson, 1996). Livelihood diversification is widespread and is found in all locations, as well as across farm sizes and across ranges of income and wealth.

Available evidence on rural household income portfolios verifies the prevalence of livelihood diversification. The true picture is not one of farming combined with just the odd bit of wage work on a neighbour's farm, or in a nearby rural town centre. Most rural families have truly multiple income sources. This may indeed include off-farm wage work in agriculture, but it is also likely to involve wage work in non-farm activities, rural non-farm self-employment (e.g. trading), and remittances from urban areas and from abroad.

Studies show that between 30% and 50% of rural household income in sub-Saharan Africa is typically derived from non-farm sources (Sahn, 1994;

Reardon, 1997). In some regions, e.g. southern Africa, this can reach 80-90%. In South Asia, the average proportion is around 60%, reflecting in part the unequal land ownership structure in that region and the dependence of many landless or near landless families almost wholly on non-farm income sources for survival.

## Types of diversification

Diversification occurs for many different reasons. Underlying trends and processes include: rural population growth; farm fragmentation; and declining returns to farming compared to other activities (which in itself may occur due to rising real production costs or declining real prices or a combination of both). Household survival strategy reasons include risk reduction, overcoming income instability caused by seasonality, improving food security, taking advantage of opportunities provided by nearby or distant labour markets, generating cash in order to meet family objectives such as the education of children and, sometimes, the sheer necessity of survival following personal misfortune (e.g. accident, ill health or eviction) or natural and human disasters (e.g. drought, flood, civil war).

The distinction is often made between diversification for reasons of necessity and diversification by choice (Hart, 1994). In reality, there is a continuum of circumstances and reasons for diversifying income sources that vary for different families in different times and places. Clearly, extreme misfortune is more likely to result in people making involuntary decisions to diversify rather than voluntary ones.

It is useful for policy purposes to distinguish income sources between different categories and sub-categories. A basic division is between natural resource-based activities and non-natural resource-based activities or income sources. The former include collection or gathering, food cultivation, non-food cultivation (e.g. export crops), livestock keeping, pastoralism, and non-farm activities that depend on natural resources, such as brick making, weaving, thatching, and so on. The latter include rural trade (marketing of inputs and outputs), other rural services (e.g. vehicle repair), rural manufacture, remittances (urban and international), and other transfers such as pensions deriving from past formal sector employment.

A complementary way of categorising income sources often used by economists is to distinguish farm from off-farm and non-farm income sources (Saith, 1992). Some definitions follow:

### Farm income

This refers to income generated from own-account farming, whether on owner-occupied land or on land accessed via cash or share tenancy. Farm income, broadly defined, includes livestock as well as crop income, and comprises both consumption-in-kind of own farm output as well as the cash income obtained from output sold. In all cases, reference is to income net of cash outlays on production.

## Off-farm income

Off-farm income typically refers to wage or exchange labour on other farms (i.e. within agriculture). It may also include, although classifications sometimes differ in this respect, income obtained from local environmental resources such as firewood, charcoal, house building materials, wild plants, and so on.

## Non-farm income

Non-farm income refers to non-agricultural income sources. Several sub-categories of non-farm income are commonly identified. These are:

- non-farm, rural wage or salary employment
- non-farm, rural self-employment
- rental income obtained from leasing land or property
- urban-to-rural remittances arising from within national boundaries
- other urban transfers, e.g. pension payments to retirees
- international remittances arising from cross-border and overseas migration.

**Migration is one of the most important methods of diversifying rural livelihoods**

Migration is one of the most important methods of diversifying rural livelihoods, and it takes several different forms (Stark, 1991). Migration means that one or more family members leave the resident household for varying periods of time, and in so doing are able to make new and different contributions to its wellbeing (although such contributions are not guaranteed by the mere fact of migration). Some different types of migration are described briefly as follows:

## Seasonal migration

This refers to temporary migration according to agricultural season. It is typically associated with movement away in the slack season and the return of migrants for the peak periods of labour input in the agricultural calendar (mainly land preparation and harvesting).

## Circular migration

This refers to temporary migration that is not necessarily tied to seasonal factors in agriculture, and that may be for varying durations (sometimes dictated by cyclical needs for labour in non-farm labour markets). Circular migration implies that migrants routinely return to the resident household and regard that as their principal place of domicile; in other words, they do not set up permanent living arrangements in the places they go for temporary work.

### Permanent migration (rural–urban)

This implies that the family member makes a long-duration move to a different location, typically an urban area or a capital city, and sets up domicile at destination. In this instance the contribution to the rural resident household takes the form of regular or intermittent remittances back home. Clearly the capability to remit depends on the type and security of the livelihood of the migrant in the urban environment.

### International migration

The family member moves either temporarily or permanently abroad. There are many different variants of international migration corresponding to the distance travelled, the permanence of the movement, the type of work obtained in the destination country, and so on.

Remittances often feature strongly in rural income portfolios. For example, in Botswana in 1985–86, they corresponded to 24% of rural household incomes (Valentine, 1993). A comparative study of rural incomes undertaken in 13 countries in the 1980s found that around 15% of rural household incomes in Pakistan, Bangladesh and Sri Lanka was accounted for by remittances (von Braun and Pandya-Lorch, 1991). For these countries, remittances mainly stem from the temporary international migration of members of rural families to the Persian Gulf. For Pakistan this order of magnitude is confirmed by a more detailed study of rural incomes conducted over more than one annual cycle (Adams and He, 1995).

## Methods for investigating diversification

Most available evidence on rural household incomes results from large-scale, formal sample surveys, typically undertaken by central statistical offices of developing countries. Such surveys are primarily conducted for macroeconomic policy purposes; they constitute the basis for calculating cost-of-living indices, as well as contributing to the estimation of national accounts data. In this sense, the information they contain on the composition of rural household incomes is an incidental by-product of data collected for other purposes.

Practitioners in the field and specialist researchers would rarely wish to emulate the procedures of these countrywide surveys, due to logistical and cost reasons. Nor are they likely to find the data collection and processing of such surveys particularly helpful for getting at the detail of local livelihood strategies because one-visit collection of data on incomes is prone to numerous defects. The same is true more generally with respect to utilising secondary data sources, i.e. data collected for other purposes, as the basis for livelihoods analysis. Some common problems are:

- The timing of one-visit surveys (e.g. middle of the dry season, during the crop-growing period, just after harvest, one month after harvest, etc.) can make enormous differences in reported income.

- Many surveys collect data only from the household head, thus the cash earnings of other income-earning members of the household are inaccurately estimated or ignored.

- Some surveys report farm net income as if it corresponds to total household income, thus perpetuating the idea that small farmers depend solely on farming for their livelihoods.

- Many surveys fail to enquire whether there are absent household members who normally contribute income to the household.

- Non-farm self-employment poses particular difficulties for its contribution to net income because data is required on both revenues and costs, and recall in this area tends to be understandably inaccurate.

**A combination of participatory methods and small-scale sample surveys is likely to prove the most cost-effective means of determining the livelihood strategies of rural households**

For local and project purposes, a combination of participatory methods and small-scale sample surveys is likely to prove the most cost-effective means of determining the livelihood strategies of rural households. These two methods serve different and complementary purposes. Participatory methods are utilised to discover the broad patterns of activity that characterise livelihoods at village level. The chief sources of village income can be discussed in focus groups, and livelihood dynamics can be explored by seeking recollection of how these sources may have changed, say, over the past five or ten years. Aspects on which participatory methods can shed light include village infrastructure and services, gender differences in patterns of activity and, most importantly, identification of households into broad income groups as perceived by participants in discussion.

Participatory methods are insufficient on their own to distinguish the livelihood strategies of the poor from those of the better-off members of village society. For this, a small-scale household survey is required. This should take into account in its design the various factors already mentioned that can lead to inaccurate knowledge about income portfolios. With sample surveys of this kind there is an important trade-off between data accuracy, on the one hand, and sample representativeness on the other. The former requires the livelihoods of small numbers of households to be investigated in great detail while the latter requires large sample size. In practice, a compromise must be achieved between these two positions; a well-planned participatory component can be utilised to reduce the need for a large sample size, thus allowing more accurate data to be collected for small numbers of respondents.

The collection of income data is a sensitive matter that requires the building of trust between researchers and the households that are chosen for sample survey work. There are, of course, ways round this problem, such as identifying a research coordinator who is resident in the village and already held in respect by village members. While not always possible for reasons of time pressure, accurate livelihood research should involve repeat visits to the same households at different points over the calendar year, both to verify recall data collected previously and to gain an insight into the seasonality characteristics of livelihood strategies. Even with one-visit surveys, repeat visits after an interval of days to follow up on matters of detail with different household members are likely to result in much better research results than can be obtained from a single visit.

## Positive and negative effects of diversification on livelihoods

In general, diversification can be said to have a positive impact on livelihoods if it makes them more secure, reduces the adverse impacts of seasonality, and helps to raise poor rural households out of the poverty trap. In other words, diversification is positive if it reduces the *vulnerability* of individuals and households to deprivation and disaster (where vulnerability is taken to mean proneness to stress and shocks). Conversely, diversification has a negative effect on livelihoods if it increases the vulnerability of households. Other factors can also enter these comparisons. A time factor is evidently important, i.e. whether the livelihood portfolio that is adopted is sustainable in the longer term (within this, the sustainable use of environmental resources, whether for gathering purposes, or for grazing, or for farming systems, is a key area of policy concern).

**Positive impacts** of diversification include consumption smoothing, risk reduction, more complete use of available household labour and skills, cash generation for investment in human or physical capital, more opportunities for women to exercise independent economic decision-making and, in some circumstances, improvement in natural environments or reduced pressure on environmental resources. Some relevant points are as follows.

### *Seasonality*

Diversification of income sources can help to ameliorate the adverse effects of seasonality on the income security of the household. Seasonality causes peaks and troughs in labour utilisation on the farm, and creates livelihood insecurity due to the mismatch between highly uneven farm income streams and continuous consumption requirements. The more that diversification involves activities the seasonal cycles of which are not synchronised with the farm's own seasons, the greater the potential for smoothing out uneven labour use and income flows.

## Risk reduction

Diversification can greatly reduce the risk of income failure confronted by the household. Reliance on income sources that are prone to annual fluctuations in outcomes, as is typical of rainfed farming systems in the tropics, places the rural household at high risk of income failure. In a similar way to seasonality, the key to risk reduction is to seek income sources that exhibit low covariate risk between them. This means that the factors that create risk for one income source (e.g. climate) should not be the same as the factors that create risk for another income source (e.g. urban job insecurity).

## Higher income

Diversification may simply achieve higher income than is possible by specialising in the single occupation of farming. It can do this by making better use of available resources and skills (see Seasonality above), and taking advantage of spatially dispersed income-earning opportunities. It can also do this by enabling the household to generate cash resources that can then be used to improve income-earning potential in the future.

## Asset improvement

Poverty is strongly associated with a lack of assets, or the inability to put assets to productive use (e.g. Moser, 1998). Assets in this context include human capital (the education and skills of household members), physical capital (e.g. farm equipment or a sewing machine), social capital (the social networks and associations to which people belong) and natural capital (the natural resource base). Cash resources obtained from diversification may be used to invest in, or improve the quality of, any or all of these classes of assets, for example, sending children to secondary school or buying equipment such as a bicycle that can be used to enhance income-generating opportunities.

## Environmental benefits

Diversification can potentially provide environmental benefits in two ways. One is by generating resources that are then invested in improving the quality of the natural resource base (the Machakos case in Kenya is often held up as an example of the investment of urban wage earnings in environmental rehabilitation). The second is by providing options that make time spent in exploiting natural resources, such as gathering activities in forests, less remunerative than time spent doing other things.

## Gender benefits

It is possible for diversification to improve the independent income-generating capabilities of women and, in so doing, also improve the care and nutritional status of children (since it is reasonably well established that cash income in the hands of women tends to be spent proportionally more on family welfare than cash income in the hands of men). For this to occur, activities need to arise in rural areas that are accessible to women. This usually means a location close to sites of residence and types of work for which women will have access to qualifications that are equal to or better than those of men.

The **negative effects** of diversification are often the converse of the positive ones, and reflect the different circumstances that arise historically in different locations. Diversification may have negative effects on rural income distribution, agricultural productivity, diversion of resources into unproductive networking (Berry, 1989) and adverse gender effects. Some points are as follows:

## Income distribution

Diversification can be associated with widening disparities between the incomes of the rich and poor in rural areas. This occurs because the diversification options of the better off are in more highly paid and secure labour markets than those that are open to the poor. For example, the rich may be able to secure permanent full-time jobs for family members in government or business, while the poor are only able to secure part-time and casual work at low wage rates. This in turn reflects the different asset positions of rural families, with those possessing high levels of human capital (education and skills) being in a better position to take advantage of opportunities that arise than those who are not so well endowed (Dercon and Krishnan, 1996). The same is true of all the different forms of wealth, including cattle held for wealth purposes.

## Farm output

Some types of livelihood diversification may result in the stagnation or decline of output on the home farm. This typically occurs when there are buoyant distant labour markets for male labour. These may stimulate the exit from agriculture of the male, the young and the educated, resulting in depletion of the labour force required to undertake peak farm production demands, such as land preparation and harvesting. This occurred in southern Africa in the 1970s and 1980s when many rural households came to depend on remittances from migrants to urban areas in South Africa for their food security (Low, 1986). It has also been observed in fast-growing Asian economies (e.g. Indonesia) where abandonment of rice paddies occurred due to the abundance of non-farm wage work in towns and cities (Preston, 1989).

## Adverse gender effects

Adverse effects on the gender balance of the household and, specifically, on the role and status of women are associated with the type of diversification that is also held to have adverse effects on agriculture. Where it is male labour that is predominantly able to take advantage of diversification opportunities, then women may be even more likely to be relegated to the domestic sphere and to eking out a livelihood from subsistence food production. A high level of male migration is also associated with the prevalence of female-headed households in rural areas. However, previous assumptions that such households are inevitably disadvantaged compared to male-headed households have not been substantiated by empirical research (Lipton and Ravallion, 1995).

**The positive effects of diversification outweigh the negative effects**

From a poverty reduction perspective the positive effects of diversification outweigh the negative effects. The positive effects tend to be generalised beneficial impacts of wide applicability (e.g. risk reduction; mitigating seasonality) while the negative effects typically occur when labour markets happen to have worked in particular ways in particular places. The conclusion is that removal of constraints to, and expansion of opportunities for, diversification are desirable policy objectives because they give individuals and households more options to improve livelihood security and to raise their own living standards (Ellis, 1998).

## Scope for external intervention

There is wide scope for intervention in support of rural livelihood diversification, and for improving the probability that diversification will have generally beneficial effects on rural welfare, rather than the negative effects that are sometimes attributed to it. Such intervention does not mean increasing the role of the state in particular economic sub-sectors, nor does it mean manipulating prices and costs in order to achieve specified outcomes. Rather it is about improving the institutional context of private decision-making by, for example, reducing risk, increasing mobility, minimising barriers to entry (e.g. licensing regulations) and ensuring fairness and transparency in the conduct of public agencies. It is also about helping the poor to identify opportunities, and facilitating them to improve their assets and income-generating capabilities.

Many policies that are conducive to income diversification by the poor fall outside the arena of natural resource policy. These include: macroeconomic policies (including stabilisation, adjustment, privatisation and market liberalisation); good governance policies designed to improve transparency, predictability and fairness in the operations of state agencies; infrastructure policies and projects including rural road construction and rural electrification; and education policies and programmes.

Market liberalisation has been shown to play a positive role in improving the diversification options of rural families, by reducing the profile in the economy of state and parastatal agencies that formerly curtailed diversity and constrained opportunities and outcomes. For example, a meticulously conducted participatory study done in a cross-section of Tanzanian villages in the early 1990s discovered that increased options for non-farm income generation were regarded by villagers as the single most significant change in their lives, resulting at that point from new economic policies (Booth *et al.*, 1993). Level of education has also been shown to have a substantial impact on the diversification capabilities of individuals and families.

## Criteria for natural resource policies and projects

From an NR policy point of view, the adoption of a livelihood diversification perspective should be seen as complementary to conventional NR priorities and as providing a framework within which to situate them:

- NR policy is fundamentally about improving the productivity of resources in agriculture, including livestock
- NR policy is also about people's interactions with off-farm environmental resources for livelihood purposes, and it seeks to secure sustainable natural resource use in this respect.

**No matter how diverse the livelihoods of rural families are, crop and livestock production continues to constitute a predominant component of their incomes**

These policy priorities remain sound. It is recognised that no matter how diverse the livelihoods of rural families are, crop and livestock production continues to constitute a predominant component of their incomes, either directly or indirectly (i.e. via trading, processing, input supply, and so on). Moreover, agricultural performance remains fundamental to food security, locally and nationally, in countries that cannot afford to make regular use of international markets for large-scale food imports.

Nevertheless, the past neglect of livelihood considerations has sometimes resulted in NR policies and projects that have been insensitive to local priorities, mistaken in their assumptions about the availability of time (e.g. people not turning up for extension meetings) and misdirected towards the better-off in rural communities rather than the rural poor.

Reference to livelihood criteria could result in projects that are more attuned to the livelihood strategies pursued by the poor, and therefore more accurate in their targeting of the poor rather than better-off social groups. As we have seen, diversification plays an important role at household level precisely in achieving objectives of reducing vulnerability and raising incomes. These efforts by households themselves should be recognised and supported in NR policies whenever it is appropriate and feasible to do so.

A livelihood approach starts off by focusing on people, their assets and their activities, rather than on sectors and their performance (which is the conventional point of entry to policy). The approach yields a number of generalised statements about the livelihoods of the rural poor that could potentially be utilised to formulate a set of 'livelihood criteria' to be taken into account in evaluating the merits of natural resource project proposals, and for seeking to strengthen the poverty reduction content of policy or project formulation and implementation. A tentative list of points contributing to such livelihood criteria for natural resource policies is as follows.

- Remoteness is typically associated with greater poverty and fewer livelihood options, and therefore it may be valid to target remote locations rather than those places already well integrated into diverse economic activities. However, remoteness may also mean fewer absolute numbers of poor people, so this is not an unambiguous criterion.

- There is a high degree of correlation between poverty and lack of assets, especially lack of access to land as an asset, but also human capital (especially education), physical capital, financial capital (credit), and so on. For this reason, projects that target individuals or families who already possess assets are likely to improve the incomes of those who are already better off, rather than those of the truly poor. Indeed, farm policies may have this effect sometimes due to the not always correct suppositions:

  - that the poor are mainly poor farmers

  - that there are multiplier effects of rising farm income beneficial to the assetless poor.

  This point is illustrated by the rural Pakistan case (Adams and He, 1995) where the poor are livestock keepers rather than cultivators, and past farm policies have invariably supported crops more than livestock. It is also true that people who already possess assets typically find it easier to substitute one type of asset for another or to use their assets to substitute one type of activity for another. Therefore, it is the assetless, or those who have difficulty in making use of their assets, who need to be assisted in poverty reduction policies.

- The ability to substitute is always worth considering in a wide variety of project situations; for example, if a project objective were to reduce the pressure on a forest used for gathering purposes by local communities, then the substitution possibilities must be identified, supported and promoted. Substitution between activities is therefore a key feature of recognising the role of diversification in livelihood security.

- Poverty reduction requires facilitating the widening of choices and options. Being poor is often a case of being trapped with no options, therefore attention must be paid to actions that increase flexibility, encourage mobility and reduce any regulatory inhibitions on activities, movement and permissible courses of action.

These livelihood criteria can be summarised under the four headings of **location**, **assets**, **substitution** and **options**. To this list should be added **knowledge** about the livelihood strategies of the constituency that a policy or project is supposedly designed to help. Perhaps one of the key conclusions to emerge from livelihood research is that you cannot proceed by making untested assumptions about the survival strategies of rural families. You cannot, for example, just assume from appearances that a particular rural social group is mainly dependent on the production of a particular crop or farming system for its livelihood. Investigation is likely to show that livelihood strategies are a great deal more complicated than that and, most importantly, there will certainly be big differences between the poor and the better off with regard to which sources of income are most important in their respective livelihood strategies.

## Key References

Adams, R.H. and He, J.J. (1995) *Sources of Income Inequality and Poverty in Rural Pakistan.* Research Report No.102, Washington D.C.: International Food Policy Research Institute.

Bryceson, D.F. (1996) 'Deagrarianization and Rural Employment in Sub-Saharan Africa: A Sectoral Perspective', *World Development* 24(1) pp 97-111.

Ellis, F. (1998) 'Household Strategies and Rural Livelihood Diversification', *Journal of Development Studies* 35(1), forthcoming.

Moser, C.O.N. (1998) 'The Asset Vulnerability Framework: Reassessing Urban Poverty Reduction Strategies', *World Development* 26(1) pp 1–19.

Reardon, T. (1997) 'Using Evidence of Household Income Diversification to Inform Study of the Rural Non-Farm Labor Market in Africa', *World Development* 25(5) pp 735–47.

von Braun, J. and Pandya-Lorch, R. (eds) (1991) *Income Sources of Malnourished People in Rural Areas: Microlevel Information and Policy Implications.* Working Paper on Commercialization of Agriculture and Nutrition No.5. Washington D.C.: International Food Policy Research Institute.

## Other references

Berry, S. (1989) 'Social Institutions and Access to Resources', *Africa* 59(1) pp 41–55.

Booth, D., Lugangira, F. *et al.* (1993) *Social, Cultural and Economic Change in Contemporary Tanzania: A People-Oriented Focus.* Stockholm: SIDA.

Cain, M. and McNicoll, G. (1988) 'Population Growth and Agrarian Outcomes', in Lee, R.E., Arthur, W.B., Kelly, A.C., Rodgers, G. and Srinivasan, T.N. (eds) *Population, Food and Rural Development.* Oxford: Clarendon Press, pp 101–117.

Dercon, S. and Krishnan. P. (1996) 'Income Portfolios in Rural Ethiopia and Tanzania: Choices and Constraints.' *Journal of Development Studies* 32(6) pp 850–75.

Hart, G. (1994) 'The Dynamics of Diversification in an Asian Rice Region', in Koppel, B. *et al.* (eds) *Development or Deterioration?: Work in Rural Asia.* Boulder, Colorado: Lynne Reinner, pp 47–71.

Lipton, M. and Ravallion, M. (1995) 'Poverty and Policy', in Behrman, J. and Srinivasan, T.N. (eds) *Handbook of Development Economics Vol.IIIB*, Amsterdam: Elsevier, pp 2551–657.

Low, A. (1986) *Agricultural Development in Southern Africa: Farm Household Theory and the Food Crisis.* London: James Currey.

Preston, D.A. (1989) 'Too Busy to Farm: Under-Utilization of Farm Land in Central Java', *Journal of Development Studies* 26(1).

Sahn, D.E. (1994) 'The Impact of Macroeconomic Adjustment on Incomes, Health and Nutrition: Sub-Saharan Africa in the 1980s', in Cornia, G.A. and Helleiner, G.K. (eds) *From Adjustment to Development in Africa: Conflict, Controversy, Convergence, Consensus?.* London: Macmillan.

Saith, A. (1992) *The Rural Non-Farm Economy: Processes and Policies.* Geneva: International Labour Office, World Employment Programme.

Stark, O. (1991) *The Migration of Labor.* Cambridge, Mass.: Basil Blackwell.

Valentine, T.R. (1993) 'Drought, Transfer Entitlements, and Income Distribution: The Botswana Experience', *World Development* 21(1) pp 109–126.

# 5 Rural–Urban Linkages and Sustainable Rural Livelihoods

*Cecilia Tacoli*

## Introduction

Most development theory and practice is implicitly based on the dichotomy between 'rural' and 'urban' areas, populations and activities. This is reflected in the division of policies along spatial and sectoral lines, with urban planners usually concentrating on urban nodes and giving scant attention to agricultural or rural-led development, while rural development planners tend to ignore urban centres and define rural areas as consisting only of villages and their agricultural land.

This, however, does not reflect the reality of households' livelihoods, which often include both rural and urban elements. For example, many urban enterprises rely on demand from rural consumers, and access to urban markets and services is crucial for most agricultural producers. In both rural and urban areas, a significant proportion of households rely on income diversification and on the combination of agricultural and non-agricultural income sources.

Rural–urban interactions can be divided into two categories. In the first category are linkages across space (such as flows of people, goods, money and information and wastes). In the second category are 'sectoral interactions', which include 'rural' activities taking place in urban areas (such as urban agriculture) or activities often classified as 'urban' (such as manufacturing and services) which take place in rural areas.

Rural–urban linkages are influenced and often intensified by current transformations at the macro-level, including structural adjustment and economic reform, which have affected both urban and rural populations. Job insecurity and general increases in prices in the urban areas make it more and more difficult for urban dwellers to support their relatives in home areas (Potts and Mutambirwa, 1998). Trade liberalisation and the growth of export-oriented agriculture have also resulted in the marginalisation of small farmers who must turn to non-agricultural rural employment or migrate to the towns. However, rural–urban linkages also vary according to local historical, political, socio-cultural and ecological factors. Spatial development policies which have attempted to integrate rural and urban dimensions have often failed because they were based on inaccurate generalisations about the relationship between the two.

## Definitions of 'rural' and 'urban'

The division between 'urban' and 'rural' policies is based on the assumption that the physical distinction between the two areas is self-explanatory and uncontroversial. However, there are three major problems with this view. The first is that demographic and economic criteria used to define what is 'urban' and what is 'rural' can vary widely between nations, making generalisations problematic (Box 1).

A second problem is that of the definition of urban boundaries. In south east Asia's Extended Metropolitan Regions, agriculture, cottage industry, industrial estates, suburban developments and other types of land use coexist in areas with a radius as large as 100 km. The population in such areas is highly mobile with many people involved in circular migration and commuting (Firman, 1996). In sub-Saharan Africa, agriculture still prevails in peri-urban areas, but significant shifts in land ownership and employment patterns are taking place, often at the expense of the poor, both rural and urban (Box 2).

The third problem in the definition of the boundaries between 'rural' and 'urban' areas lies in the fact that urban residents and enterprises depend on an area significantly larger than the built-up area for basic resources and ecological functions. In general, the larger and wealthier the city, the more its industrial base and its wealthy consumers will draw on such resources and ecological functions from beyond its surrounding region (McGranahan *et al.*, 1996). The concept of a city's 'ecological footprint' was developed to quantify the land area on which any city's inhabitants depend for food, water and other renewable resources (such as fuelwood), and the absorption of carbon to compensate for the carbon dioxide emitted from fossil fuel use (Rees, 1992). The concept makes clear that any city will be dependent upon the resources and ecological functions of an area considerably larger than itself (although urban areas

---

**Box 1: Variations in the definition of urban centres**

Asia remains a predominantly 'rural' continent; two-thirds of its population lived in rural areas in 1990. However, if both India and China were to change their definition of urban centres to one based on a relatively low population threshold of 2,000 or 2,500 inhabitants – as used by many Latin American and European nations – a large proportion of their population would change from being classified as 'rural' to an 'urban' classification. Given the fact that India and China have a high share of Asia's population, this in turn would significantly change Asia's level of urbanisation – and even change the world's level of urbanisation by a few percentage points (UNCHS, 1996).

---

**Box 2: Land use conversion in the Philippines**

In Manila's extended metropolitan region, large swathes of rice land have been converted to industrial, residential and recreational uses. Alternatively, land may simply lie idle, with cattle grazing on grassed-over rice fields whose owners await either development permits or more propitious market conditions. Although the 1988 Land Reform Law protects from conversion lands eligible for redistribution from landlord to tenant farmer, it has in fact accelerated the process of land conversion. This is because landlords keen to avoid losing their land have converted it to non-agricultural uses, and in many cases tenant farmers have been evicted and the land left idle (Kelly, 1998).

---

with limited industrial bases and low-income populations will have much smaller and generally more local ecological footprints than large and prosperous cities).

## Flows of people

Internal migration is often seen as essentially rural-to-urban and as contributing to uncontrolled growth and related urban management problems in many large cities in the South. This has resulted in many policies to control or discourage migration. Seldom is migration actually restricted by such policies. Rather, efforts are made to render cities inhospitable (for example by bulldozing informal low-income settlements) or to make it difficult for new migrants to secure property rights to land or access to public services. These measures generally have little impact aside from lowering welfare, especially for the poor.

In fact, most of the growth in urban population is due to natural increase within the community. Further, since rural-to-urban migration is most common where economic growth is highest (migrants tend to move to places where they are likely to find employment opportunities), this movement is not in reality as problematic as it is made out to be (UNCHS, 1996). In addition, secondary urban centres, have recently attracted new investment and industries which would previously have been directed to large cities, especially in Latin America. As a consequence, they have also increased their role as destinations, which takes the pressure off the larger cities.

Despite widely held beliefs that flows are always rural-to-urban, migration from urban to rural areas is also increasing. This type of movement is often associated with economic decline and increasing poverty. In sub-Saharan Africa, significant numbers of retrenched urban workers are thought to have returned to rural 'home' areas where the cost of living is lower (Potts, 1995). Seasonal waged agricultural work in rural areas can also provide temporary employment for low-income urban groups (Kamete, 1998). Temporary and seasonal movement such as this is not reflected in census figures, and can make 'static' enumerations of rural and urban populations unreliable.

Complexity in migration direction and duration is matched by complexity in the composition of the flows, which reflect wider socio-economic dynamics. The number of migrant women has increased in many countries in the South (although there are important regional variations). The age and gender of those who move and those who stay can have a significant impact on source areas in terms of labour availability, remittances, household organisation and agricultural production systems. In some cases, those who leave retain control over the decision-making about natural resources and production. This can limit the impact of policy and project interventions at village level.

## Multi-spatial households

Household membership is usually defined as those who 'share the same pot', under the same roof. However, the strong commitments and obligations between rural-based and urban-based individuals and units show that in many instances these are 'multi-spatial households', in which reciprocal support is provided across space. For example, remittances from urban-based members can be an important income source for the rural-based members, who in turn may look after their migrant relatives' children and property. These linkages can be crucial in the livelihood strategies of the poor, but are not usually taken into consideration in policy-making (Box 3).

## Flows of goods

Exchanges of goods between urban and rural areas are an essential element of rural–urban linkages. The 'virtuous circle' model of rural–urban development emphasises efficient economic linkages and physical infrastructure connecting farmers and other rural producers with both domestic and external markets. This involves three phases:

---

**Box 3: Multi-spatial households**

In Old Naledi, a low-income settlement of Gaborone (Botswana), a third of all households own cattle and half retain land in their home village. This proportion does not decline with the length that people stay in the city. Rural assets have both monetary and social value and serve as a safety net for low-income households with uncertain livelihood prospects in the city. Despite the fact that most of these urban-based households have no other assets, they are not eligible to relief or aid in case of asset loss as these measures are designed exclusively for rural dwellers (Krüger, 1998).

In Durban (South Africa), maintaining both an urban and a rural base also provides a safety net for low-income city dwellers in times of economic hardship or political violence. However, housing and rural development programmes do not acknowledge such multi-spatial, extended households: eligibility to subsidies and grants is based on the size of the co-resident household (either in town or in the countryside) and the funds can be used in only one of the two locations. Since urban housing subsidies are more widely available this may encourage urban-based members of multi-spatial households to cut their rural links (Smit, 1998).

---

**Box 4: Market access and control in Senegal's charcoal trade**

In Senegal, forests are officially owned by the state and managed by the Forest Service which allocates commercial rights to urban-based merchants through licences, permits and quotas. Village chiefs control direct forest access, ultimately deciding whether to allow merchants' woodcutters into the forests. Despite their control, villagers reap only a small portion of the profits from commercial forestry. More substantial benefits accrue to merchants and wholesalers who, through their social relations, control access to forestry markets, labour opportunities and urban distribution, as well as access to state agents and officials. Local control and management of natural resources is therefore weakened because of a lack of economic incentives (Ribot, 1998).

---

1.  Rural households earn higher incomes from the production of agricultural goods for non-local markets, and increase their demand for consumer goods.

2.  This leads to the creation of non-farm jobs and employment diversification, especially in small towns close to agricultural production areas.

3.  Which in turn absorbs surplus rural labour, raises demand for agricultural produce and again boosts agricultural productivity and rural incomes (Evans, 1990; UNDP/UNCHS, 1995).

However, spatial proximity to markets does not necessarily improve farmers' access to the inputs and services required to increase agricultural productivity. Access to land, capital and labour may be far more important in determining the extent to which farmers are able to benefit from urban markets. In Paraguay, despite their proximity to the capital city, smallholders' production is hardly stimulated by urban markets as their low incomes do not allow investment in cash crops or in production intensification to compensate for their lack of land (Zoomers and Kleinpenning, 1996). Patterns of attendance at periodic markets also show that distance is a much less important issue than rural consumers' income and purchasing power in determining demand for manufactured goods, inputs and services (Morris, 1997).

Markets are also social institutions in which some actors are able to enforce mechanisms of control which favour access for specific groups and exclude others (Box 4). Grain markets in south Asia tend to be dominated by large local merchants who control access to the means of distribution (transport, sites, capital, credit and information); even in the petty retailing subsector, caste and gender are major entry barriers (Harriss–White, 1995).

## Sectoral interactions

The growth of urban agriculture since the 1970s has long been understood as a response to escalating poverty and rising food prices or shortages, often exacerbated by structural adjustment and economic reform. Recent research shows that its nature may be changing and that, at least in low-income nations, a significant proportion of high- and middle-income urban farmers engage in commercial production (Mbiba, 1995). More needs to be learned about how this may affect access to urban food markets for producers, especially smallholders, from surrounding rural areas.

**The increase in non-agricultural rural employment is an on-going process in most countries in the South**

The increase in non-agricultural rural employment, or deagrarianisation, is an ongoing process in most countries in the South. There are several reasons for this. Among them, environmental degradation, population growth and land subdivision make it difficult for large numbers of farmers in many regions to rely solely on agriculture. Access to non-agricultural rural employment is mediated by culturally specific formal and informal networks, which may be based on income, political and/or religious affiliation, ethnicity, household type, gender and generation. This can constrain some groups' access to the opportunities provided by deagrarianisation and occupational diversification.

## Urban centres and rural development

Since the 1970s, comprehensive rural–urban development frameworks have been formulated as an explicit attempt to promote rural development, and with the implicit aim of curbing migration to large cities. Integrated Rural Development has contributed to the view of rural development as holistic and multi-faceted and as comprising non-agricultural as well as agricultural activities. However, IRDPs rarely have explicit urban components and where spatial dimensions are included, they are usually limited to marketing functions.

Other attempts take urban centres as their starting point. In the 'urban functions in rural development' (UFRD) approach, the strategy for promoting rural development is to develop a network of small, medium-sized and larger centres, each providing centrally located functions (such as services, facilities and infrastructure) hierarchically organised (Rondinelli and Ruddle, 1978). Rural development is expected to be stimulated by filling in the supposedly missing functions (for example, banking services) through selective investment in rural towns (Box 5). Translating this model into practice has been problematic for three main reasons.

- 'Urban functions' are assumed to benefit the entire surrounding region and all rural households, irrespective of social and economic status – issues of access and control are not considered.

- The methods for selecting key towns for investment are not clear, and tend to focus only on the attributes of the towns themselves, with no consideration of the rural potential.

- The model is based on generalisations which do not account for the rich variety in the roles of urban centres, which are determined by both the rural and regional context.

---

### Box 5: Application of the UFRD approach in the Philippines

This USAID-funded programme was carried out in the Bicol Region in the late 1970s. A study conducted ten years later found that the selected towns were not performing the 'missing' functions and were themselves stagnating. Among the main reasons were that:

❍ the identified functions did not support rural development but rather the urban-based military and civil service personnel

❍ transport linkages to larger towns did not encourage the marketing and commercial functions of local towns, which were by-passed, and

❍ since agricultural productivity did not increase, rural household expenditures for non-agricultural goods and services did not rise and did not stimulate the 'virtuous circle' of urban and rural expansion (Koppel, 1987).

---

The underlying conceptual problem is the assumption that it is an absence of 'central places' that constrains development, rather than factors such as ecological capacity, land-owning structures, crop types and control on crop prices or access to markets (all of which in turn are shaped by rural–urban interactions within the specific regional context).

A third position on the role of small towns in rural development can be defined as 'intermediate' (Hardoy and Satterthwaite, 1986). Drawing on empirical case studies from Africa, Asia and Latin America, it shows that universal generalisations and prescriptions, which form the basis of most spatial planning models, are not valid. Centralised policies, which do not take into account the peculiarities and specifics of small towns and their regions, may not be efficient. Real decentralisation of decision-making with investment and resource-raising at the local level may allow the articulation of local needs and priorities and stimulate both rural and urban development (Box 6). However, wider socio–economic issues such as inequitable land-owning structures and government crop purchasing policies and taxation are also likely to affect small towns and, by extension, migration to larger cities.

---

### Box 6: Positive links between rural and urban development

The Upper Valley of the Rio Negro and Nequen in Argentina shows how rapid growth in agricultural production can be accompanied by rapid growth in employment linked to agriculture and urban growth. The Upper Valley is linked by railway to Buenos Aires, giving local farmers access to both national and international markets. In the 1950s the area acquired provincial status, which increased the power and resources available to the local government. The land-owning structure is relatively equitable. Most of the land is cultivated by farmer-owners with sufficient capital to invest in intensive production, mainly fruit trees. The growing number of prosperous farmers has provided a considerable stimulus to local urban growth, with a chain of small centres developing along the railway. Urban-based enterprises were stimulated by demand from agricultural producers both as forward linkages (cold storage plants, industries producing packaging material, plants for processing into juices, jams, dried or tinned fruit) and as backward linkages (production of inputs such as fertilisers and pesticides, or tools and machinery) (Manzanal and Vapnarsky, 1986).

---

# Methods for investigating rural–urban linkages

**It is important to identify bottlenecks which prevent positive interactions**

Rural–urban linkages can follow quite different paths. For local and project research, it is important to identify bottlenecks which prevent positive interactions. This can be done through the analysis of the patterns of different flows (of people, of goods and of the related flows of money and information) and subsequently through the analysis of their combined impact on rural–urban linkages. This holistic approach requires that both the rural and the urban components of the flows' trajectories are included in the analysis. For example, migration should be examined in terms of both labour supply and labour demand. In flows of goods, access to market price information and to the actual marketplaces should be considered.

The trajectories of the flows are not usually limited to within the regional boundaries of a town and its hinterland. Migrants can go to a variety of places, including international destinations, and goods and services can be sold and purchased in many different locations. From the perspective of a rural household, the pattern of flows is thus more likely to resemble a network involving multiple linkages with a number of villages and towns, rather than revolving around a single urban centre (Douglass, 1998). The focus should therefore be on regional networks rather than on dyadic relations between a single village and a single centre. The initial demarcation of these networks can be based on the existing flows of goods and people between settlements.

Secondary data are not a reliable source of information, especially for population flows, since circular and temporary migration are not usually recorded in censuses nor in annual household registration data. A combination of participatory methods, small-scale household surveys and interviews with key informants is likely to be the most efficient approach for local, project-related research. Participatory methods can help in the initial mapping of the flows, and in focus group discussions on the reasons behind the patterns identified. Stratified household surveys allow a clearer understanding of how the nature of local rural–urban linkages affects the livelihoods of different groups. Key informants can provide useful information on policies and practices which may not emerge directly from interviews with village respondents.

In the analysis of flows of goods, it may be useful to use commodity chain analysis, which consists of: (i) identifying the actors involved at all different stages of the chain (production, processing, exchange, transport, distribution, final sale, end use); (ii) evaluating income and profit at each level through the analysis of prices and quantities of goods handled by the different actors; (iii) evaluating the distribution of income and profit within each group along the chain, and where benefits are invested (locally or in more distant urban centres); and (iv) using the distribution of these benefits to trace out the mechanisms by which access to benefits is maintained and controlled (Ribot, 1998).

# Rural–urban linkages and sustainable rural livelihoods

The positive impact of rural–urban linkages on rural livelihoods is summarised in the 'virtuous circle', where rural and urban development are mutually dependent and integrated. However, rural–urban linkages should not be assumed to be beneficial in all circumstances. In some cases, they can increase inequality and the vulnerability of those groups with least assets.

Especially where land ownership is highly unequal, government policies and subsidised credit institutions set up in small towns tend to benefit already privileged urban elites and large farmers. When inputs and services for agricultural development are locally available, those small farmers who cannot afford to buy them tend to lose their land to large farmers who are reinvesting the profits from their increased production.

Non-agricultural rural employment can be an 'accumulation strategy' for farmers with assets and access to urban networks. For these groups, profits from urban-based activities are often reinvested in agricultural production, resulting in capital and asset accumulation. For other groups, however, engaging in non-agricultural rural employment may be determined by lack or loss of land, capital or traditional labour opportunities. Moreover, social marginalisation can limit access to non-agricultural activities, and individuals and households with limited access to social networks (often female-headed households or widows living alone) may be forced to find employment in unprofitable occupations as a 'survival strategy' (Baker, 1995). The least remunerative of these activities do not reduce vulnerability and may rely on excessive extraction from the natural resource base (Box 7).

Migration as a livelihood strategy is also mediated by access to assets. Those who move tend to be young, physically fit and often better educated, that is they have high levels of human capital. They also tend to have access to urban-based social networks. The elderly and the poorest people do not usually migrate (and labour availability in peak agricultural seasons can become scarce). Over time, migration may erode village-based networks as migrants become part of urban-based networks and remittances tend to decrease (Fall, 1998).

---

**Box 7: Poverty, non-agricultural activities and natural resources**

The cumulative effect of famines in northern Darfur (Sudan) has engendered a number of coping strategies among villagers, including trade, handicraft production, internal and international migration. However, these are not accessible to those with few assets for whom the main activity is the collection of grass (as fodder for camels and donkeys) and fuelwood, which they sell to petty traders in small village markets. Given the semi-desert nature of the region, the environmental costs of this activity – which accelerates the deterioration of the area's overall natural resource base – are significant (El Bashir Ibrahim, 1997).

---

Migrant women tend to send larger remittances to home areas than men, although an important reason for moving is often to escape family constraints. The renegotiation of gender roles resulting from women's migration is, however, not always reflected in an increase in control over their own remittances. In many cases women who stay in home areas also have limited control over remittances sent by male relatives. This partly reflects culturally specific gender relations, but also in many cases women's lack of access to assets. Depending on specific locations and groups, projects facilitating the productive use of remittances may have the potential to contribute to poverty reduction (Box 8).

## Implications of rural–urban linkages for NR and poverty reduction policies

### Why should NR policies and projects take into account rural-urban linkages?

A first reason is that understanding the scale and nature of rural–urban linkages is essential in order to locate rural livelihoods and the rural economy within the wider regional context. Positive rural–urban interactions and the 'virtuous circle' of development are fostered by backward and forward linkages between agricultural production and industry and services. However, policies encouraging these mutually reinforcing linkages need to overcome the traditional separation between rural and urban planners. They also need to avoid generalisations and be grounded in the specifics of the regional context.

Political and administrative decentralisation involving real decision-making power and financial autonomy is more likely to overcome planning dichotomies and to identify local needs and priorities. This needs to be supported by the national government, which should also provide infrastructure and basic services. Incentives for localised and diversified foreign investment would help to avoid the weaknesses of investment in single resources and crops.

Balanced rural–urban regional development requires an equal distribution of benefits among the rural population, since increases in

---

**Box 8: Remittances and agricultural production**

In Swaziland, poor agricultural production was traditionally explained as the outcome of men's migration to South African mining areas and of the inability of women adequately to carry the responsibility of production. However, a more crucial factor was the unavailability of new agricultural technologies. This began to change in the 1970s when returning migrants bought second-hand tractors with their savings. Remittances from mine wages were used by women to hire tractors, therefore compensating for the lack of male labour. This has resulted in an increase in agricultural production and in the number of family fields under cultivation (Simelane, 1995).

**Inequalities in access to assets are the main reason why there are very few actual examples of 'virtuous circle' development**

rural household income and expenditure are the springboard for the expansion of many urban-based enterprises. Inequalities in access to assets are the main reason why there are very few actual examples of 'virtuous circle' development. To strengthen the poverty reduction element of natural resource policies and projects, the potential of rural–urban linkages in widening choice and options should be taken into account. Increasing people's options also involves recognising the diversity of needs and priorities within any low-income population. This diversity is not only a result of different income levels but also because of differences in social relations (gender, age and ethnicity).

The following is a tentative list of issues related to rural-urban linkages to keep in mind in the formulation of NR policies and projects.

- Agricultural production is assumed to benefit from proximity to urban markets. However, the opportunities for household income increase are mediated by the household members' assets (physical, human and financial) as well as by their social capital and the mediating processes which determine access to markets. Projects aiming to increase agricultural production should also consider possible bottlenecks in commercialisation, which can include merchants' monopolistic practices and competition from other areas as well as lack of information about markets and prices.

- It should not be assumed that reinforcing the physical infrastructure connecting rural and urban areas is necessarily beneficial (because it reinforces local interactions) or negative (because it extracts resources from the region bypassing local centres in favour of larger cities). A low intensity of rural–urban linkages can be the result of specific socio-economic conditions in a given rural area (which may also affect different groups in different ways), as well as of poor transportation systems.

- Linkages with more than one urban centre are likely to be more successful for rural development as they increase the range of income diversification opportunities and the number of potential markets open to people. This is also because in many cases different flows (for example of people and of goods) have different spatial patterns. The understanding of these patterns and of the reasons why some groups may be excluded from some or all rural–urban linkages can give indications of priorities for policy and project interventions.

- Migration is an important element of livelihood strategies. In many cases, it is more useful to understand households as 'multi-spatial' rather than 'rural' or 'urban', and to encourage the positive linkages between spatially distant members by recognising urban-based members' claims on rural assets and facilitating their contribution to the rural economy, for example through the productive investment of remittances.

● However, in some instances the household members who 'stay behind' in the rural areas have little decision-making power as to the management of local resources, as control remains with the migrant members. This is particularly the case for women, although there are a range of factors in play, such as culturally specific gender roles and relations, gender divisions of labour within households, land tenure and women's workloads. This should be taken into account when targeting extension messages in rural areas.

In summary, rural–urban linkages play an important role in the ways in which livelihoods are constructed, although the traditional dichotomy between 'rural' and 'urban' development theory and practice has underplayed their significance. However, while rural and urban relations should be seen as mutually reinforcing, generalisations about the nature of rural-urban linkages across different locations and in terms of how they affect different groups must be avoided. Within specific regional contexts, the potential for rural–urban linkages to contribute to poverty reduction cannot be separated from issues related to assets and mediating processes. These determine whether livelihoods which straddle the rural–urban divide are best understood as 'accumulation strategies' or as 'survival strategies'.

## Key references

Baker, J. and Pedersen, P.O. (eds) (1992) *The Rural–Urban Interface in Africa: Expansion and Adaptation*. Uppsala: The Scandinavian Institute of African Studies.

Bryceson, D.F. and Jamal, V. (eds) (1997) *Farewell to Farms: De-agrarianisation and Employment in Africa*. Africa Studies Centre, Leiden, Research Series 1997/10. Aldershot: Ashgate.

Douglass, M. (1998) 'A Regional Network Strategy for Reciprocal Rural-Urban Linkages: An Agenda for Policy Research with Reference to Indonesia', *Third World Planning Review* 20(1) pp 1–33.

*Environment and Urbanization* (10)1, April 1998, special issue 'Beyond the Rural–Urban Divide'.

Hardoy, J. E. and Satterthwaite, D. (eds) (1986) *Small and Intermediate Urban Centres: Their Role in National and Regional Development in the Third World*. London: Hodder and Stoughton in association with IIED.

## References cited

Baker, J. (1995) 'Survival and Accumulation Strategies at the Rural–Urban Interface in Northwest Tanzania', *Environment and Urbanization* 7(1) pp 117–132.

Douglass, M. (1998) 'A Regional Network Strategy for Reciprocal Rural–Urban Linkages', *TWPR* 20(1) pp 1–33.

El Bashir Ibrahim, H. (1997) 'Coping with Famine and Poverty: The Dynamics of Non-Agricultural Rural Employment in Darfur, Sudan', in: Bryceson, D.F. and Jamal, V. (eds) *Farewell to Farms: De-agrarianisation and Employment in Africa*. Aldershot: Ashgate, pp 23–40.

Evans, H.E. (1990) 'Rural–Urban Linkages and Structural Transformation', *Report INU 71*, Infrastructure and Urban Development Department. Washington D.C.: The World Bank.

Fall, A.S. (1998) 'Migrants' Long-Distance Relationships and Social Networks in Dakar', *Environment and Urbanization* 10(1) pp 135–146.

Firman, T. (1996) 'Urban Development in Bandung Metropolitan Region: A Transformation to a Desa-Kota region', *Third World Planning Review* 18(1) pp 1–22.

Hardoy, J. E. and Satterthwaite, D. (eds) (1986) *Small and Intermediate Urban Centres: Their Role in National and Regional Development in the Third World*. London: Hodder and Stoughton in association with IIED.

Harriss-White, B. (1995) 'Maps and Landscapes of Grain Markets in South Asia', in Harriss, J., Hunter, J. and Lewis, C.M. (eds) *The New Institutional Economics and Third World Development*. London: Routledge, pp 87-108.

Kamete, A.Y. (1998) 'Interlocking Livelihoods: Farm and Small Town in Zimbabwe', *Environment and Urbanization* 10(1) pp 23–34.

Kelly, P. (1998) 'The Politics of Urban–Rural Relationships: Land Conversion in the Philippines', *Environment and Urbanization* 10(1) pp 35–54.

Koppel, B. (1987) 'Does Integrated Rural Development Really Work? Lessons from the Bicol River Basin', *World Development* 15, pp 205–220.

Krüger, F. (1998) 'Taking Advantage of Rural Assets as a Coping Strategy for the Urban Poor', *Environment and Urbanization* 10(1) pp 119–34.

Manzanal, M. and Vapnarsky, C. (1986) 'The Development of the Upper Valley of Rio Negro and its Periphery Within the Comahue Region, Argentina', in Hardoy, J.E. and Satterthwaite, D. (eds) (op.cit).

Mbiba, B. (1995) *Urban Agriculture in Zimbabwe*. Aldershot: Avebury.

McGranahan, G., Singsore, J. and Kjellén, M. (1996) 'Sustainability, Poverty and Urban Environmental Transitions', in Pugh, C. (ed.) *Sustainability, the Environment and Urbanization*. London: Earthscan, pp 103–133.

Morris, A. (1997) 'Market Behaviour and Market Systems in State of Mexico', in van Lindert, P. and Verkoren, O. (eds) *Small Towns and Beyond: Rural Transformation and Small Urban Centres in Latin America*. Amsterdam: Thela Publishers, pp 123–32.

Potts, D. (1995) 'Shall We Go Home? Increasing Urban Poverty in African Cities and Migration Processes.' In: *The Geographic Journal* 161:3, 245-264.

Potts, D. and Mutambirwa, C. (1998) '"Basics Are Now A Luxury": Perceptions of the Impact of Structural Adjustment on Rural and Urban Areas in Zimbabwe', *Environment and Urbanization* 10(1) pp 55–76.

Rees, W. (1992) 'Ecological Footprints and Appropriate Carrying Capacity: what Urban Economics Leaves Out', *Environment and Urbanization* 4(2) pp 121–30.

Ribot, J.C. (1998) 'Theorizing Access: Forest Profits Along Senegal's Charcoal Commodity Chains', *Development and Change* 29, pp 307–341.

Rondinelli, D. and Ruddle, K. (1978) *Urbanization and Rural Development: A Spatial Policy for Equitable Growth*. New York: Praeger.

Seppala, P. (1996) 'The Politics of Economic Diversification: Reconceptualizing the Rural Informal Sector in Southeast Tanzania', *Development and Change* 27, pp 557–78.

Simelane, S.H. (1995) 'Labour Migration and Rural Transformation in Post-Colonial Swaziland', *Journal of Contemporary African Studies* 13(2) pp 207–226.

Smit, W. (1998) 'The Rural Linkages of Urban Households in Durban', *Environment and Urbanization* 10(1) pp 77–88.

United Nations Centre for Human Settlements (UNCHS) (1996) *An Urbanizing World: Global report on Human Settlements 1996*. Oxford: Oxford University Press.

UNDP/UNCHS (Habitat) (1995) 'Rural-Urban Linkages: Policy Guidelines for Rural Development.' Paper prepared for the Twenty-Third Meeting of the ACC Sub-Committee on Rural Development, UNESCO Headquarters, Paris, 31 May–2 June 1995.

Zoomers, A.E.B. and Kleinpenning, J. (1996) 'Livelihood and Urban–Rural Relations in Central Paraguay', *Tijdschrift voor Economische en Sociale Geografie* 87(2) pp 161–74.

# ENTRY POINT PAPERS

# 6 Biodiversity and Sustainable Rural Livelihoods

*Izabella Koziell*

---

*'A social problem rooted in a biological world'* (Swanson, 1997).

## Introduction

This chapter discusses the DFID approach to biodiversity, in the context of the goal to reduce by one half the number of people living in extreme poverty by 2015. Following an introduction to the concept of biodiversity as a resource, the chapter discusses how biodiversity should be viewed by the bilateral programme in support of sustainable rural livelihoods. Finally, the chapter discusses how this relates to the wider issue of the global value of biodiversity.

## What is biodiversity?

Biodiversity is described as the **variety** of living organisms and is often considered at three levels: genetic, species and ecosystem (Convention on Biological Diversity, 1993; WRI, 1992; McNeely *et al.*, 1990; Wilson, 1989).

Biodiversity has resulted from a gradual accumulation of differences between individual organisms throughout four billion years of evolution.[1] In our time span, biodiversity is therefore a non-renewable resource. Once lost, this diversity cannot be renewed. In Sri Lanka, for example, the number of rice varieties has dropped from 2,000 in 1958 to less than 100 today (WCMC, 1992). In contrast, rice — considering biomass irrespective of biodiversity — remains a renewable resource (Swanson, 1997).

The distinction between biodiversity and biomass is important but the relationships are not always simple or clear. A reduction in biodiversity may or may not affect biological productivity, stability or ecological processes (WRI, 1989). For example, the productivity of a maize monoculture can be higher than from a diverse production system per unit area — but will require higher inputs and may be much more susceptible to disease.

North America, Madagascar and Australia have lost a large share of their vertebrate megafauna within the recent past, yet there is, as yet, scant evidence of profound ecosystem instability (Myers, 1996). Ecosystem processes, such as carbon sinks, can be maintained either by a tract of biodiverse rainforest or a uniform plantation of eucalyptus trees. However, a eucalyptus plantation would probably provide less cycling of minerals and soil nutrients and support fewer plants and animals (Myers, 1996).

The focus of this chapter (and the associated Linking Policy and Practice in Biodiversity (LPPB) project, see Box 1) will be on the specific contribution of biodiversity as a resource – rather than biomass – to sustainable rural livelihoods.

## How does biodiversity relate to sustainable rural livelihoods?

The sustainable rural livelihoods approach has shifted the emphasis towards first considering people, and then examining how they manipulate different capital stocks (natural, physical, social, financial and human) to augment their livelihoods. Biodiversity represents a part of natural capital.[2] Natural capital provides the material, energy, processes and information which people combine to produce and accumulate other capital stocks – physical, human and financial – from which are derived positive livelihood outcomes. Thus, biodiversity should be seen as a *means* of contributing to sustainable rural livelihoods, rather than an end in itself.

**Biodiversity should be seen as a *means* of contributing to sustainable rural livelihoods, rather than an end in itself**

Both wild and domesticated biodiversity hold significant social, aesthetic, cultural and economic values for human societies. Some of the generic economic values are displayed in Table 1.

Some of these categories have direct use to people, and benefits arising are more easily measurable and quantifiable, e.g. financial returns gained from harvesting a stand of timber. Others are less easily quantifiable, because they provide functional values, e.g. the contribution of forest diversity to watershed protection, or depend upon potential future rather than short-term benefit, or are 'global' and cannot be captured by, or allocated to, any one individual group of people.[3] The implications of this are discussed in the final section of the chapter.

The use values can be more easily realised through a range of management activities that can involve combinations of approaches along a spectrum

---

**Box 1: Linking Policy and Practice in Biodiversity (LPPB) Project**

The LPPB project aims to improve and clarify our understanding of the inter-relationships between biodiversity and development, particularly at the bilateral country programme level, in order to assist DFID in its decision-making. It also aims to clarify linkages between local, national and global concerns. The project will consider both wild and domestic biodiversity across a range of productive sectors.

**Table 1: Categories of potential economic values assigned to biodiversity**

| Use Values | | Examples |
|---|---|---|
| Direct Use | Outputs that are directly consumable or tradable | Harvested products for consumptive use (e.g. firewood, fuel, fodder, game meat, cash crops, timber, fish, ivory and medicinal plants) and non-consumptive use (e.g. ecotourism and recreation) |
| Indirect Use | Outputs that provide functional benefits | Ecological functions, flood and storm protection, waste assimilation, microclimatic functions, nutrient cycles, photosynthesis, carbon stores, soil production |
| **Non Use Values** | | **Examples** |
| Option Values | Future direct and indirect values | Maintenance of biodiversity for future direct and indirect use and non-use |
| Bequest Values | Use and non-use value of environmental legacy | Prevention of irreversible change in habitats |
| Existence Values | Value gained from continuous knowledge of existence | Cultural and spiritual assets, worth of wildlife species, natural areas, and overall biodiversity as objects of intrinsic and stewardship value |

After *Pearce and Moran* (1994)

from total *protection* to total *conversion*[4] of biodiversity. These management activities offer a series of options for *use* of biodiversity, some being more appropriate than others within the specific ecological and socio–economic context. Both conversion and protection of biodiversity can bring different benefits – and different costs – to different people. It is important to clarify *who* is likely to receive benefits, and *who* is likely to suffer the costs, in both the shorter and longer term.

## *Benefits of conversion*

Over the millennia, people have been converting natural capital to other forms of capital stock. Biodiversity provides the range of species and varieties, the careful selection of which has enabled the successful expansion of those species and varieties that are particularly appropriate for converting to food, fuel, shelter, clothing and other goods. Such manipulations have provided the basis for wealth accumulation and appropriation of other capital assets, albeit not always on an equitable basis.[5] As a result, countries that have 'converted' biodiversity are often rich materially in comparison to those that have not.[6] It is therefore understandable that 'unconverted' countries are keen to follow similar and safely 'proven' development paths.

## Costs of conversion

Despite the uncertainties that surround the measurement of biodiversity, there is now ample evidence to show that biodiversity is declining. While decline associated with conversion has provided distinct benefits to certain groups of people, it can also be associated with heavy livelihood losses, particularly to those who are politically and socially marginalised, or the 'poorest of the poor'. These groups have often continued to remain directly dependent on biodiversity for both on-farm and off-farm livelihood activities. Loss of this biodiversity undermines their production choices, food security and increases exposure to risk. In this context, it is not generally the loss of a single species that is meaningful, but the loss of large components of biodiversity. For poor and marginalised groups, protection and maintenance of, and improved access to, biodiversity can often contribute more to sustainable livelihoods than conversion.

## The benefits of maintaining and protecting biodiversity

Protection and sustainable use of biodiversity can also provide unique values (Box 2). The challenge lies in ensuring these values can be captured and retained by local people as well as broader groups.

## Costs associated with maintaining areas of high biodiversity

In addition to the opportunity cost of forgone gain from conversion (to monoculture, for example), costs include livestock and crop losses from wild animal encroachment and predation, weeds and pest infestation. In

---

**Box 2: Potential benefits provided by maintenance or sustainable use of biodiversity**

A diversity of species provides a range of economic and investment opportunities.

o   Food security is improved by a range of varieties which help reduce the risk of loss due to pests, and increase tolerance to climatic stress.

o   Land can have greater biomass output over longer periods of time when biodiverse (non-diverse farming systems succeed by economies of scale, and over shorter periods of time – often requiring high levels of inputs to sustain yields).

o   Protection is provided against epidemic pathogens – the more genetically uniform a population is, the more vulnerable it is to epidemic disease.

o   Genetic information is available to plant breeding and pharmaceutical industries, the outputs of which contribute to food security and improved human health.

o   Exposure to environmental risk is reduced through supporting ecosystem processes which protect poor people from variables such as drought and flood.

o   Nutrition and health are improved by providing a source of medicines and vitamins for humans and livestock.

o   A range of unique social and cultural identities which have developed through the establishment of different people–landscape interactions are maintained.

some situations, it is the *activities* designed to maintain biodiversity which have impacted negatively upon livelihoods. For example, the establishment of protected areas has sometimes been associated with resettlement programmes, human displacement and restrictions on access to local resources. Even where protected areas bring tourism, gains from tourism often benefit outsiders rather than local communities. Such protected area programmes have sometimes led to serious conflicts between local communities and government park departments and an escalation in the costs of protection.[7] Finally, the banditry, poaching and smuggling associated with 'wilderness' areas have occasionally had significant negative impacts.

## How should DFID support the contribution of biodiversity to sustainable rural livelihoods?

**The focus should be on maximising social and economic benefits that arise out of the protection, sustainable use or conversion of biodiversity, and seeking their fair and equitable distribution**

DFID is committed to eradicating poverty. Thus, certainly in the context of the bilateral programmes and the sustainable rural livelihoods approach, the focus should be on maximising social and economic benefits that arise out of the protection, sustainable use or conversion of biodiversity, and seeking their fair and equitable distribution.

The shift in emphasis of the sustainable rural livelihoods approach implies the term 'win–win' should no longer be understood to mean that the purpose is both poverty reduction and biodiversity maintenance. The *purpose* of the bilateral programme should be poverty reduction. A 'win–win' situation occurs where maintenance of biodiversity is the best *means* of achieving poverty reduction. In this context:

- Protectionist interventions for maintaining biodiversity will be of relevance only where the benefits to local people arising from protection exceed those arising from an alternative activity. In Bangladesh, for example, local people establish 'brush parks' which create protected habitats for breeding stock by restricting fishing. Such a mosaic of protection and use of biodiversity has applications in other sectors, but the link between maintaining a reservoir of biodiversity and supporting local livelihoods must be demonstrable.

- Between the extremes of total protection and entire conversion, most options will involve a degree of partial conversion (involving some loss of biodiversity) and sustainable use. Once again, such activities should be supported only where they result in greater benefits for poor people than other alternatives. For example, in Java, during the pre-colonial era, large urban populations were supplied successfully by the garden farming system which was extremely biodiverse, encouraging integration of both domestic and wild elements (Christanty *et al.*, 1986). Examples of sustainable use of wild biodiversity are found in community-based wildlife management programmes.

- Conversion, which may reduce biodiversity, will also continue to be assessed against what it contributes to sustainable rural livelihoods. DFID should aim to ensure the equitable distribution of benefits, and also that conversion of biodiversity-rich areas for wider benefit does not undermine people's welfare within that locality.

## What are the trade-offs to consider in the management of biodiversity for development?

In the section above, we argue that biodiversity should be considered as a resource which can contribute to sustainable rural livelihoods in many different ways, directly and indirectly, in the short and long term. We point out that the greatest challenge lies in ensuring, and maintaining, objectivity over decisions regarding effective use of biodiversity for poverty reduction. Such an approach entails questioning some of the general assumptions that continue to be made regarding relationships between biodiversity decline and human development. It involves ensuring that decisions are framed within the specificity of the local or regional context. And it involves recognising that there are difficult trade-offs (or generally combinations of trade-offs) to make in such decisions. These include:

- long-term vs. short-term imperatives
- quantifiable value vs. non-quantifiable value
- anticipated value vs. actual value
- local value vs. global value.

How should DFID make these choices?

### *Long-term vs. short-term imperatives*

Sustainable rural livelihoods demand sustainable use of resources. For example, DFID would not promote conversion to a less diverse system for short-term gain if such a system was unsustainable.

However, the short-term needs of poor people and governments cannot be ignored. Vulnerability, need or greed, may lead people to take decisions based on a short-term view. Too much unpredictability lies between the now and the long-term future. For example, colonisers in forest margins may choose farming methods – such as rearing cattle – which are heavily supported by government incentives, and which otherwise would not be economically viable and are unsustainable in the long term.[8] Turning forest into farmland may support a family for two years, but after that the only option may be to burn more forest (Blench, 1998). How should DFID and partner governments assist in making such choices?

## Quantifiable value vs. non-quantifiable value

When considering management options for reducing poverty through direct use of biodiversity, economic benefits are more easily measurable. But how does one quantify the value of protecting a watershed? More difficult still, how does one measure the spiritual or cultural value of biodiversity to local people? How do we weigh the measurable against the unmeasurable when making management choices?

## Anticipated value vs. actual value

Closely related to the two categories above, is the question of anticipated values. For example, there may in the future be great value in bioprospecting. But technological improvements in drug development may make these values worthless – or what value exists may be captured by agents other than local people. How should DFID balance such *potential* benefit against the *certain* benefit of, for example, converting that biodiverse system?

## Local value vs. global value

We need to recognise that our own concerns about climate change, endangered species and preserving 'the natural order of things' may be significantly different to the priorities of most poor people. This does not mean our purpose (i.e. reducing poverty) is different; the differences manifest themselves in how we choose to achieve that purpose. Global biodiversity benefits, as defined by us, cannot be allocated to any individual group of people. Therefore, the costs of maintaining global biodiversity should not be transferred onto poorer groups.

The bilateral programme has the remit of reducing poverty in partner countries. Ideally, global concerns such as these would not therefore enter bilateral decisions; these are issues for multilateral and international funding. However, bilateral programmes may sometimes find themselves serving the global – in addition to the local – good. In such cases, the programme must be sure that livelihoods of local people, or the effectiveness of the programme in reducing poverty, are not compromised in any way.

# Key References

Glowka, L. *et al.* (1994) *A Guide to the Convention on Biological Diversity*. IUCN Environmental Policy and Law Paper No.30, IUCN Biodiversity Programme, 1994.

McNeely, J. *et al.* (1990) *Conserving the World's Biological Diversity*. Gland and Washington D.C.: IUCN, WRI, Conservation International, WWF-US, World Bank.

Pearce, D. and Moran, D. (1994) *The Economic Value of Biodiversity*. London: IUCN, Earthscan Publications.

Swanson, T. (1997) *Global Action for Biodiversity*. London: IUCN, Earthscan Publications.

Wilson, E.O. and Peter, F.M. (1988) *Biodiversity*. Washington, D.C.: National Academy of Sciences.

WCMC. (1992) *Global Biodiversity: State of the Earth's Living Resources*. London: Chapman and Hall.

# Other references

BCPC (1998) *Saving the Planet with Pesticides, Biotechnology and European Farm Reform*. London: British Crop Protection Council.

Blench, R. (1998, forthcoming) *Timor Mortis Conturbat Me: Extinction Theory and the Loss of Biodiversity*.

Christianty, L., Abdoellah, O.S., Marten, G.G. and Iskandar, J. (1986) 'Traditional Agro-Forestry in West Java: the Perangkan (homegarden) and the *Kebun-Talun* (annual-perennial rotation) cropping systems', in

Marten, G.G. (ed.) *Traditional Agriculture in Southeast Asia: A Human Ecology Perspective*. Boulder and London: Westview Press, pp 132–58.

Ehrlich, P.R. and Ehrlich, A.H. (1981) *Extinction: The Causes and Consequences of the Disappearance of Species*. New York: Random House.

FAO (1996) *Global Plan of Action for the Conservation and Sustainable Utilisation of Plant Genetic Resources for Food and Agriculture*. Rome: FAO.

Hawkes, J.G. (1983) *The Diversity of Crop Plants*. Cambridge, MA: Harvard University Press.

Heywood, V.H. and Watson. R.T. (eds) (1995) *Global Biodiversity Assessment*. Cambridge, UK: Cambridge University Press.

Leader-Williams, N. and Albon, S. (1988) 'Allocation of Resources for Conservation' *Nature* 336 pp 533-535

Lovejoy, T.E. (1988) 'Diverse Considerations', in Wilson, E.O. (ed.) *Biodiversity*, E.O. Wilson. Washington D.C.: National Academy Press.

Myers, N. (1996) 'Environmental Services of Biodiversity', *Proceedings of National Academy of Sciences, USA* 93, pp 2764–9.

Myers, N. (1993) 'Biodiversity and the Precautionary Principle', *Ambio* 22(2–3) pp 74–9.

Owen-Smith, N. (1988) *The Influence of Very Large Body Size on Ecology.* Cambridge, UK: Cambridge University Press.

Perfect, J. (1991) 'Biodiversity: How Important A Resource?', *Outlook on Agriculture* 21(1) pp 5–7.

Pletscher, D.H. and Hutto., R.L. (1990) 'Wildlife Management and the Maintenance of Biological Diversity', *Western Wildlands* 17(3) pp 8–12.

Poole, P.J. (1993) 'Indigenous Peoples and Biodiversity Protection', in Shelton, H.D. (ed.) *The Social Challenge of Biodiversity Conservation.* Working Paper No.1. Washington D.C.: The Global Environment Facility.

Posey, D.A. (1996) 'Protecting Indigenous Peoples' Rights to Biodiversity', *Environment* 38(8) p. 6.

Pretty, J. (1998) *The Living Land.* London: Earthscan Publications.

Redford, K.H. and Sanderson, S.E. (1992) 'The Brief, Barren Marriage of Biodiversity and Sustainability?', *Bulletin of the Ecological Society of America* 73(1) pp 36–8.

Reid, W.V., Barber, C. and Miller, K.R. (1992) *Global Biodiversity Strategy: Guidelines for Action to Save, Study and use Earth's Biotic Wealth Sustainability and Equability.* New York: World Resource Institute.

Reid, W.V. and Miller, K.R. (1989) *Keeping Options Alive-The Scientific Basis for Conserving Biodiversity.* Washington, D.C.: World Resources Institute.

Repetto, R. and Gillis, M. (1988) *Public Policies and Misuse of Forest Resources.* Cambridge, UK: Cambridge University Press.

Shiva, V.P.A., Schucking, H., Gray, A., Lohmann, L. and D. Cooper (eds) (1991) *Biodiversity: Social and Ecological Perspectives.* New Jersey: Zed Books.

Smith, C.L. (1994) 'Connecting Cultural and Biological Diversity in Restoring Northwest Salmon', *Fisheries* 19(2) pp 20–26.

Swanson, T. (1998, forthcoming) *Conserving Global Biological Diversity Through Alternative Development Path.*

Tisdell, C.A. (1995) 'Issues in Biodiversity Conservation Including the Role of Local Communities', *Environmental Conservation* 22(3) p. 216.

UNEP (1994) 'Measures for Conservation of Biodiversity and Sustainable Use of its Components', *Global Biodiversity Assessment.* Nairobi: UNEP.

Wilson, E.O. (1989) 'Threats to Biodiversity', *Scientific American* 261, pp 108–116.

Wilson, E.O. (1989) *The Diversity of Life.* Cambridge, MA: Harvard University Press.

WRI (1992) *Global Biodiversity Strategy: Guidelines for Action to Save, Study and use Earth's Biotic Wealth, Sustainably and Equitably.* Paris: World Resource Institute, World Conservation Union, and United Nations Environment Program.

# Endnotes

1   So far only 1.6 million species have been identified. Estimates vary from five to 50 million, with the more conservative estimates ranging around 10 million (Ehrlich and Ehrlich, 1981; Wilson, 1989). The vast majority of these species are small organisms.

2   Natural capital refers to the stocks of plants, animals, insects and fish, and the ecosystems of which they are part, minerals, atmosphere and water (Pretty, 1998).

3   The measurement of non-use values has proved very difficult, given that they are generally motivated by moral concern, prediction and altruism – which do not have a monetary value. The uncertainties surrounding economic valuation of non-use values has resulted in some inaccurate claims over the potential value of bioprospecting, ecotourism etc.

4   Where conversion means modification of a biodiverse system, wild or domesticated, to a less biodiverse system.

5   Development gains experienced by countries from conversion are significant in terms of agricultural yields, income growth and general development status. For example, countries which have raised crop yields fastest have generally reduced births per woman fastest e.g. Zimbabwe (BCPC, 1998).

6   The countries with greatest 'species richness' range between 1–7% of OECD average per capita income, McNeely *et al.* (1990).

7   Leader–Williams and Albon (1988) estimated that in Africa expenditures of up to $200/km are required for protection of large mammals (e.g. rhino), implying that adequate protection of simply one mammal would consume the entire parks budget for many countries!

8   In several parts of Amazonia government incentives, such as direct clearance and land title grants and cattle market support, create individual incentive for burning and clearing for conversion to ranching (Repetto and Gillis, 1988).

# 7

# The Integration of Livestock Interventions into a Sustainable Rural Livelihoods Approach

*Livestock in Development*

## Introduction

Background research for the DFID White Paper on International Development reviewed the relationship between livestock and the poor in developing countries. The aim was to examine the arguments for and against continued support to livestock interventions in the light of DFID's sharpened poverty focus. The review (Holden *et al.*, 1997) concluded that livestock are important to the majority of the rural poor in developing countries, contributing in many and diverse ways to rural livelihoods (see Box 1). It recommended placing support to the *livelihoods of poor livestock keepers* at the centre of future livestock–related development interventions – that is to say, focusing on the needs of poor people who keep livestock as opposed to livestock and their products, or places where livestock production is of greatest importance.

---

**Box 1: Contributions of livestock to the livelihoods of the rural poor**

Livestock support the livelihoods of the poor in many diverse ways, simultaneously fulfilling several different functions. They can represent:

❍ an important source of cash income from the sale or hire of animals or their products

❍ one of the few assets available to the poor and women (which can be crucial in maintaining household survival in times of crisis, and can be accumulated when possible and sold when needed)

❍ a central component of farming systems (provision of draught power and manure is important when the purchase of substitutes in sufficient quantities is often impossible – livestock also contribute to sustainable resource use through the effect of their manure on soil quality and water retention)

❍ a means of allowing the poor to capture private benefits from common property resources

❍ a source of livelihood security by diversifying risk and buffering crop yields, particularly in drought-prone environments

❍ the difference between survival and abject poverty for pastoralists, share-croppers, marginal farmers or others whose livelihoods are dependent on access to livestock

❍ a source of food, transport, fuel, access to social support networks, cultural well-being and a variety of other functions.

---

The framework presented in the introductory chapter to this book suggests that sustainable rural livelihoods are derived through access to five types of capital assets: natural, physical, financial, human and social capital. Conventionally, livestock projects have concentrated on delivering such capital assets directly, through technical and service projects. The next section reviews the impact of this type of intervention on the poor.

## Technical and service projects

Projects focusing on the development and direct delivery of technology and livestock services to livestock keepers represent the majority of donor interventions in the sector. Some 93% of DFID funds allocated to livestock projects since 1990 have been for projects that include such a technical or service component. They have typically aimed to provide the following types of benefits:

- better disease control through national and international vaccination campaigns, improved disease surveillance systems, the provision of clinical and diagnostic services, and the development of new disease control technology

- new production resources, including animals on credit, fodder plants and draught power equipment

- higher productivity through the use of improved breeds, feed processing and different production techniques

- access to markets through government livestock marketing corporations, the development of livestock abattoirs and investment in infrastructure, and

- information on improved production and marketing techniques.

### *Lessons*

**A review of donor experience encompassing around 800 projects by most of the main funding agencies revealed little evidence of a sustainable impact on the poor**

A review of donor experience encompassing around 800 projects by most of the main funding agencies (including multilateral agencies, bilateral donors, and NGOs) revealed little evidence of a sustainable impact on the poor (see Table 1). Many of these projects were not aimed at the poor, and it is therefore unsurprising that they did not impact on them. However, those that did target the poor have also been largely unsuccessful at reaching them. The reasons can be summarised as follows:

- technology, goods or services have been developed but are not delivered to the poor either because (i) the project failed to achieve its aims or because (ii) local organisations were incapable of delivering services in the absence of project support

## Table 1: Donor experiences with technical and service projects

| Organisation | Project types and number | Conclusion |
| --- | --- | --- |
| The World Bank (Walshe, 1993) | 1985 review of 330 smallholder livestock projects | Projects performed unsatisfactorily overall, particularly in Africa, having a cattle bias, and design influenced by livestock systems in developed countries and larger commercial producers. |
| | 1981 review of 67 livestock projects in dry tropical Africa | Ranching projects failed dismally; marketing, slaughtering and processing were abysmal; veterinary and off-range fattening were good. |
| | 1982 review of 60 dairy projects | Positive about Latin America, India and Kenya; Problems in much of east Africa, south Asia except India, and east Asia. |
| Netherlands Development Cooperation | Review of a random sample of 23 out of 94 livestock projects from the 1970s and 1980s | Early projects supported high technology dairying, often on a large scale. These projects were unsuccessful, producing little in the way of positive results (NDC, 1992; Konstapel and Nell, 1993). |
| Swiss Development Cooperation | Review of 25 livestock projects from 1960s to 1980s | Success limited for many projects; where benefits emerged, they rarely reached the poor (von Sury, 1990). |
| Danida | Overview of experience with livestock projects | A number of problems encountered, similar to those experienced by the World Bank, ADB and Netherlands. Some success, but doubts whether the poor benefited (Danida, 1997). |
| EC DG1 | Review of eight representative EC livestock projects in Asia | Early projects were of weak design, poor relevance and low sustainability; mostly technical (Vandersmissen and Symoens, 1997). |
| USAID | 1978 review of African drylands projects | Review found many areas where improvements were needed; projects were frequently ill-fated (Atherton, 1984; Scoones, 1995; Blackburn, 1993). |
| Asian Development Bank | Review of livestock projects | Gloomy picture, with many weaknesses in early projects (ADB, 1991; Timon, 1993). |
| ILRI | Review of 30 African livestock projects over 15 years | More than 75% performed poorly (ILRI, 1995). |

- poor livestock keepers have not adopted the technology or made use of the service because it is inappropriate for their needs and circumstances, and/or

- poor livestock keepers have not benefited even where technologies are delivered and adopted, either because wealthier farmers or traders have captured the project benefits, often to the detriment of the poor, or because the technology has proved difficult for the poor to sustain.

**Where technical projects have been successful, it has usually been because they have operated within a wider policy environment that was especially supportive of their activities**

Where technical projects have been successful, it has usually been because they have operated within a wider policy environment that was especially supportive of their activities. For example, a highly successful FAO project in China (on urea-treated straw for beef production) was supported by the government with sufficient staffing and infrastructure at village level, with political support and with subsidised urea and credit (Dolberg and Findlayson, 1995)

Given the heavy investment in technical projects, the paucity of evidence demonstrating sustainable impact on the poor is disappointing.

## Underlying causes

Many of the reasons for the weak performance can be traced to problems within organisations concerned with livestock development, which cause them to be less effective at benefiting the poor. The underlying causes of failure include that:

- delivery organisations do not have a pro-poor policy

- the state formulates policy and legislation which discriminates against the poor (for example, inappropriate land tenure legislation)

- delivery organisation staff have inadequate skills and poor motivation

- insufficient funds are allocated to public services, leading to budget shortfalls which curtail activities

- excessive state presence inhibits the progress of alternative delivery organisations

- delivery and research organisations are staffed by people who lack skills to consult with and understand poor livestock keepers' objectives, constraints and options, and therefore their needs

- delivery and research organisations use top-down planning procedures that preclude the development of client-oriented programmes, and

- research organisations have weak links with delivery organisations so many technologies are not demand-led and remain 'on the shelf'.

In recognition of these problems, many donors have attempted to address weaknesses within organisations involved in livestock development. We term these 'organisational' projects, and consider their record at impacting on poor livestock keepers in the next section.

# Organisational projects

Organisational projects seek to improve the skills, management, planning or information systems of an organisation. Some 49% of DFID funds allocated to livestock-related projects since 1990 contain some element of organisational development. Typically, they:

- provide training for government organisations (such as state veterinary services, laboratories, universities, animal research and extension) so that they are better able to address the needs of poorer livestock clients through the adoption of decentralised planning and farmer participatory approaches

- introduce new extension systems (such as training and visit) to state organisations, or

- introduce new disease surveillance, epidemiology and economic techniques to improve disease control planning.

## *Lessons*

Many organisational projects have had acceptable performance during their lifetime, but the benefits have diminished once projects have ended. The reasons for this fall into two main categories.

(i) The organisation does not provide services that are economically valuable; reduced demand (from the public or private sectors) once project support is withdrawn renders them financially nonviable and dysfunctional. For example, many veterinary diagnostic laboratories are under-used by fee-paying farmers and, in the absence of public support, quickly fall into disuse (Kenyon and Nour, 1991, cited in Majok and Schwabe, 1996).

(ii) The organisation does not make use of the new skills because its institutional framework does not encourage its members to change their behaviour. Farmer-first research approaches have quickly been abandoned by state research organisations in which the scientific reward system penalises research conducted in an unorthodox way (Jordan *et al.*, 1998).

**This is an opportunity to consider a new paradigm for donor livestock interventions**

How then should donors proceed? There are immediate opportunities to improve the planning and implementation of most projects, to sharpen the poverty focus, to increase the client focus. However, this is also an opportunity to consider a new paradigm for donor livestock interventions, a subject to which we now turn.

# An institutional reappraisal of livestock development

New Institutional Economics draws our attention to the importance of institutions in modelling human behaviour. Institutions are defined as 'the "rules of the game" that shape the way we behave as individuals and as a society' (North, 1990). Institutions include formal rules (which are embodied in legislation), or informal rules that govern our behaviour and expectations. There are hierarchies of institutions. International institutions govern international trade: national institutions, such as a country's statute book, apply to all citizens of the nation. Social institutions, such as the definition of gender roles, may apply nationwide or to a small section of society. Local institutions, such as those governing collective action, apply to a limited number of people.

It is important to distinguish between institutions and organisations, because of their influence on each other. While organisations influence the institutional framework – for example, the state is responsible for a country's national legislation – institutions in turn shape organisations, by defining what they seek to do.

## *Underlying causes of organisational failure*

Poor organisational performance can be largely attributed to the nature of the institutional framework under which the organisation operates. Institutional frameworks commonly do not support client-focused delivery of services. For example, research centres reward their staff for conducting new research, but not for the impact of the research on the poor. Researchers therefore have little incentive to invest in participatory client-led research.

The lack of a poverty focus within organisations usually reflects the fact that the international and national institutional frameworks within which they operate do not support pro-poor development. For example, international trading laws discriminate against poor livestock keepers and national property rights rarely support the use of communal grazing by the poor. The distribution of veterinary medicines is often limited to channels which do not suit the needs of the poor and national subsidies and taxes support non-poor livestock keepers.

Professional values and norms similarly favour the development of commercial livestock production which has higher levels of marketed output. Many professionals have neither the skills nor the interest to work with the livestock systems in which the poor are involved.

Local informal institutional frameworks are also frequently loaded against the poor. In the context of livestock projects, wealthier farmers have appropriated common land and so denied poorer households access to fodder (Thomas-Slayter and Bhatt, 1994); market traders have colluded to fix prices against the interests of the poor (Seabright, 1992; Harriss-White, 1995).

To summarise, many technical projects have failed because of organisational weaknesses, which in turn have arisen because of domestic and international institutional frameworks that do not make poverty reduction the key priority. The implication is that no widespread and sustainable improvement in the livelihoods of the poor can take place until institutions are reformed to be supportive of poverty reduction. It would appear, then, that projects which address institutional aspects of livestock development might improve the chances of achieving a sustainable impact on poor livestock keepers. The next section considers donor experience to date in efforts to reform institutions.

**No widespread and sustainable improvement in the livelihoods of the poor can take place until institutions are reformed to be supportive of poverty reduction**

## Institutional projects

Institutional projects go beyond organisational projects by attempting to reform not just the skills, management, planning or information systems of an organisation, but also the underlying institutions which influence how that organisation behaves. Just 10% of DFID funds for livestock projects are allocated to projects with institutional components. However, few of these projects attempt to reform national or social-level institutions that influence organisational behaviour. Instead, most are pitched at an organisational or local level, that is they introduce new sets of rules to organisations. Institutional projects have therefore typically aimed to:

- develop farmers' associations and cooperatives that are able to provide services to their members (including supply of veterinary inputs, maintenance and development of water supplies, and the processing and marketing of animal products) or facilitate collective action for grazing or other natural resource management activities

- create new private sector enterprises or roles, such as community-based animal health workers who are able to deliver veterinary services to poor livestock keepers

- establish credit and savings groups or work with formal financial organisations to develop new lending procedures which make credit available to those without personal financial collateral, and/or

- rationalise the delivery of state services (e.g. through privatisation), in order to focus on selected functions and improve the delivery of the others through ceding responsibilities to non-state organisations.

### *Lessons*

Many institutional projects are new and have yet to stand the test of time. Nevertheless, existing evidence of their ability to impact positively on the poor appears encouraging. For example:

- An Oxfam pastoral development project in Kenya raised average pastoral incomes by some $424 per annum per household through the development of pastoral and credit associations. The project is estimated to have an internal rate of return of over 50%, demonstrating that institutional interventions with poor pastoralists in arid lands can yield significant economic benefits (Odhiambo *et al.*, 1998).

- The Grameen Bank in Bangladesh has reduced the transaction costs of lending to the poor by adopting group-based lending with peer pressure to monitor and enforce contracts. It has reached two million households in more than half the villages in Bangladesh, with approximately 50% of loans targeting livestock. The overall repayment rate exceeds 95%, which is remarkable given its primary focus on poor women (Qureshi *et al.*, 1996; Dolberg, 1996).

- An ITDG project supported private-sector community-based animal health workers to deliver veterinary drugs and advice to small-scale livestock farmers in semi-arid Kenya. The animal health workers cost $200 each to train, but yielded benefits to their community valued at $3,840 per annum. These benefits were still being obtained ten years after the project had come to an end (Holden, 1997).

However, many of these projects are likely to prove unsustainable in the long term, because the changes the project is trying to bring about are often incompatible with the wider institutional environment within which they operate. For example:

- Many community-based animal health projects have doubtful futures because these organisational forms of service delivery contravene legislation that restricts the right to deliver animal health services to registered veterinarians (Butcher, 1994).

- Herder associations have successfully established viable service delivery functions, but have had less success with range management. This is because many projects have failed to achieve adequate participatory processes due to an inability to overcome deeply embedded authoritarian cultures and the social structure of the groups themselves (de Haan *et al.*, 1997).

**Continued competition from the public sector remains a constraint to private sector development in many countries**

- Some projects have introduced new rules that have been resisted by vested interests. The Pan African Rinderpest Campaign, for example, prepared regulations on the respective roles of the private and public sectors. The legal frameworks have been strongly resisted by veterinarians working for government who currently engage in private practice as government employees. Continued competition from the public sector remains a constraint to private sector development in many countries (EC, 1997).

National laws unrelated to livestock may also inhibit projects. NGOs have become increasingly involved in credit delivery in Bolivia since the 1980s. In order to expand their activities to meet demand, the NGOs find they need to resort to accessing public funds or to mobilisation of savings. However, if they do so, they fall under different banking laws, which require them to maintain very high levels of assets to cover the risk of their lending operations to the poor (Birbuet and Cornacchia, 1996).

Very few projects have attempted to address the problems of the wider/ higher institutional environment which compromise the sustainability of poverty-focused projects. As a result there are few examples from which to draw conclusions regarding impact on the poor. However, one example of an institutional project, which is considered to have been highly successful in many (though not all) aspects, is 'Operation Flood' in India. This project organises milk marketing through 75,000 village-level cooperatives, whose ten million members link to a national milk supply grid. A key element of the success of the programme has been the way in which it dealt with cheap (subsidised) milk imports, which competed unfairly with local producers. A government policy decision restricted the importation of subsidised milk powder to the National Dairy Development Board (which used funds generated to support local cooperatives). The result was a major increase in domestic milk supply (World Bank, 1997).

A contemporary DFID livestock project with a strong institutional element is the DELIVERI project in Indonesia. This aims to introduce a client-oriented approach to the state livestock services by changing the institutional framework – both formal and informal – of the delivery organisation. Likewise, new EC projects in Asia now also include institutional components to strengthen policy-making and veterinary legislation (Vandersmissen, 1997).

Institutional projects are concerned with creating an enabling environment in which pro-poor livestock development is able to take place. A poverty-focused enabling environment is characterised by combinations of institutions that create incentives for organisations to focus on reducing poverty. The need for such an approach is indicated by the evidence given in this chapter.

(i)   Many technical and service projects have been ineffective at reaching the poor because of organisational problems.

(ii)  Organisational projects have in turn been limited by the social, organisational, national and international institutions – both formal and informal – which determine the behaviour of organisations.

(iii) Institutional projects have tended to focus only on a lower level of institution and have generally neglected the higher-level institutions which have a critical effect on whether they are able to fulfil their potential and achieve a sustainable impact on the poor.

Given the significance of institutions in shaping organisations, and the role of organisations in providing technology and services to the poor, projects with national- or social-level institutional components have the potential for widespread positive impact on poor livestock keepers.

# Implications for DFID

The key lesson to emerge from our review of project experience is the importance of institutions in defining success. Institutions shape the development and behaviour of organisations and therefore influence whether or not they act in the interests of the poor. Many projects have been in conflict with incompatible institutional frameworks, and this has been part of the reason why some of the projects which have attempted to reach the poor have not succeeded, or have proved to be unsustainable.

Donor investment in institutional reform has been limited and usually pitched at an organisational level, through the formation of associations and farmer groups. Since the organisational and institutional context may have a crucial bearing on the outcome of projects, a practical implication is that institutional barriers to development should be considered when planning any new project. A supportive institutional framework will increase the focus on the poor and will enhance the sustainability of projects. Where the institutional framework is not supportive it may be possible to internalise the problem within the project by linking the project to these wider issues.

On occasions this will not be feasible, for example, when the problem is set at a level beyond the influence of a national-level project or is so deeply rooted or widespread that it is not easily changed. On these occasions, there may be a need for a higher-level project to be put in place to address the issue specifically. Alternatively project managers should recognise the likely constraint to project success and plan to reduce the effect if possible. In this latter case, the importance of our analysis is to allow potential problems to be recognised in advance, so that plans can be made to take measures to address them if appropriate.

**Traditional country-programme projects will not be able to address all areas of institutional reform**

However, it is also important to recognise that traditional country-programme projects will not be able to address all areas of institutional reform; many national-level institutions are effectively determined by higher-level international institutions. Given the cascade of linkages between one level of institution and another, it becomes highly relevant for a donor to invest in institutional reform at an international level (not tied to a particular country programme) in order to address constraints to poor people's livelihoods identified at the lowest level.

A **decision tree** has been produced to illustrate the type of questions a donor might ask in order to determine the need for interventions in the livestock sector, and to identify the key issues that need to be addressed. This may be found in the full version of this report (LID, 1998). The decision tree highlights links between poverty reduction and institutions at all levels and illustrates how interventions may be pitched at several of these levels.

- International-level institutional reform, through organisations such as the WTO and its veterinary advisory body the OIE, would aim to create a level playing field for poor livestock keepers.

- National and social institutional reform requires support for poverty reduction from the highest-level rule-makers. Only then do state organisations have the authority to revise policy and legislation to support pro-poor growth, which in turn provides an incentive for subsequent institutional reform at an organisational level. Donor support for poverty reduction is therefore likely to have most impact in countries with a high-level commitment to poverty reduction. Elsewhere, impact may be localised and have limited prospects for sustainability.

- State-level institutional reform will frequently be needed to help government institutions better reflect a pro-poor policy. However, such institutional reform at high organisational level brings with it immense challenges in terms of overturning long-held views and professional norms, vested interests, and the sometimes legitimate, multiple – and opposing – interests of a production-oriented state organisation. The implication is that the process will require substantial investment in time and consultation to create genuine ownership of both the process and product of reform.

There are implications for DFID's considerable research budget. Not only must donor-funded research be more poverty-focused, but institutional reform is also necessary to provide the incentives to ensure that more appropriate research is conducted.

**Donors should review their own institutions to ensure that they are compatible with poverty-focused development**

Finally, donors should review their own institutions to ensure that they are compatible with poverty-focused development based on the promotion of sustainable rural livelihoods. In an era of multi-donor sectorwide approaches to development intervention, any single donor's voice (such as DFID's) is considerably diluted and it is the combined position of the donor consortium that influences the nature and direction of a reform 'project'. This implies that DFID should invest as much in influencing the strength and cohesiveness of the donor position as it does in bringing its influence to bear with the partner organisation itself.

In conclusion, we argue that where institutions affecting livestock development do not support poverty reduction, any projects are likely to be fundamentally limited in both their impact on the poor and the sustainability of the systems they establish. Solutions rest with strategies that create an institutional framework that is supportive of poverty reduction. There remains an important role for 'lower-level' projects in the conventional sense, but they must be explicitly linked to – and inform – the institutional reforms that are necessary to create an environment that is supportive of poverty eradication.

# Key References

de Haan, C., Steinfeld, H. and Blackburn, H. (1997) *Livestock and the Environment: Finding a Balance.* Report of a study sponsored by the Commission of the European Communities, the World Bank and the governments of Denmark, France, Germany, The Netherlands, United Kingdom and United States of America. Brussels: European Commission Directorate General for Development.

Holden, S., Ashley, S. and Bazeley, P. (1997) *Livestock and Poverty Interactions: A Review of the Literature.* Discussion Paper for DFID Natural Resources Policy and Advisory Department. Crewkerne: Livestock in Development.

Livestock In Development (1998) *Strategies for Improving DFID's Impact on Poverty Reduction: A Review of Best Practice in the Livestock Sector.* A policy research paper undertaken for DFID's Natural Resources Policy and Advisory Department. Crewkerne: Livestock In Development.

Mack, S. (ed.) (1993) *Strategies for Sustainable Animal Agriculture in Developing Countries: FAO Animal Production and Health Paper 107.* Proceedings of the FAO expert consultation on strategies for sustainable animal agriculture in developing countries, Rome, Italy, 10–14 December, 1990. Rome: FAO.

North, D. (1990) *Institutions, Institutional Change and Economic Performance.* Cambridge: Cambridge University Press.

Scoones, I. (ed.) (1995) *Living with Uncertainty: New Directions in Pastoral Development in Africa.* London: Intermediate Technology Publications.

# References Cited

Asian Development Bank (1991) 'Sector Paper on Livestock.' *Staff Paper* 4. Manila: ADB Agriculture Department.

Atherton, J.S. (1984) 'The Evolution of a Donor Assistance Strategy for Livestock Programs in sub-Saharan Africa', in Evangelou, P. and Simpson, J.R. (eds) *Livestock Development in Sub-Saharan Africa.* Boulder: Westview Press, pp 163–74.

Birbuet, G., and Cornacchia, S. (1996) 'Les ONG specialisées dans le financement rural en Bolivie – l'expérience de l'ANED', *Revue Tiers Monde* 37(145) pp 203–212.

Blackburn, H. (1993) 'An Overview of Livestock Development Funding by The United States Agency for International Development', in Blackburn and de Haan (eds) (1993), pp 47–53.

Blackburn, H. and de Haan, C. (eds) (1993) 'Livestock Development Projects; Past, Present and Future.' Proceedings of an informal meeting of donor representatives involved in livestock development, organised by USAID and the World Bank, Paris, France, 4–6 December 1992. Washington D.C.: USAID/World Bank.

Butcher, C. (1994) 'Extension and Pastoral Development: Past, Present and Future', *Pastoral Development Network Paper* 37d. London: ODI.

Danida (1997) *Livestock: Danida Sector Policies*. Copenhagen: Ministry of Foreign Affairs.

de Haan, C., Steinfeld, H. and Blackburn, H. (1997) *Livestock and the Environment: Finding a Balance*. Report of a study sponsored by the Commission of the European Communities, the World Bank and the governments of Denmark, France, Germany, The Netherlands, United Kingdom and United States of America. Brussels: European Commission Directorate General for Development.

Dolberg, F. and Findlayson, P. (1995) 'Treated Straw for Beef Production in China', *World Animal Review* 82(1) pp 14–24.

Dolberg, F. (1996) 'Feed Resources for Landless and Small Farmers in Asia: Research Requirements based on studies in Vietnam, India and Bangladesh.' *Staff Working Paper* 19. Rome: IFAD Technical Advisory Division.

EC (European Commission) (1997) *Evaluation of the Pan-African Rinderpest Campaign. Final Report*. Brussels: EC, DGVIII.

Harriss–White, B. (1995) 'Maps and Landscapes of Grain Markets in South Asia', in Harriss, J., Hunter, J. and Lewis, C.M. (eds) *The New Institutional Economics and Third World Development*. London: Routledge.

Holden, S. (1997) *Economic Impact of Community-Based Animal Health Workers in Kathakani, Kenya*. Crewkerne: Livestock in Development.

Holden, S., Ashley, S. and Bazeley, P. (1997) *Livestock and Poverty Interactions: A Review of the Literature*. Mimeo. Crewkerne: Livestock in Development.

ILRI (International Livestock Research Institute) (1995) 'Livestock Policy Analysis', *ILRI Training Manual 2*. Addis Ababa: ILRI.

Jordan, T., Chema, S., Holden, S. and West, C. (1998) *KETRI/DFID Trypanosomiasis Research Project - Phase III. Final Review*. Nairobi: British Development Division East Africa.

Kenyon, S.J. and Nour, A. (1991) 'Animal Disease Diagnoses Laboratories: What are their Functions in a Less Developed Country?' Presented at the Centre for African Studies symposium on *Technology, Culture and Development in the Third World: Lessons and Examples from Africa*, Ohio State University, Ohio, USA, 23–25 May 1991.

Konstapel, C.D and Nell, A.J. (1993) 'Livestock Production in the Netherlands' Development Cooperation Programme', in Blackburn and de Haan (eds) (1993) pp 10–18.

Majok, A. and Schwabe, C. (1996) *Development among Africa's Migratory Pastoralists*. Westport: Bergin and Garvey.

NDC (Netherlands Development Cooperation) (1992) 'Livestock Production in Developing Countries.' *Policy Document 1*. The Hague: Ministry of Foreign Affairs.

North, D. (1990) *Institutions, Institutional Change and Economic Performance.* Cambridge: Cambridge University Press.

Odhiambo, O., Holden, S., and Ackello-Ogutu, C. (1998) *OXFAM Wajir Pastoral Development Project: An Economic Impact Assessment.* Nairobi: OXFAM.

Qureshi, S., Nabi, I., and Faruqee, R. (1996) *Rural Finance for Growth and Poverty Alleviation in Pakistan. Financial Report.* Washington, D.C.: The World Bank: Agriculture and Natural Resources Division, South Asia Region.

Scoones, I. (1995) 'New Directions in Pastoral Development in Africa', in Scoones, I. (ed.) *Living with Uncertainty.* London: Intermediate Technology Publications, pp 1–37.

Seabright, P. (1992) 'Quality of Livestock Assets Under Selective Credit Schemes: Evidence from South Indian Data', *Journal of Development Economics* 37, pp 327–50.

Thomas-Slayter, B. and Bhatt, N. (1994) 'Land, Livestock and Livelihoods: Changing Dynamics of Gender, Caste and Ethnicity in a Nepalese Village', *Human Ecology* 22(4).

Timon, V.M. (1993) 'Strategies for Sustainable Development of Animal Agriculture – An FAO Perspective', in S. Mack (ed.) *Strategies for Sustainable Animal Agriculture in Developing Countries: Proceedings of the FAO Expert Consultation held in Rome, Italy, 10-14 December, 1990.* Rome: FAO, pp 7–22.

Vandersmissen, A. (1997) 'Strengthening Livestock Services in South East Asia: A Contribution to the Regional Control of Foot and Mouth Disease.' Presented at the third meeting of the OIE sub-commission for foot and mouth disease, Manila, Philippines, 24–28 February 1997.

Vandersmissen, A. and Symoens, C. (1997) 'Factors Influencing the Efficiency of Development Projects in Animal Production and Health Services: Some Lessons from Cooperation with Livestock Services in Asia.' Paper presented at the workshop on systematic improvement of the efficiency of public and private livestock services in Asia, Bangkok, Thailand, 22–26 April 1997.

von Sury, F. E. (1990) 'Guidelines of SDC in the Field of Livestock Production. A Sectoral Policy Regarding Future SDC projects'. Bern: Agriculture Service, Swiss Development Cooperation.

Walshe, M. J. (1993) 'Investment for Sustainable Livestock Development in Developing Countries', in Mack, S. (ed.) *Strategies for Sustainable Animal Agriculture in Developing Countries: Proceedings of the FAO Expert Consultation Held in Rome, Italy, 10–14 December, 1990.* Rome: FAO, pp 163–74.

World Bank (1997) 'The Impact of Dairying Development in India: The Bank's Contribution', *Evaluation Report 16848-IN.* Washington D.C.: World Bank.

# 8 Ethical Trade and Sustainable Rural Livelihoods

## Natural Resources and Ethical Trade Programme, NRI

## Introduction

This chapter explores the actual and potential contribution ethical trade can make to the achievement of sustainable rural livelihoods. It is an edited version of a report based on case studies of different approaches to ethical trade in renewable natural resources (see Table 1 and Case Studies). The report also draws on the experience of the Natural Resources and Ethical Trade Programme (NRET), the Soil Association and others involved in ethical trade.[1] Analysis is in the context of the sustainable rural livelihoods framework.

## What is ethical trade?

Ethical trade is the trade in goods produced under conditions that are socially and/or environmentally as well as economically responsible. There is no definitive approach to ethical trade. Rather, ethical trade is a generic term applicable to a variety of initiatives which apply sets of social/ environmental values to aspects of the production and marketing process. These initiatives include: fair trade schemes; in-house codes of practice; organic production; environmental codes; forest certification; and the ethical sourcing initiatives of major western retailers.

### Ethical trade and sustainability

It can be argued that the values espoused by the various ethical trade initiatives are all elements of sustainability. Indeed, some would argue that the existence of ethical trade is a necessary condition for sustainability, something that cannot be achieved unless we find a 'more holistic and ethical approach to doing business' that values social and environmental impact and restructures North–South relations (Welford, 1995). Others

**Table 1: Case studies**

| Initiative | Commodity | Location |
|---|---|---|
| Fair trade and organic farming | Cotton | Uganda |
| Fair trade | Minimally processed fruit and vegetables | Uganda |
| Fair trade | Bananas | Ghana |
| Certified forests | Forest products | Mexico |
| Organic farming | Fruit and vegetables | Uganda |

Additional primary data was obtained on fair trade cocoa (Ghana), organic horticulture (Ghana), and organic cotton (Kenya and Zimbabwe).

would go even further than this and suggest that international trade itself is unsustainable.[2] Further investigation is therefore required if we are to understand whether ethical trade and sustainability are headed on a path of convergence or collision.

## Ethical trade and natural resources

The development of ethical standards has close links with the renewable natural resources area. Organic farming standards have existed for over 50 years, certification of sustainably managed forests began in the early 1990s, and in the mid–1990s the first fair trade product – coffee – became widely available. More recently, ethical standards for manufacturing industry have gained a higher public profile, though new initiatives continue to be developed in the natural resources area (e.g. for horticulture and fisheries).

## Types of ethical trade initiative

There are four main functioning ethical initiatives relevant to rural areas:[3]

- forest certification
- fair trade
- organic agriculture
- cut flowers.

**Table 2: Shared elements in existing ethical trade initiatives**

Custodian body to set ethical standards.

Third-party verification of compliance with standards.

Use of label or logo to show compliance with standards.

Transparency regarding certification process and access to findings.

This project has looked at the first three, of which only fair trade addresses trading relations *per se*. The other initiatives are concerned with the conditions under which traded items are produced (although organic production and forest certification do provide a means of accessing particular markets). Though these initiatives developed independently, they share common elements, as shown in Table 2. They also differ in significant respects (Table 3).

## The ethical market place

The overriding factor affecting ethical trade is the market. Both fair trade and organic agriculture have distinct markets. The fair trade market for products from developing countries accounts for US$300–500 million in retail sales each year in Europe and the USA. The world organic market is worth US$11 billion; US$500 million by value of the goods sold come from developing countries. Certified forest products compete in the same market as conventional products; according to some estimates, certified

---

### Table 3: Divergent elements of ethical trade initiatives

| Description | Comment |
|---|---|
| Focus | Fair trade has a primarily social emphasis; some schemes include environmental responsibility criteria.<br>Forest certification mixed social and environmental emphasis.<br>Organic primarily environmental emphasis but some social criteria depending on scheme. |
| End product | Only organic agriculture has a distinguishable end product (i.e. without chemical residues). The physical end products of forest certification and fair trade are not distinguishable from their conventionally produced equivalents. |
| Ethical premiums | Organic products currently sell at a premium price. Products sold on the fair trade market have a social premium. Little evidence except in niche markets of a green premium for certified forest products. |
| Access to markets | Marketing is integral to fair trade; incidental to organic and forest certification. |
| Capacity building | Involvement in capacity building for producers is integral to fair trade.<br>Not part of forest certification.<br>Part of organic certification depending on the certification body (e.g. Soil Association). |
| Different certification periods | Organic and fair trade annual.<br>Forest certification 5-yearly with 3 intermediate audits. |
| Certifiers | IFOAM* requires a change in individual certifiers after a given period. Forest certification and fair trade encourages use of the same certifiers. |

\* IFOAM: International Federation of Organic Agricultural Movements

---

forest products (mostly from developing countries) will account for 15% of the timber market in certain countries by 1999.

**Demand for ethically produced items currently outstrips supply**

Demand for ethically produced items currently outstrips supply, and fair trade and organic markets are growing at 10–25% per year, though growth is from a very low base (fair trade accounts for only 0.01% of global trade). Projections for organic markets are optimistic. Some estimate that organic produce will account for 15% (by value) of the world food market by 2006, though this estimate appears to assume an unusual adoption curve, whereby current price premiums for organic produce (sometimes greater than 50%) will persist despite expansion in production and in the number of consumers.

This brings us to the question of whether ethical produce will ever extend its appeal beyond affluent consumers. While prices remain high, this is unlikely. However, some argue that producer prices for certain commodities can be raised – the main objective of ethical trade schemes – without unduly raising consumer prices, as the producer price represents a relatively small element of the total price (see Robins and Roberts, 1997).

However, conjecture about the ultimate size of the ethical market may be a red herring, at least in some sectors, because of the ethical criteria that are starting to be developed by major retailers/importers. For some products within the next few years, it may no longer be a question of how large the ethical market is because the ethical market may have become *the* market, something already evidenced from the application of ethical criteria to the sourcing of fresh produce.

## The ethical premium

A key attraction of ethical trade lies in the premium prices ethical products can command. In principle, the social premium paid by consumers (3 cents per kilo for bananas from Latin America and Ghana) is passed on to producer organisations and is earmarked for social development activities for their members.

Organic trade does not try to regulate how income from the sale of organic produce is distributed, but the green premium the organic market attracts allows buyers to pay higher farm-gate prices to producers. Although some producers are clearly benefiting from this, there are also cases in which buyers are retaining a large share of the premium for themselves.

Forest certification has not been promoted on the basis of any price premium, though many people – especially producers outside the scheme– have this expectation. The value of the scheme is that it provides market access to small producers who do not meet the volume requirements for the conventional timber trade.

**Figure 1: Stakeholders in ethical trade**

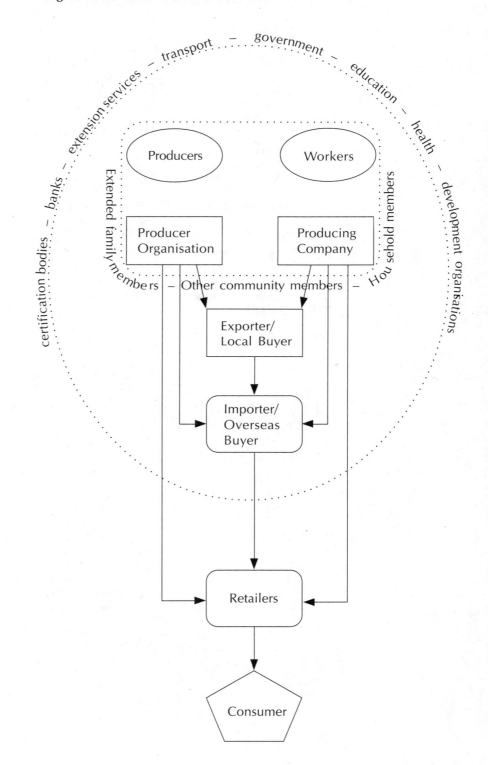

# Roles and actors in ethical trade

## *Private sector*

There are a large number of stakeholder groups which affect ethical trade (Figure 1). Not surprisingly many of these are in the private sector. Private sector organisations are involved not only in production but also in import/export, certification processes, banking/credit, transport, storage, retailing, market promotion and technical services. The constraints faced by those involved are not always unique to ethical trade but rather are generic to export trade from developing countries (Table 4).

## *Marketing organisations*

Ethical trade takes place through a variety of different marketing organisations, not all of which were established with the intention of

---

**Table 4: Constraints to the private sector's role in ethical trade development**

| | |
|---|---|
| Retailers | Consumer expectations regarding quality and price<br>Insufficient quality and quantity of produce<br>Erratic supply<br>Cost of ethical auditing of producers<br>Too many standards/codes |
| Importers | Insufficient quality and quantity of produce<br>Erratic supply<br>Cost of ethical auditing of producers<br>Too many standards/codes |
| Exporters/Traders | Limited knowledge of export markets<br>Excessively lengthy supply chains<br>High cost of loans<br>Suspicions of public sector and development agencies<br>Price fluctuations<br>Poor infrastructure |
| Certification bodies | High cost of certification (particularly if done by foreign consultants)<br>Limited in-country capacity |
| Banking | Reluctance to invest in agriculture<br>Poor organisation of producer and trader groups<br>Weak understanding of ethical objectives |
| In-country processing industries | Poor infrastructure (e.g. power, roads, storage)<br>Low quality standards<br>Limited knowledge of export markets<br>Unsupportive policy environment<br>High cost of loans<br>Inappropriate technology and poor skills base |
| In-country service | High cost of loans<br>Unsupportive policy environment<br>Poor skills base<br>Poor infrastructure |

supplying the ethical market. In many cases, the buyers do not have a conventional marketing background and are driven as much by moral as commercial values. These 'ethical entrepreneurs' can be highly imaginative in bringing new products to the market, as is the case in Quintana Roo (Mexico) where non-traditional timber species have been exported since forest certification. However, new buyers usually have fewer resources to invest than conventional marketing organisations. This limits their capacity to enter the added-value end of the market (e.g. pre-packing). There are also problems of scale as low turnover makes it difficult to cover the costs of capital equipment.

Produce from ethical trade schemes is not, though, sold exclusively to ethical market sectors. In some instances in the case studies, producers complained that they had no way of knowing into which market (and therefore at what price) buyers were selling. They felt that buyers were holding back this information in order to deny them an ethical premium.

## Public sector

Ethical trade has grown without significant public sector involvement. It has, however, benefited from trade liberalisation, supportive export trade policies and investment in infrastructure – not least government's ability to bring about political stability. In the longer term the success of ethical trade is likely to depend on effective public–private sector collaboration.

## Development organisations

It is difficult to find an example of ethical trade that has not been influenced in some way by international development programmes. Donor agencies have facilitated grants, loans and technical support. The role of NGOs and trade unions has also been crucial.

The involvement of development organisations has not, however, always been positive. There is a 'honey pot' tendency whereby development organisations have channelled resources to ethical trade scheme participants to the exclusion of others. Equally, development organisations tend to focus on production rather than market promotion, and there are instances of this destroying the market through over-supply.

## International trade regulation

The World Trade Organisation's (WTO's) view of ethical trade – which will be fundamental to the future development of this type of trading relationship – is a cause for concern within parts of the ethical trade movement. Initially it was feared that the WTO would view ethical standards as a form of non-tariff barrier, a view that has been shared by some developing countries. The WTO is due to review this situation, but the Dutch and British governments are currently of the opinion that WTO will not intervene if ethical standards remain voluntary.

Other policies have had a more immediate impact. For instance, the EU Banana Protocol under the Lomé Convention has been a significant factor in the development of fair trade bananas. On the one hand, it has added significantly to the cost of fair trade bananas which are imported from Ghana and Latin America; on the other hand, it may have the potential to protect fair trade bananas from the Caribbean.[4] EU organic regulations have assisted the organic market, but the fumigation required under the USA's quarantine regulations effectively destroys the organic status of some imported fresh produce.[5]

## Western consumers

Ethical trade has been heavily influenced by consumer values in areas such as consumer health, environmental sustainability, producer well-being and animal welfare (Christian Aid, 1997). What this means is that for the first time the western consumer could become a direct stakeholder in international development. This is a positive step, but it is not without its problems. It introduces the possibility of ethical criteria being introduced as a response to western consumer rather than southern producer concerns. As mainstream retailers and importers become more involved in ethical sourcing they are becoming aware of this hazard. They are, however, reluctant to run the risk of NGO or media opprobrium and consequent loss of sales by pointing this out. In the longer term, though, there is a fear that consumer misconceptions, if not corrected, will damage the credibility of ethical trade (for instance, by the inclusion of inappropriate criteria for assessing ethical performance or through consumer reluctance to embrace concepts of sustainable use).

**For the first time the western consumer could become a direct stakeholder in international development**

## Assets required to engage in ethical trade

### Natural capital

Natural capital requirements to participate in ethical trade vary according to the commodity and scheme. Many ethical trade schemes require some form of long-term tenure because they involve perennial crops (e.g. fair trade coffee, bananas, cocoa), or require verifiable land management practices over a minimum period (e.g. five years for organic farms). The requirements of forest certification also favour those with secure access rights, though this need not take the form of private ownership (community-owned and managed forests have been certified in Mexico, Papua New Guinea and the Solomon Islands).

---

### Case Study 1: Solar-dried fruit

Fruits of the Nile (FON) was established in 1990 and started regular trading in 1993. It is a Ugandan-registered company exporting sun-dried fruit for the health food and fair trade markets.

FON started with the aim of improving rural livelihoods. It hit on solar drying after exploring various options that could diversify income-generating opportunities, add value at the community level, use simple and affordable technology, be transportable using existing infrastructure, reduce perishability, and not have a negative effect on other African economies. Fruit drying was finally chosen because of the potential of the solar-drying technology.

The company sources from about 100 groups and individuals. From 50 kg at the outset, FON now exports 36–40 tonnes annually with a net export value of about US$130,000.

---

The amount and type of land required depends on the commodity. Although there are commercial farms, forests and plantations producing for the ethical market, there are also smallholders with less than one hectare of cultivable land producing for both fair trade and organic markets. Indeed, some argue that organic agriculture, being more labour intensive, is more suited to small-scale farming.[6]

**Ethical trade can also benefit those without direct access to natural resources**

Ethical trade can also benefit those without direct access to natural resources. The landless are able to work on plantations, and some outgrower schemes provide people with access to land. Where ethical trade is in minimally processed items, such as solar-dried fruit, it is also possible for those without cultivable land to participate as long as they have access to raw materials, for which they will require financial resources.

## Financial capital

The amount of financial capital required to produce for ethical trade markets again depends on the commodity. Many schemes have built upon existing endowments so that much of the start-up investment, for instance in land preparation and planting materials, has already been made. The exceptions to this are where investment in processing equipment is required, or where plantations have had to be established.

---

### Case Study 2: Community-managed forests

In 1995 Quintana Roo in Mexico was the first community-managed forest to be certified under the Forest Stewardship Council. The 86,000 ha of forest had been returned to community ownership in the 1980s, and the 832 *ejidos* which own the forest were encouraged to join together in co-operatives to improve technical and managerial support.

Quintana Roo was already selling to ethical buyers prior to certification thanks to a long programme of assistance from the Mexican government, GTZ and American environmental NGOs. Certification was strongly supported by Mexican NGOs and government agencies. Most of the timber is sold domestically or to conventional export markets, but certification has helped Quintana Roo timber to access ethical markets, particularly markets for non-traditional timber in the USA.

* An *ejido* is an area of land and the people who have rights to that land.

---

However, production for ethical markets does incur additional expense, most importantly for certification. This can cost as much as US$10,000 for organic produce and US$13,000 for a community-managed forest. In reality, though, few small producers appear to incur certification costs directly, as they are met by buyers or development agencies. For fair trade, the cost of producer assessment seems to be included in the fee paid by European buyers to use the fair trade label.

## Human capital

### Skills–base

Forest certification requires improved knowledge about forest management, and organic agriculture is knowledge-intensive rather than input-intensive (it requires more design and management). This makes human resource and institutional development an important component of support to ethical trade, and buyers and development organisations have often been involved in the necessary training and extension (e.g. the introduction of plantation bananas in Ghana and of organic farming techniques and solar drying technology in Uganda).

Formal education can be required for certain aspects of ethical trade. In addition to the skills associated with conventional export trading, those involved must have the capacity to fulfil comprehensive documentation and monitoring procedures in order to demonstrate good management. Weak producer capacity in this area has led to many buyers or third parties taking on this role.

### Labour

Participation in ethical trade – and particularly organic production – can increase labour demands, as compared to conventional production and trade. Additional labour is required for tasks such as drawing up forest inventories and increased manual weeding. As a result, organic agriculture has been most successful where labour is readily available and affordable.

Access to the labour required may be affected by gender, age and marital status (see, for example, Blowfield, 1994). For instance, women are less likely to have access to family labour than men, older people are more able to access family labour than younger ones, and non-married people have less access than married ones. This has impacts on different groups' ability to become involved in ethical trade. Women, in particular, have been constrained from participating due to the multiple tasks they have to perform within the household.

**Organic agriculture has been most successful where labour is readily available and affordable**

## Social capital

Land tenure is an indigenous institution that significantly affects participation in ethical trade. Even on plantations where theoretically anyone can work, some local leaders have insisted that preference be given to their own people, perhaps as part of the lease agreement for the land. This can be positive in that it allows local people (some of whom may have been displaced by the plantation) to obtain work. But any inequities in the indigenous institution will also be carried over (for instance, where traditional land tenure disfavours access by women or migrants).

Non-traditional institutions, such as political and religious groups, can also affect participation in ethical schemes.

## *Physical capital*

The amount and type of physical capital required for ethical trade depends more on the commodity and production system than on any particular requirements of the ethical market. It is fair to say that ethical trade demands no more than a machete and no less than a container vessel. For instance, a banana plantation requires multi-million dollar investment in packing stations, irrigation, cableways, etc., but smallholder organic ginger cultivation requires only access to land, organic fertiliser and planting material. Smallholder cotton production represents an intermediate point as it requires land, seed and labour as well as access to stores and ginneries.

At the same time, lack of physical capital accounts for the failure of some producers and buyers to exploit opportunities in the ethical market place. For instance, poor-quality sawmills have hampered sales of certified timber; poor packing and presentation may have cost Fruits of the Nile an important overseas contract; and inadequate storage and transport facilities have resulted in the rejection of Ghanaian bananas by the Swiss fair trade market.

**Schemes are affected by the objectives of their particular branch of ethical trade, the commodities with which they work, and the national context in which they operate**

## Features of ethical trade

As the case study boxes show, there is no definitive approach to ethical trade. The numerous schemes are affected by the objectives of their particular branch of ethical trade, the commodities with which they work, and the national context in which they operate. Nonetheless, it is possible to identify common themes that link the approaches.

---

**Case Study 3: Organic farming**

Suntrade is a buyer and exporter of organic horticultural produce from Uganda. Over seven years its annual exports have expanded from 1 to 104 tonnes, sent mostly to Switzerland but also to the Netherlands, UAE, South Africa and the UK. It is currently buying from smallholders in different parts of the country; certification is organised and paid for by Suntrade. Conversion to organic farming has been relatively easy for producers because years of domestic conflict meant that farmers had little access to high-input agriculture.

Produce is air-freighted, something made viable by the relatively low air costs from Kampala and the green premium on organic produce. Unlike other case studies, Suntrade has had no development agency support.

---

## *Short and transparent trading chains*

The range of stakeholders in any ethical trade scheme can be seen from Figure 1. At the core of the scheme are the producers, producer organisations (which may also be involved in marketing), local marketing organisations and overseas buyers.

The length of the production–marketing chain is important for a number of reasons. First, fair trade organisations have blamed traders and long trading chains for poor farm-gate prices. Therefore, fair trade tries to 'cut out the middle man' by encouraging overseas buyers to deal directly with producers (who are often encouraged to form groups or cooperatives for this purpose). In the case of fair trade bananas, the fair trade plantation companies are actually part-owners of the sole importer of fair trade bananas in Europe.

Second, the ability to show where, when and how a given item was produced is vital to the integrity of the trade. This requires auditable chains of custody or traceability mechanisms. These can be jeopardised by unduly long supply chains. Ethical trade chains are therefore often more tightly vertically integrated than those in conventional trade.

**Fair trade tries to 'cut out the middle man' by encouraging overseas buyers to deal directly with producers**

## *Fair prices and prompt payment*

Producers are normally paid in cash on receipt of the produce by the buyer. For large-volume transactions this can involve considerable pre-financing by the buyer. Documented cash transactions are part of building buyer–producer trust – a principle of fair trade which is also evident in organic and sustainable timber trade. Buyers often commit themselves to purchasing everything that is produced, so long as minimum quality standards are met. Fair trade prices are normally guaranteed for up to a year, which again helps develop trust.

Price guarantees and promises to buy produce are not without their problems; indeed, they can threaten the viability of an entire marketing venture. Strong foreign exchange rates and weak local currencies have in recent times provided buyers with a cushion against fluctuating world prices. However, ethical buyers cannot go on buying at above world prices

---

**Case Study 4: Fair trade bananas**

Volta River Estates Ltd (VREL) is a Ghanaian-registered plantation company formed in 1988. Disease wiped out its plantations, and when it started to export once more it was hit by the EU Banana Protocol under which countries such as Ghana were compelled to buy licences to access EU markets.

A chance meeting with Dutch fair trade organisations led to VREL supplying the EU fair trade market in 1996 under the Oké label. In 1993 the company had 23 workers, 140 ha of partly uncultivated land and a host of labour and local problems. By the end of 1997, after a year of selling to the fair trade market, it had 280 ha under production, had largely resolved its labour problems and was employing 900 people. In the words of one VREL manager, 'Fair trade saved VREL.'

---

---

### Case Study 5: Organic and fair trade cotton

Organic cotton has been promoted in various African countries by the SIDA-funded Export Promotion of Organic Products from Africa project (EPOPA). In Uganda, EPOPA supported the Lango Farmers' Cooperative Union (LFCU) which buys from groups of farmers organised into 156 'Primary Societies'. Since 1996, LFCU has sold to Farmers Fair Trade, owned by a Dutch-based trading company that specialises in fair trade.

In the first three years, the number of farmers growing organic cotton rose from 200 to over 5,000, and production grew from 70 to 900 tonnes. Today there are over 7,000 farmers involved. Farm-gate prices are over 60% higher than for non-organic cotton.

---

indefinitely, as Farmers Fair Trade in Uganda discovered in its short-lived sesame trading enterprise. If buyers are unable to take producers' output, then this jeopardises another common feature of ethical trade schemes: exclusive contracts (see below).

One strategy to stabilise prices is to move into markets in which consumers are willing to pay an ethical premium. At present, quality problems have meant that these niche markets remain mostly under-supplied. However, there can be rationing in such markets; when one fair trade buyer was caught by over-supply, it insisted that its producers cut back on volume, instigating a quota system in order to maintain unit prices to producers.

## Exclusive contracts

Close relationships between buyers and suppliers are often cemented through exclusive contracts. These are a crucial factor in the success of ethical trade. Without firm contracts with their suppliers ethical buyers are unable to develop stable markets or to ensure that the cost of auditing/certification will be recouped. However, until buyers have proven their reliability, it is in the producers' interests to have a choice of outlets and not to tie themselves to a particular buyer. Thus, there can be a conflict of interests.

Traditional traders have often restricted producers' marketing options through the use of tied loans. Although none of the case studies provides a model alternative, producer–buyer relations are strongest when the buyer also provides access to credit, technical support and assistance with institution-building. Relationships and trust are also strengthened when the buyer operates a policy of transparency about prices and market conditions. This does not always happen, particularly when it comes to the social/ ethical premium.

The case studies showed that producers of fairly traded dried fruits in Uganda were unaware of any social premium that their buyers were receiving (although Fruits of the Nile does provide considerable technical and managerial support to producers as part of its overall programme). Lagona Farmers' Cooperatives Union, also in Uganda, does not run a social development programme for its cotton producers, and some producers complained that they were not being paid at all. Volta River Estates (in Ghana) acknowledges that it should use the social premium for its workers, but at present the premium is being used by the buyer, Agrofair, to purchase the European import licences required under the EU Banana Protocol.

## Catalysts and viability

Each of the case study schemes has depended on a catalyst – the normally overlooked individual or organisation that exceeds the requirements of their particular role in order to make the scheme work (Table 5). In both the small and large schemes examined, individuals have invested significant sums of their own money to keep their schemes afloat. Many schemes also depend upon 'subsidy' in the form of development grants, technical assistance and soft loans. This, though, brings into question their long-term financial viability, which is an issue that merits further research.

**Many schemes depend upon 'subsidy' in the form of development grants, technical assistance and soft loans**

## Auditing of performance

Common to all ethical trade initiatives is the measurement of performance against the standards of a standard–setting body (e.g. FLO (Fair trade Labelling Organisations International), FSC (Forest Stewardship Council) or IFOAM (International Federation of Organic Agricultural Movements)). However, there can be problems with the way ethical auditing is developed. Ethical criteria tend not to be the result of stakeholder consultation, but of western consumers' concerns. (The experiences of international development in fostering participatory approaches have not yet been absorbed into auditing practice.) The resulting values may therefore reflect neither producer opinion and priorities nor the practical problems faced along the production–marketing chain.[7]

Another concern is that, in fair trade, the standard-setting bodies are run by fair trade organisations which themselves have interests in licensing labels, verification, production and buying. This situation might have been justified when the movement was new, but if such vertical integration were

---

### Table 5: Catalyst organisations in case studies

| Scheme | Catalyst organisation |
| --- | --- |
| Quintana Roo community forests | Plan Piloto Forestal (Mexico–Germany technical co-operation project) |
| Ghana fair trade bananas | Volta River Estates Limited |
| Uganda organic horticulture | Suntrade |
| Uganda fair trade dried fruit | Fruits of the Nile |
| Organic and fair trade cotton | Farmers Fair Trade |

**Table 6: Ethical trade initiatives' contribution to components of sustainable rural livelihoods**

| SRL Component | Fair trade | | Organic farming | | Forest certification | |
|---|---|---|---|---|---|---|
| | *Stated in criteria* | *Evident from case studies* | *Stated in criteria* | *Evident from case studies* | *Stated in criteria* | *Evident from case studies* |
| Increased livelihood opportunities | Implicit | ✓x | No | ✓ | No | ✓ |
| Poverty reduction | Implicit | ✓x | No | ✓ | No | ✓ |
| Fostering participation | Yes | ✓ | Partial | ✓x | Implicit | ✓ |
| Development of human capital | Yes | ✓ | Implicit | ✓ | No | ✓ |
| Development of social capital | Yes | ✓ | No | ✓x | Implicit | ✓ |
| Development of physical capital | No | ✓ | No | ✓ | Implicit | ✓ |
| Sustainable natural resource management | Yes | ✓ | Yes | ✓ | Yes | ✓ |

to be found in, for instance, a multinational company, it would undermine the credibility of the auditing system.

# Outcomes

A summary of the outcomes of ethical trade for components of sustainable rural livelihoods is found in Table 6. Table 7 shows how the schemes meet selected DFID Policy Information Marker System (PIMS) objectives.

## *Livelihood opportunities*

Ethical trade is able to increase livelihood opportunities for a range of socially differentiated actors. The type and variety of opportunities is largely a factor of the commodity, but ethical trade has established markets for the produce of smallholders and landless workers, and has introduced new products from certain marginalised producers to the market. In some cases, the requirements of ethical trade have led to increased employment opportunities (for instance, through manual weeding under organic farming and the creation of new functions in forest management). Increased incomes have also led to the creation of new opportunities (e.g. in transport, petty trading).

However, ethical trade's definition of poverty is much less precise than that of international development organisations. Some schemes may favour poor community members, but this is not something that is valued when

## Table 7: Ethical trade performance against selected DFID Policy Information Marker System (PIMS)

| PIMS marker | PIMS score | Comments |
|---|---|---|
| Macro-economic policy: new trade and investment | P | |
| Fiscal reform: import liberalisation | 0 | Import liberalisation in Western countries a requirement for ethical trade. |
| Social policy: policy to redress aspects of social disadvantaged | 0 | Weak targeting of disadvantaged. |
| Strengthening legal/regulatory frameworks | P/S | Fair trade encourages improved worker representation and labour rights. All initiatives enhance Civil Society Organisations' capacity to monitor codes of conduct. |
| Sector policy: improved access of poor to micro-finance | S | Many schemes facilitate access to micro-finance. |
| Sector policy: improved opportunities for poor to market and export crops | P | |
| Sector policy: enhanced access of poor to education, health and other basic services | S/0 | Many schemes have enhanced access of certain sections of the poor. |
| Private sector capacity building, and investment to overcome market failures | P | |
| Access of poor to land, resources and markets | P/0 | Most clearly stated in fair trade, but evident in other initiatives, particularly in access to markets. Impact lessened by weak poverty focus and failure to consider impact on non-participants. |
| Good governance | S/0 | Some schemes make positive contribution to empowerment and democratic accountability in producers' groups. |
| Removal of gender discrimination | 0 | Women have equal rights within schemes, but overall gender impact not considered. Many schemes unsuited to women's needs and conditions. |
| Mobilise business sector in poverty elimination and sustainable development | P | |
| Rights of the child | P/0 | Fair trade has explicit criteria on child rights. |
| Training and skills development | S | |
| Food security | 0 | Focus on export crops may reduce subsistence farming and reduce food security. |

P = principal objective; S = significant objective; 0 = not an objective schemes are assessed. Ethical auditing measures the impact of production on producers, not on non-participants. Therefore, the reasons why women, for instance, are less likely than men to be able to work on ethical trade schemes is not monitored nor factored into management strategies. Likewise whether participation in an ethical trade scheme increases the labour burden of others in the household, or restricts the time and labour producers have available to pursue other productive and reproductive activities is not considered.

Setting up ethical trade schemes can involve some people losing access to natural resources, an impact that again is not measured. Equally, increased incomes from participation in the schemes may lead to expansion at the expense of non-participants and wealth gaps may grow within communities as a result of schemes.

This is not to say that ethical trade schemes do not benefit marginalised people. There are, for instance, schemes that have increased women's livelihood opportunities and allowed those with little access to land to obtain more secure livelihoods. In addition, one feature of most ethical trade schemes studied is that participation may bring with it access to credit (at low interest rates), grants or inputs from buyers/exporters or development agencies.

It is also notable that ethical trade schemes are working successfully in remote areas and areas in which there has been political instability. Because organic agriculture does not depend on external inputs, producers in countries hit by war or weak economies have been able to participate (e.g. Uganda, El Salvador, Mozambique). Forest certification in Mexico and the reversal of land degradation through organic farming may also have helped to reduce outward migration from rural areas.

## *Poverty reduction*

The overall impact of ethical trade on poverty reduction depends on four factors:

### (i) Increased income

Increased remuneration is a stated aim of fair trade. Organic and certified forest schemes can also provide increased income because higher prices are paid and/or market access is better (Table 8).

### (ii) Type and timing of payment

Fair trade insists that producers are paid upon delivery of their product and that payment is in cash (in-kind payments are sometimes used by traders to lower the real farm-gate price paid). However, the timing of payment varies according to the harvesting characteristics of the commodity. Timber and cotton yield infrequent, large sums while horticultural products provide smaller but more regular sums that may be more beneficial to household sustainability.

### Table 8: Comparison of prices between ethical trade and conventional products

| Item | Ethical market price | Conventional export market price | Local market price |
|---|---|---|---|
| Apple banana[+] | 3.00 | 1.70 | – |
| Cavendish banana[♦] | 0.47 | 0.35 | 0.12 |
| Cotton | 2.64* | 1.65 | – |
| Dried pineapple[♦] | 2.64 | 1.85 | – |
| Ginger[+] | *0.60 | – | 0.15 |

1997 prices US$/kg, CIF London unless otherwise stated.
♦ Fair trade  + Organic  * Farm-gate price

### (iii) Impact on others

In some instances, increased earnings from ethical trade have encouraged greater use of hired labour or created new wage-earning opportunities. However, increased earnings are not always passed on to the producers' own suppliers. For example, pineapple and banana growers in Uganda who supply produce for solar drying for the fair trade market receive the local price for their produce, and labourers on organic farms are no better paid than labourers on other farms. Equally, the best wage-earning opportunities derived from ethical trade may be made available to family members, thereby maintaining or increasing social and economic gaps.

### (iv) Distribution of benefits

Ethical trade encourages export crop cultivation, the earnings from which are typically controlled by men. This export focus can lead to women having less opportunity for their own farms and less control over income, depending upon their socially determined negotiating positions. The case studies provide examples in which women have been both advantaged and disadvantaged by male household heads' participation in ethical trade. In neither case was this impact assessed by the ethical trade scheme.

## *Human capabilities*

### Human capital

Increased incomes are often invested in formal education for children. Furthermore the presence of ethical trading schemes increases the opportunities for informal training and education, not least because schemes attract NGO and government development projects. In some case studies, schemes have played a role in improving health facilities for producers and the community at large. Better health and education are also promoted by the year-round incomes producers receive.

Ethical trade schemes also encourage the development of human capital by introducing people to the market, new skills and a range of new partnerships. Although women are less likely than men to participate in ethical trade, where they do it has led to greater respect, responsibility and active participation in the cash economy. Ethical trade has also provided opportunities for younger people as managers of their own businesses, as officials in producer groups, or as union and company officers on plantations.

Away from the producer level, ethical trade has fostered a body of national expertise developing new skills in areas which are important for expanding the export sector.

## Social capital

It is a common feature of ethical trade schemes that they are influenced by existing social capital formations such as land tenure systems, ethnic/cultural groupings and the household. The role of indigenous institutions can be in providing access to natural resources, in determining who participates in ethical trade schemes, and in controlling the distribution of benefits. Yet none of the schemes investigated measures its interaction with these institutions or actively encourages them.

Indeed, initiatives such as fair trade that promote the development of social capital, typically prescribe alternative, exogenous institutional forms such as cooperatives and trade unions. Some form of producer group is necessary in order to reduce the cost of certification/assessment, and in some cases to provide a producer-owned link with buyers. But cooperatives in the case studies are all facing difficulties, and in several instances producers are establishing informal, more localised groups, sometimes built on indigenous institutions, to take over the functions of the cooperatives.

Independent trade unions are a requirement on fair trade plantations. In Ghana, backed by union-friendly national legislation, the union has negotiated a collective bargaining agreement and been active in protesting against the EU Banana Protocol.

## Participation

The development of formal institutions has fostered producer participation, particularly in fair trade and forest certification schemes. Through increased awareness of prices, markets, export issues or forest management, producers have acquired new skills and responsibilities. However, attempts to achieve economies of scale by creating large producer groups have tended to lessen the sense of ownership and control, and may be a reason for the poor functioning of cooperatives.

**Participation is noticeably absent in the setting of ethical criteria and indicators**

One area where participation is noticeably absent is in the setting of ethical criteria and indicators and the management of standards. There is a contradiction at the heart of ethical trade where on the one hand western stakeholders wish to support developing country producers and their environment, but in order to do this they demand complicated monitoring systems over which producers have little influence. Ethical trade consequently may come across as being paternalistic, and as promoting standards that may not represent the values or priorities of the producers themselves.

## Vulnerability and resilience

The contribution ethical trade makes to reducing vulnerability depends on the extent to which benefits from participation help communities and their natural resource base as a whole. By promoting more responsible environmental management, initiatives assume a positive environmental impact. However, in the case studies there was little awareness of why certain practices were being adopted. In some instances producers were even unaware that they were participating in a specific scheme.

**Ethical trade may reduce the opportunities open to non-participants**

As discussed elsewhere, the distribution of benefits is unequal and in some instances ethical trade may reduce the opportunities open to non-participants. Participants often gain improved access and familiarity with the market, although sometimes this comes at the expense of subsistence production opportunities. Ultimately, whether this is a net benefit depends on the resilience of the trading organisations that serve the ethical market, and there is good reason to doubt the viability of some schemes.

Producers are also at risk if they commit to a particular ethical market but then fail certification/assessment. In only one of the case studies had a thorough analysis of the likely impact and benefits of the scheme on local people been conducted prior to start-up, and despite examples of ethical trade schemes having to pull out of certain markets, producer vulnerability is not monitored.

## Sustainable use of the natural resource base

In forest certification and organic farming, enhancing natural resource sustainability is the major concern, and each has well-developed sets of criteria and indicators. In the past, there was little attempt to accommodate indigenous knowledge systems into criteria. Recently, though, the Forestry Stewardship Council has started to give greater emphasis to local conditions and local participation.

In the case studies, producers did not need to make significant changes to existing practices in order to meet organic or sustainable forest management criteria. There are also reasons to doubt the consistency with which criteria have been adhered to; some producers appear to have chosen one organic certifier over another on the grounds that less strict requirements would be imposed.

All ethical trade initiatives measure impact at the local level and do not consider broader issues related to production. For instance, the impact of road and air transport, the energy used to produce packaging or chemical inputs, and the energy used by sawmills or cotton ginneries are beyond the limits of environmental auditing requirements for most ethically traded products. Consequently, it is impossible to say whether environmentally acceptable production for the ethical market has a net positive or negative impact on natural resources.[8]

## Conclusions

Ethical trade initiatives, whether explicitly or implicitly, are concerned with sustainability. While questions can be asked about some of the criteria and indicators emphasised, sets of ethical standards today provide evolving tools for measuring social and/or environmental impact.

Schemes using these standards are creating new livelihood opportunities and increasing the income levels of many participants. For these participants, ethical trade schemes bring considerable benefits in terms of human and social capital development, and provide access to new markets. They allow participants to attract new sources of investment, credit and donor funding. They are also able to function in remote areas and where there has been recent instability. However, there are actual and potential negative impacts, particularly among those unable or unwilling to participate, and initiatives are weak in targeting certain disadvantaged groups.

A major achievement of ethical trade schemes is that they form a catalyst that brings together diverse stakeholders in developing and developed countries, many of whom may not have previously considered themselves to have had a development function. New partnerships are evolving throughout the production–marketing chain. These are vital to the success of the trade. Development organisations have had to become more market-aware, and this in turn has led some of them to adopt a more holistic view of development rather than a narrow production focus. Nevertheless, these partnerships have not been unproblematic. Development organisations must learn more about how trade is conducted, and the influence of western ethical values should be balanced by more participation on the part of developing country producers. At the same time, the knowledge and skills gained by international development professionals (e.g. in participatory approaches) should be brought to bear in the ethical trade area.

The economics of the ethical market are not properly understood. Future projections have tended to emphasise the positive sometimes at the expense of basic marketing economics theory. The ethical premium may not persist as mainstream markets adopt ethical criteria, and production and demand become more balanced. However, producer prices are often a small component of the retail price, so reduced margins need not result in poor

**Development organisations must learn more about how trade is conducted**

127

returns for producers. Of greater concern is the viability of ethical buyers, many of whom are dependent on subsidies (often in the form of development assistance), and the question of alternatives open to producers should a particular buyer withdraw.

Ethical trade is already affecting the thinking of western buyers and retailers. However, it should be noted that the restrictive trade practices highlighted by ethical trade lobbyists as the cause of poor producer prices are, at least in the export market, becoming a thing of the past due to trade liberalisation and the adoption of transparent, traceable trading systems even in conventional export trade. For producers, the long-term value of ethical trade is most likely to derive from the assistance they obtain for developing human and social capital, and for improving natural resource management, rather than from higher prices or better contracts.

The future development of ethical trade depends greatly on the nascent ethical sourcing initiatives of mainstream retailers and importers. The large corporations are learning from existing ethical initiatives, but they also have their own demands. They are unlikely to be as tolerant of production inefficiencies as many current ethical buyers, and may favour commercial farms or plantations over small producers who require more investment if they are to be competitive. However, wage labour opportunities on plantations can be equally attractive to some poor rural people as own production.

Ethical trade by itself is not an answer to sustainability, and this chapter highlights some of its weaknesses as well as its strengths. But, if approached wisely, ethical trade can be an important component in building sustainable rural livelihoods for certain people. Its ultimate impact will depend upon: increasing efficiency; improving targeting of socially differentiated actors; increasing developing country stakeholder involvement in developing initiatives; ensuring commercial viability of key organisations; increasing western consumer awareness of development issues; and adopting sustainable marketing systems. The ongoing partnership-building process described in this paper provides a basis for addressing these constraints in order to optimise the contribution trade can make to developmental goals.

## Key references

Blowfield, M.E. (1994) *Labour Decision-Making in Smallholder Perennial Tree Crop Production: Studies from Ghana and Indonesia.* Report No. R2137(s). Chatham: Natural Resources Institute.

Christian Aid (1997) *Change at the Check-out? Supermarkets and Ethical Business.* London: Christian Aid.

NRI (1997) *Potential for Fair Trade and Organic Bananas from the Caribbean.* Report for Department for International Development. Chatham: Natural Resources Institute.

Robins, N. and Roberts, S. (1997) *Unlocking Trade Opportunities: Case Studies of Export Success from Developing Countries.* London: International Institute for Environment and Development.

Welford, R. (1995) *Environmental Strategy and Sustainable Development: The Corporate Challenge for the 21st Century.* London: Routledge.

## Endnotes

1  The report was prepared by Mick Blowfield, Annabelle Malins, Bill Maynard and Valerie Nelson with additional inputs from Nick Fereday. Case studies were conducted by Mick Blowfield, Annabelle Malins, Bill Maynard, Stephanie Gallet and Valerie Nelson. The work was supplemented by a review of organic agriculture's developmental impact by David Crucefix.

2  See for instance the work of the SAFE Alliance.

3  Other initiatives are in the start-up phase. The Marine Stewardship Council is in the process of developing standards for sustainable fisheries, and African horticultural producers are developing the first regional set of standards for fresh horticultural products. Major retailers and importers are developing ethical sourcing standards but, with the exception of The Body Shop, none of these is in operation at the present time. We chose not to include The Body Shop in the case studies because: (i) it is well- documented elsewhere; (ii) ethical sourcing accounts for a small amount of the company's total trade (e.g. the well-known trade in shea butter is only 30 tonnes per annum); and (iii) the ethical systems are similar to those found in other initiatives (e.g. fair trade).

4  For a more detailed analysis of the EU Banana Protocol and its implications for organic and fair trade, see NRI, 1997.

5  For a more detailed description of the impact of policy and regulations in developing countries on environmental sustainable trade, see Robins and Roberts, 1997.

6  However, it should be noted that commercial farms are increasingly exploring organic production. For example, the organic sector in South Africa is now dominated by large farmers.

7  For instance, poor prices or late payment to producers may be because of late payment by wholesalers to exporters. If the ethical chain is to function, then performance criteria must be adhered to throughout the chain.

8  Some companies have introduced life-cycle assessment to monitor the cradle-to-grave environmental impact of their products. These techniques are difficult to apply to initiatives that assess a single commodity which may pass through several processes and companies before reaching the retail market.

# 9 Research and the Sustainable Rural Livelihoods Approach
## *DFID Natural Resources Research Department*

## Is research an entry point?

The term 'research' describes a process of systematic investigation leading to an increase in the sum of knowledge. Research is based on the collection and analysis of data which are processed to create knowledge. The subsequent application of knowledge to effect a desirable outcome is the process of development. Thus every development paradigm is ultimately dependent upon the creation and application of new knowledge or the application of existing knowledge in new ways. The Sustainable Rural Livelihoods approach is unlikely to be different.

Whether research, and the knowledge it generates, can be considered as an entry point into the sustainable livelihoods approach is debatable, since it would risk the perception that knowledge is a commodity with an intrinsic value of its own. Knowledge achieves its main developmental value when applied to effect a desirable outcome. In the case of the SRL approach, the creation of new knowledge about the five characteristic capital assets of a rural livelihood system may be an essential investment; it will certainly be an underpinning process, informing and improving the quality of other interventions.

Indeed, the DFID White Paper *"Eliminating World Poverty – A Challenge for the 21ˢᵗ Century"* makes the point that "knowledge, research and technology underpin all our work" (para 2.42). The Paper goes on to state that: "The elimination of poverty and protection of the environment requires improved access to knowledge and technologies by poor people". This is a clear recognition that poverty reduction is only possible where existing knowledge is made more easily accessible, and relevant new knowledge is created (where necessary) to address a problem or an opportunity in development.

The ability of practitioners and academics to apply the sustainable livelihoods approach may be dependent on a more complete understanding of the natural, human, social, physical and financial assets available to rural communities. Such knowledge is essential to the success of a development process which sets out to improve poor people's access to these assets and their control over them. It seems self evident that the better the state of knowledge, the greater the confidence with which poverty reduction can be addressed.

Any asset-based entry point into the sustainable rural livelihoods approach has the potential for unplanned, possibly unrecognised, impacts in other parts of the rural system, and on other livelihood assets. One function of research is to establish a level of understanding which can avoid or mitigate such impacts, such that SRL interventions may be equitable and sustainable.

## Why is research needed?

**At present, the Sustainable Rural Livelihoods approach exists as an hypothesis ... an important task for research is to test and subsequently transform the hypothesis into proven principles**

When considering the contribution which research and knowledge systems can make to the success of the SRL approach, one must recognise that the very concept is itself a research product, emerging from a series of studies investigating new paradigms of development which might more effectively eliminate rural poverty. At present, the Sustainable Rural Livelihoods approach exists as an hypothesis – that the integrated management of livelihood assets in rural areas is a universally applicable means of eliminating rural poverty. An important task for research is to test and subsequently transform the hypothesis into proven principles which can, with confidence, be applied in practice.

Application of the SRL concept implies the use of existing knowledge in innovative ways: the measurement and comparative analysis of assets and the generation of new understanding about the constraints to effective utilisation of these assets by the poor. As a general rule, research tends to add dimensions of complexity to the implications of taking any particular course of action. The risk-averse approach to the application of the SRL concept is to start slow, making incremental interventions and play it long, recognising the complexity of the asset base and the extreme variability of its parameters.

The analytical content of such an approach would be rather limited, essentially focused on *ex-post* measurement of cause and effect followed by a series of iterations to adapt the emerging model to differing patterns of assets. This approach focuses on operationalising the SRL concept and generating understanding by observation. An alternative approach is to improve understanding of the asset base and develop a suite of options from which choices can be made according to local circumstances, recognising that these may change from time to time.

Such an approach is implicit in Renewable Natural Resource (RNR) systems research, where the difference between actual and potential performance of natural, human and social capital within a particular

**Where knowledge of the behaviour of assets within any livelihood system is incomplete, the unplanned impacts arising from the application of new knowledge can be considerable**

community or production system is exploited to generate a range of outcomes. Where knowledge of the behaviour of assets within any livelihood system is incomplete, the unplanned impacts arising from the application of new knowledge can be considerable. For example, the successful introduction of high yielding varieties (HYV) of rice into India and Bangladesh in the mid-1960s was accompanied by debate over the possible exacerbation of inequalities and adverse consequences for the poor. Indeed, the water management conditions which maximised the benefits of HYV rice for many did create adverse consequences for some fishery dependent communities of poor people whose livelihoods were affected by a consequent decline in the natural capital to which they had access (see Box 1). A systems-based approach, implicit in SRL, can minimise or mitigate such impacts.

## What kind of research is needed?

Although there already exists some considerable understanding of the five asset streams thought to be important to a sustainable livelihood, it will almost certainly be necessary to generate new knowledge, particularly about their interactions under conditions of change. Interventions to generate a sustainable livelihood will be most effective when there is sound understanding of the assets and their interrelationships.

The SRL approach will, therefore, require new knowledge of financial, social and human capital (social sciences), of natural capital (environmental sciences) and an understanding of physical capital (engineering sciences). It will also require an understanding of the variability within these capital assets and the interactions between them such that the potential effects of interventions on livelihoods can be predicted.

---

**Box 1: Research into livelihood interactions in Bangladesh**

Floodplain systems are characterised by the co-location of common property and private property means of production of aquatic and terrestrial resources in seasonal and spatial cycles. Livelihoods dependent on flood plain systems are highly vulnerable to unplanned impacts of management interventions. For example, the control of river flooding in Bangladesh for the production of HYV rice caused a decline in environmental quality and a loss of biodiversity. It also reduced fish production from the open access fisheries. Livelihoods were affected and rural poverty increased in affected locations. Current research being undertaken by DFID is focused on an analysis of social, human and natural capital in a major floodplain area in Bangladesh. The researchers are modelling the complex system of physical, social and economic interactions of a large rural population, substantially dependent for their livelihoods on the natural capital represented by the floodplain. The aim is to assess how individual livelihood strategies affect the floodplain environment and have collateral impacts on other producer and social groups. Through gaining a better understanding of the inter-relationships between natural, human and social capital, those responsible for development planning will be better able to create the conditions in which rural livelihoods can be made more secure.

---

Research to achieve this understanding will be demand-led and, to some extent, location-specific. There may be a substantial component of adaptation. It seems likely that the research effort must be focused at three levels:

(i) *strategic research* studies which have the objective of increasing understanding of the SRL concept and its possible applications

(ii) *applied research* to generate understanding of the livelihood assets available to any particular target group and the behaviour of these assets when one or more are changed

(iii) *adaptive research* to transform applied social or biological knowledge into products essential to the improvement of specified rural livelihoods.

Such different categories of research, in the several relevant disciplines required for comprehensive understanding, highlight a need for effective coordination and management of integrated studies.

Many applications of the SRL approach will focus on communities of poor people, with the aim of reducing vulnerability and other expressions of poverty. The three main routes to the elimination of rural poverty by application of new knowledge are through:

- changes in production by poor people

- changes in consumption by poor people

- changes in employment of poor people.

The manipulation of assets to produce these outcomes is highly complex. Investment in research to produce relevant knowledge must be balanced between: studies focused on the rights, interests and needs of poor people; inclusive studies which focus on issues of equity and access and developing a general understanding of the opportunities and services of benefit to the whole rural community; and enabling studies which provide knowledge in support of the policies and context for poverty elimination.

## How should such research be funded?

The generation of new knowledge relevant to the creation of sustainable rural livelihoods could emerge from either public or private sector initiatives. Private sector investment in research of relevance to developing countries has historically been modest. However, in recent years, the increasing pace of biotechnological discoveries and the ability to capture intellectual property rights has encouraged a much more active private sector research agenda.

Since the objectives of private sector-funded research are measured in terms of profit and influence, the products must be 'owned' for a period which is sufficiently long to generate the commercial benefit sought.

Private sector investment is not attracted by knowledge which is non-excludable or non-subtractable (this would include much work on common property resources). Although these factors do not rule out the use of products arising from private initiatives within a SRL approach, they do suggest that the whole area of sustainable rural livelihoods is unlikely to be a specific focus for private sector investment in research.

Public sector investment is essential to cover such market failure and to support those who can neither fund their own knowledge needs nor utilise the products of private sector research. Public investment is particularly needed to address issues of policy and regulation of resource use.

Private sector research is often conducted with limited community participation and with the greatest effort devoted to technology development and subsequent marketing. Public sector research, conversely, usually follows the current fashion of wide participation by intended beneficiaries. The effort devoted to technology development is limited, whilst marketing is often completely absent. Marketing is replaced by 'dissemination', a process which makes the knowledge widely available through various channels, with varying success.

**The essential characteristics of successful SRL research will be the creation of reliable and enduring partnerships between researchers in different disciplines and between institutions representing different stakeholders**

The essential characteristics of successful SRL research will be the creation of reliable and enduring partnerships between researchers in different disciplines and between institutions representing different stakeholders (particularly the institutions which will use knowledge directly to the benefit of rural livelihoods). These research-based relationships will almost certainly be supported with public funds, but the work must be demand-led, and carefully planned to achieve closely specified outcomes.

Public sector investment in research is often challenged, either at a general or a programme-specific level. Efforts to evaluate the benefits of investment in research have met with difficulty. The attribution of impact to the use of new knowledge is extremely difficult where the objectives of a research programme are complex, as would be the case in the context of sustainable rural livelihoods. One therefore falls back on general assessments of economic returns to investment in research, several of which suggest that figures of 30–60% can be anticipated in the natural resources sector. Such returns are unlikely to be different in studies focused on SRL, given that the problems and solutions, and institutional mechanisms for their application, are essentially those governing research performance at present.

## How can SRL research be implemented by DFID?

DFID currently invests in research through one of two mechanisms. The creation of knowledge required to resolve location-specific problems and efforts to strengthen national capacity to generate new knowledge is supported with bilateral technical cooperation (TC) funds managed by DFID country programme managers. Such work tends to be adaptive and applied rather than strategic. Although the structure of bilateral TC projects is completely flexible and responsive, country programme research projects have tended to be sectorally narrow. There is no history of broad-based interdisciplinary research effort in geographic programmes, though there is no barrier to the design and implementation of such projects.

The creation of knowledge required to improve understanding of strategic issues is the target for sectoral technical cooperation funds managed by DFID professional departments. Such work has traditionally, by definition, been sectoral. In relatively recent times, following the adoption by some professional departments of development objectives to guide their investment in research, a substantial element of interdisciplinarity has emerged within these sectoral research programmes.

The management of research in DFID is based on development cooperation procedures and financial instruments, which have not to date been designed to facilitate the intersectoral and multidisciplinary efforts needed to effect a coordinated approach to sustainable rural livelihoods. Some other development agencies have adopted structures and procedures which explicitly promote broad-based research programmes focused on developmental themes and concepts. One such is the Canadian International Development Research Centre (IDRC) which manages fifteen geographically focused thematic programmes, each supporting a portfolio of related interdisciplinary projects investigating key constraints.

DFID's effort to develop the new knowledge required to implement the sustainable livelihoods approach will be mainly focused at the applied research level, probably in the awkward gap between the strategic programmes on which sectoral support is focused and the adaptive programmes on which the country programme support is, in practice, focused. Some of DFID's sectoral research programmes have sought to move downstream from the strategic level more directly to influence developmental processes. Such programmes implement research on strategic issues which respond to location-specific demand, the results of which are demonstrated by application at local level. However, such approaches are not uniform within DFID and intersectoral coordination to address the knowledge needs of rural livelihoods development may not be easy.

It would seem more appropriate to establish a thematic programme, based on funds specifically allocated to the SRL approach. Such funds should be under the control of a professional manager charged with drawing relevant strategic knowledge from existing sectoral programmes and integrating this with new knowledge from interdisciplinary research studies in order to generate understanding of the interactions between the

**In relatively recent times a substantial element of interdisciplinarity has emerged within these sectoral research programmes**

five asset streams identified in the SRL framework. This approach would mirror the RNR Systems approach, which the RNR Research Strategy Natural Resources Systems Programme is designed to support. Like SRL, the RNR systems approach is based on an hypothesis that development is more cost effective and has more sustainable outcomes when an integrated, interdisciplinary approach is adopted to resolve problems in rural development. A thematic research programme would contribute significantly to confirmation of that hypothesis.

DFID has recently established a central Knowledge Policy Unit to advise on generic knowledge issues, to lead the strategic direction of DFID support for knowledge generation, and to maximise the impact of knowledge programmes on DFID's development objectives. As part of its responsibility for achieving coherent intersectoral coordination – when this is essential to knowledge requirements – the Knowledge Policy Unit may establish a multidisciplinary research programme. An integrated and intersectoral approach to the generation and management of knowledge contributing to the SRL approach would clearly be a prime target for such a programme.

# 10 Aquatic Resources and Sustainable Rural Livelihoods
## Philip Townsley

## Context

### Diversity in aquatic resources

The role of aquatic resources in rural livelihoods is characterised by diversity: diversity in the resource, diversity of habitat and environment and diversity of resource users and the ways in which they exploit these resources and incorporate them into their livelihood strategies.

Appreciation of this diversity is important. Fish are often only the most 'noticeable' of aquatic resources because they pass through markets and have a recognised role in food supply. But rural households exploit a wide range of aquatic resources, many of which are unrecorded and the importance of which is rarely measured. Low-value species of fish, molluscs and shellfish, aquatic weeds and amphibians can all play important roles in the food supply and income-generation strategies of rural households.

The nature of the aquatic habitat in which resources are found has a determining effect on the ways in which those resources are used and, in many cases, on *who* uses them. The characteristics of fisheries in deeper, open-water areas, whether marine or freshwater, are very different from those of fisheries in shallow, closed waters. Swamps, rivers and estuaries, tidal areas and seasonal water bodies all have distinct characteristics which make particular demands on those exploiting the living resources in them – demands in terms of technology, level of investment, organisation of work, mobility, support mechanisms and market links. Similarly, the different aquatic resources within these habitats can have very different behavioural patterns and require radically different strategies for their exploitation depending on whether they are migratory or sedentary, where in the water column they live, breed and feed and whether they obey seasonal or other cyclical patterns.

Culture technologies of a wide range of relative sophistication can either make use of existing aquatic environments or create new or artificial ones. The levels of investment, and so the user groups for which they are appropriate, can shift considerably as a result.

The diversity in aquatic resource use is reflected in the diversity of aquatic resource user groups. 'Fishers' (i.e. people who depend on fishing for most of their livelihood) are usually only a proportion of the overall population who make use of aquatic resources.

## Capture fisheries

Fisher communities exploiting open-water fisheries have distinctive social and cultural features, marked by stratification between the owners of productive assets and labour, and dependent relations between producers and the trader/financiers who link them to markets. In many parts of Asia, rural fishers form distinct groups. They live in clearly demarcated and physically separate communities and have culturally defined links with the surrounding community. Artisanal fisher communities are frequently identified as being among the 'poorest of the poor' (IFAD, 1992) and fishing communities are often characterised by overcrowded living conditions and inadequate services, low levels of education and a lack of the skills and assets (particularly land) which would permit diversification of their livelihoods.

Less specialised groups commonly involved in fishing include tribal and indigenous groups, agricultural labourers, small-scale farmers and traders and service providers living in resource-adjacent communities who combine fishery activities with their other occupations. Seasonal variations – whether in the availability of aquatic resources, in the aquatic habitat itself or in the alternatives available – play a determining role in the importance of aquatic resources to livelihoods at any given time (Box 1).

---

**Box 1: Seasonal fisheries in Bangladesh**

Fisheries in Bangladesh follow the cyclical rise and fall of flood waters. The aquatic cycle creates numerous opportunities for different groups to make use of aquatic resources in different ways. In the *haor* of the north-east, when heavy early rains cause the first floods, fish that have survived the winter in residual water areas move *en masse* onto the floodplain to spawn. The fishery which results, the *ozaya maash*, may last only a few days or a few hours but can attract people from a wide radius to fish with the simplest of gear. Those in the right place at the right time can earn significant cash income in a very short period. At the end of the flood season, as water drains off the floodplains, new opportunities are created for people from all walks of life to catch fish which remain stranded in pools and channels. These are then emptied by hand or by pump to catch every last fish available. In some places, after water areas have been 'fished out' by professional fishers working for leasees of waterbodies, local people may be allowed to hold a *nimbais*, or group catch, to clean out the last of the remaining fish.

*Source:* FAP 6, 1992 / FAP 17, 1994

---

## Aquaculture

Aquaculture has more in common with agricultural production than with capture fisheries; fishers do not always make good aquaculturists as the entire mode of production is more akin to livestock husbandry than the hunting of wild fish. Different types of aquaculture have different resource demands. Some freshwater aquaculture requires access to land for ponds and to water supply, both of which may not be readily available to some sections of the rural poor. But aquaculture integrated with other agricultural activities can also improve the productivity of small and marginal farms or areas of land which cannot be used for traditional agricultural activities. Other culture activities involve the enclosure of areas of existing water with particular implications for tenure and access to 'common' water resources.

**Aquaculture integrated with other agricultural activities can also improve the productivity of small and marginal farms**

## Enhancement

Stock enhancement in freshwater areas is a relatively new option which involves increasing and/or diversifying the biomass in existing water areas. Some traditional means of aggregating aquatic resources can also create improved habitats for naturally occurring fish (e.g. the 'brush parks' used in floodplain areas of Asia and Africa). In marine areas, artificial reefs can be used to: protect shorelines subject to erosion; improve the aquatic habitat for reef fish; and aggregate fish. At the same time they discourage more destructive fisheries such as trawling.

## Post-harvest fisheries

The perishability of many aquatic products (particularly fish and shellfish), means that relatively well-developed and efficient marketing systems are critical. Fish marketing and support systems can fulfil numerous other important functions, notably credit provision and communications in rural areas.

Where aquatic products cannot be sold fresh, they generally require rapid processing – by drying, salting, smoking or fermentation. This generates further opportunities for employment and income-generation in resource-adjacent communities. Opportunities for women in the processing and marketing of aquatic products are important in parts of Asia and, particularly, in West Africa, where the entire post-harvest sector is dominated by women. Depending on the volume being handled and the stability of supply from producers, post-harvest handling of aquatic resources can either represent a full-time source of livelihood or be an occasional or seasonal activity.

# Factors influencing the role of aquatic resources in rural livelihoods

## Gender and age

The contribution of aquatic resources to rural livelihoods often remains 'unseen' because it is women and youth who are involved. Women often play key roles in the processing and marketing of aquatic resources but these should not obscure the important role they can also play in harvesting. Fishing as an 'occupation' is a predominantly male activity, particularly where it involves larger types of fishing gear and boats, but many 'niche' fisheries involve women. In some cases (such as some reef fisheries and shellfish collection in many areas of the South Pacific and Melanesia) women are the main actors. Much of this production contributes directly to household food supply as it often involves low-value species which are not readily saleable.

Involvement in aquatic resource use is often identified with specific periods of the household or individual development cycle. In many African lake fisheries a relatively small group of experienced fishers will often direct a larger team of mostly young males who spend a limited period working as labour on fishing crew as a means of earning cash income. In some cases fishing labour is regarded as a means of accumulating the capital required to set up a family, open up agricultural land or establish some form of business.

The involvement of children in fisheries is an area which has not attracted adequate attention to date, although the tendency of children in many artisanal fishing communities to abandon school very early to take part in fisheries is often noted. Particularly in 'marginal' aquatic habitats, such as shallow or seasonal waterbodies, the role of children in exploiting resources and providing a source of income and food for their families (while engaged in an activity commonly viewed as 'play') should not be underestimated.

## Access and tenure

Aquatic resources constitute a reserve of renewable natural capital which can be drawn on at times of need and integrated into overall livelihood strategies as required, with relatively little forward planning or investment. Indeed, aquatic resources in many parts of the world constitute a resource 'of last resort'. Open-access fisheries and other forms of aquatic resource use are fall-back options for the rural poor when loss of land or failures in access to other rural activities threaten their livelihoods. Lake fisheries on Lake Kyoga in Uganda constitute a typical example of this. Successive changes in the political and economic context – the disruption of traditional agricultural patterns by civil war and cattle raiding, the demobilisation of combatants at the end of various insurgencies, the retrenchment of

**Fishing as an 'occupation' is a predominantly male activity but many 'niche' fisheries involve women**

government services, the rising numbers of people widowed or orphaned by the AIDS epidemic – have reportedly pushed increasing numbers of people into fishing on the lake.

Aquatic resources can therefore constitute an important stabilising element in rural livelihoods for those households most vulnerable to changes in land-based activities. Linkages between landlessness, dependence on seasonal labour and dependence on aquatic resources for some or all of the year – even for households that do not regard themselves as 'fishers' – is a common pattern

Most aquatic resources are common pool resources.[1] From the point of view of rural livelihoods, it is their frequent *de facto* open-access nature for local rural people which makes aquatic resources an attractive livelihood option. However, this can also constitute a threat to sustainability. Growing population pressure and the attraction of the cash income potentially generated by fisheries (in increasingly cash-oriented local economies) tend to lead to unsustainable levels of exploitation if no forms of control are introduced.

Lack of regulation of access can have particularly negative impacts on those with more exclusive dependence on aquatic resources. Groups of fishers often have limited alternative livelihood options and this makes them particularly vulnerable to changes in the condition of and access to the aquatic resources on which they depend. From their point of view, greater control of resource use is advantageous as long as they themselves are included among those with access rights. However, such controls can often result in the exclusion of a larger group of rural people in favour of a limited community of more intensive resource users.

The rules and regulations affecting access to aquatic resources are often ill-defined and subject to different interpretations according to the interests of the actors and stakeholders involved. With the increasing competition for all resources in rural areas it can often become more and more difficult for poor rural households, whether in fishing communities or resource user groups, to maintain their rights of access in the face of interest by more influential groups.

Various forms of indigenous regulation of aquatic resource use have, in the past, ensured the sustainability of aquatic resources. Some indigenous regimes still function, most frequently in situations where water areas are clearly demarcated or restricted and the numbers of people and communities involved in using the same resource are limited. (Bodies of freshwater such as reservoirs, smaller lakes and swamps are more amenable to this form of management than marine areas). Traditional management mechanisms are not, however, always driven by concerns about resource conservation. They may well have more to do with the status of communities and individuals, with reciprocal exchange and mediation within the community and outside, and the maintenance of ceremonial and cultural values. 'Equitable'

**Traditional management mechanisms are not, however, always driven by concerns about resource conservation**

distribution of benefits, user participation in decision-making and sustainable management of the resource may represent new, and unfamiliar, priorities. The applicability of such traditional mechanisms to the emerging needs of resource management has yet to be conclusively demonstrated.

The spread of aquaculture technology has important implications for water access and tenure arrangements. Where aquaculture makes use of existing bodies of water, these areas acquire value which they may not previously have had. The areas used are often 'common property', and changes in their value can have an adverse impact on poorer rural households who may now be denied user rights. This has occurred throughout the tropics where intensive shrimp culture has 'privatised' extensive areas of coastal swamps and mangroves formerly used for the collection of firewood and small-scale fishing activities.

But it is not inevitable that the poor lose access. The development of aquaculture in rural Bangladesh has shown how rural aquaculturists can develop innovative solutions to resolve ambiguities over access and tenure on small areas of water so that these can be used for aquaculture. The benefits often flow to poor households on a sustained basis.

## Institutional arrangements

The state generally continues to play an important role as steward of aquatic resources, deciding how resources should be allocated and when they should be preserved. The uses mandated by the state have, though, often reflected relatively transient political and economic priorities rather than the needs of users and existing access arrangements. In the same way, the institutions governing aquatic resources rarely represent the complete range of users involved in the use of those resources. This has regularly been the case even in 'participatory' models of resource management. Rights to participate in decision-making are often granted according to one's level of investment in resource use. This can lead to the domination of the process by a relatively small number of gear and craft owners to the exclusion of the far larger group of fishing labourers whose relative dependence on the fishery for their livelihood may well be greater.

**Institutions governing aquatic resources rarely represent the complete range of users involved in the use of those resources**

The potential contribution of aquatic resources to rural livelihoods is often limited by a policy environment that fails to develop the kind of vertical and horizontal linkages which are especially important for the aquatic resources sector. Policy formulation skills in the sector are often limited. In addition, policies tend to focus on the most 'productive' sub-sectors – industrial and semi-industrial fisheries and intensive aquaculture – and do not cater for the needs of other aquatic resource users. The integration between different livelihood strands at the level of the rural household is rarely reflected in integration at the policy-making level, leading to contradictory policies being applied in different sectors, with negative impacts on rural livelihoods and wastage of development resources.

## *Market conditions*

Many aquatic resources (particularly fish) are commodities which are widely in demand and not easily substituted. This makes for fairly buoyant market conditions. However, relations between traders and resource users are often marked by dependence and exploitation, though it should be noted that marketing links often channel credit and goods which would not otherwise be available into rural households (see Box 2). The need for constant replacement of fishing equipment often makes the double function of fish trader and credit provider especially important.

## Interactions

The aquatic resources which are used by rural households to support their livelihoods generally come from habitats which lie at the 'end' of the water cycle and are therefore highly vulnerable to changes and processes affecting all the different stages of that cycle. This, and the inherent mobility of many aquatic resources, means that interactions are of particular importance in aquatic resource use.

Different forms of aquatic resource use generate biological, physical, social and economic interactions. Scale of operation is an important factor, with large-scale operators frequently causing negative impacts on smaller, artisanal resource users (by exploiting similar resources more efficiently and often causing significant habitat damage in the process). Markets and prices for the products of small-scale producers can be affected by the sudden fluctuations in supply caused by high-volume producers. The perishable nature of fish makes this a particular problem.

While some forms of resource use are compatible with conservation and tourism, others may directly conflict. Efforts to protect and conserve aquatic resources through the establishment of reserves and marine or coastal parks may therefore have an adverse impact upon people's livelihoods.

---

**Box 2 : Fishers and fish dealers**

The widespread perception that fish dealers generally exploit fishers has had an important influence on fisheries development. In particular it has encouraged efforts to establish fisheries cooperatives which have met with mixed success. Cases where individual dealers or cartels of fish traders actively limit fishers' choices of where to sell and at what prices are not uncommon – marketing channels for some high-priced resources such as shrimp in remote areas of South-East Asia are an example. But fish dealers are generally as dependent on fishers as vice versa and cases of monopolistic control are probably less common than is thought (Stride, 1993). Fishers often enter into dependent relations with dealers by choice in order to access flexible credit and services which are not otherwise available. Many dealers are themselves fishers who may move from one occupation to the other according to season and catches. In Bangladesh, many traditional fishers have themselves turned to fish trading as an alternative when competition on the fishing grounds with non-traditional fishers has become too fierce.

---

The culture of aquatic organisms introduces new problems, including uncertainties about the impact on local aquatic ecology and biodiversity in the event of escape. Of even greater concern is the potential impact of the spread of disease from cultured species to the wild.

The overall tendency for increasingly intensive use of aquatic resources contributes to the growing potential for conflicts between resource users. Without mechanisms for mediation or the avoidance of these conflicts, the end result can be the undermining of the sustainability of the resources themselves. Failure to recognise these interactions and accommodate them in policy formulation can frequently lead to direct competition between different policy elements related to aquatic resources.

Developments in other sectors can also have strong impacts on the natural assets on which aquatic resource users depend. Changes in the aquatic habitat can be caused by intensification of agriculture (and accompanying demands on water resources for irrigation), changes in watersheds or by industrial and urban development. These can render efforts to manage aquatic resources ineffective or irrelevant unless planning and policy are coordinated across sectors, especially in areas of intensive urban and industrial development. Decentralised planning authority, while positive from other points of view, can exacerbate the problems involved in integrating planning in different sectors.

## Trends affecting aquatic resources

### Economic liberalisation

Economic reforms aimed at the progressive liberalisation of trade and the improvement of the investment climate can have ambiguous impacts on patterns of aquatic resource use. Increased investment in commercial enterprises, whether aquaculture or capture fisheries, may create negative interactions with small-scale and artisanal operations which use the same resources or depend on the same habitat. But the development of urban demand for aquatic products can also create market niches for small-scale producers.

### Restructuring and retrenchment

The reduction of the public sector role in many economies has created opportunities for greater local-level participation in resource management. Privatisation, on the other hand, has sometimes had an adverse effect on access to common resources for sections of the rural community. The disruption of patterns of employment resulting from retrenchment within government can lead to a sharp increase in the numbers of people who depend on open-access aquatic resources, increasing competition with existing users and putting pressure on the resources themselves.

> **Box 3: Rural–urban conflicts over fisheries in Brazil**
>
> The sustainability of livelihood strategies among the *ribeirinho* communities living among the *varzea* in the Lower Amazon Floodplain is threatened by a combination of elements. Market changes have reduced demand for jute, traditionally the key element in local agricultural systems, and local people have had to depend more and more on fisheries in the *varzea* lakes. This increasing dependence has brought them into conflict with the *geleiros* (or urban-based itinerant fishers who have expanded their range of operation in order to feed growing urban markets. Building on the awareness of *ribeirinho* fishers of the need to protect their access to and control of *varzea* resources, the Mamirauà Sustainable Development Project has supported the *ribeirenho* in developing appropriate mechanisms for the management of the *varzea* lakes.

## Decentralisation

On the positive side, decentralisation shifts decision-making about the allocation of resource rights and resource use priorities closer to the level of actual resource users. But decentralisation does not eliminate the risk of capture of resource allocation mechanisms by political and economic interest groups. These groups may have concerns other than sustainability and equitable distribution of resource benefits. If they chose to maximise revenue through commercialisation of resources, the interests of local users could be damaged. Decentralisation can also cause problems for the management of resources which span administrative boundaries. The withdrawal of central government can lead to the fragmentation of control over resources and make effective management more difficult. New bodies may need to be established or existing institutions given new roles in order to achieve the comprehensive coverage required for management of mobile resources in larger water areas. Internationally shared resources create particular problems which will often require a central government role, and the creation of international institutions.

## Urbanisation

Urban markets demand reliable, high-volume supplies and tend to encourage commercial modes of exploitation very different from the extensive methods of production used by many rural resource users, although such competition can also be generated if urban-based operations widen the range which they exploit. Excessive demand for low-volume species and processed fish in urban markets can also undermine the sustainability of aquatic resources as an element in the natural capital of rural people.

# Developing and sustaining aquatic resource contributions to SRLs

In its aquatic resource activities, three principal areas of intervention are open to DFID:

- actions to ensure the sustainability of the existing contribution of aquatic resources to livelihoods
- actions to increase the contribution of aquatic resources through appropriate forms of culture and resource enhancement, and
- actions to promote an enabling environment for the above (see Table 1).

## Sustaining aquatic resource contributions to SRL

Community-led approaches to management of aquatic resources can overcome many of the problems of non-compliance and user conflict resulting from attempts to limit resource use. Management solutions developed in consultation with fishers on Lake Malombe in Malawi, and led by them, have proved sustainable and effective in regenerating the resource. Such community-led approaches should form part of a broader attempt to address the social and economic impacts of reduced resource use (e.g. the provision of alternative livelihood options). Linkages between the management of aquatic resources and the provision of rural finance, education and skills training can be supported with a view to opening up alternative options for resource-dependent communities.

**Community-led approaches should form part of a broader attempt to address the social and economic impacts of reduced resource use**

The involvement of all user groups and the explicit recognition of their different sets of interests is particularly important. Assistance in developing skills in comprehensive consultation and consensus building should be provided. Support to community-based management can also take the form of developing linkages between community-based mechanisms and formal institutions, of providing technical and financial support for community- led research, and of the identification of innovative forms of management appropriate to community-based systems. Where users of resources are spread over a number of communities, regions or even countries, management responsibility will often need to be exercised by agencies and institutions operating at higher levels. Mechanisms will be required to link the communities concerned and facilitate their participation in the higher-level bodies. Integrated management approaches, whether focused on resources (fisheries, water) or on areas (marine, coastal, catchment or lake basin) may provide an appropriate framework for creating these linkages.

## Enhancing aquatic resource contributions to rural livelihoods

The introduction of appropriate culture techniques can significantly enhance the contribution of aquatic resources to rural livelihoods. However, this will only be appropriate where the following are available:

- secure tenure for the key resources of water and/or land
- appropriate technologies, and
- adequate technical support and input supply.

## Table 1: DFID options for intervention in aquatic resources

| Types of action | Interventions | Impacts on SRLs and related issues |
|---|---|---|
| Action to ensure aquatic resource sustainability | Support to community-led approaches to resource management | + for local communities possibly − impacts on other user-groups |
| | Innovative forms of management | varies |
| | Strengthening of institutions governing aquatic resource-use: institutional skills in consultation and conflict resolution | + if attention paid to integration of poor into consultative processes |
| | Reduction of exclusive dependence on aquatic resources | + but possibly short-term − if alternatives not provided |
| | Integrated management | + |
| Action to enhance aquatic resource contributions | Identification of niches available to poor for practice of aquaculture | + if possible conflicts with other users resolved |
| | Appropriate support mechanisms and skills for pro-poor aquaculture integrated into agricultural extension | + if resources for effective extension available |
| | Appropriate post-harvest technologies to reduce losses and increase value | + |
| Actions to improve policy environment | Promote vertical and horizontal linkages in policy-making | + |
| | Support to decentralised institutions controlling natural resources | + if poor participate in new institutions |
| | Legislative reform to enhance community-level rights and responsibilities | + but possible opposition from institutions and government |
| | Legislative review to clarify tenure of and access to aquatic resources | + if attention paid to integration of needs of poor |
| | Support to forums for management of international resources | + if needs of poor taken into account |
| | Support to application of Code of Conduct for Responsible Fisheries | +, − for users of destructive small-scale gears |

In all cases, aquaculture should be seen as an integral part of rural livelihood systems and not promoted 'for its own sake'. Successes have been achieved above all where innovative techniques make use of existing resources and integrate well with other activities (e.g. CAGES and IPM in Bangladesh).[2] Potential impacts of aquaculture development on land values and access rights to common property should be taken into consideration and proper zoning regulations for aquaculture development introduced to protect catchments. Skills for assessing possible impacts and conflicts should also be developed.

The post-harvest sector also offers opportunities for maximising returns from aquatic resource use, though care should be taken to ensure that the introduction of technical solutions does not threaten the roles of those currently involved, particularly women. Changes in levels of investment required can seriously affect people's ability to participate and compete in some areas, but appropriate, low-cost solutions can raise incomes.

The enhancement of aquatic resources through stocking programmes also has potential. Linkages between such interventions and mechanisms for community-based control are likely to improve success levels and ensure that benefits reach the groups which are most in need. The appropriateness of stock enhancement also requires careful prior assessment of:

- the nature of the water areas in question
- the characteristics of resource user groups
- eventual risks to biodiversity, and
- costs and sustainability.

## *Policy environment*

To be fully effective, both the strands of intervention identified above require a policy and institutional environment which is conducive to creating horizontal linkages (between sectors, institutions, administrations and communities) and vertical linkages (between levels of political and administrative responsibility). Support to good governance and democratisation can enhance this process, but tools are also required to ensure that policy becomes more responsive to issues at the ground level.

Often it will be necessary to review and clarify legislation governing aquatic resources and their use. In order to reduce the negative interactions between large-scale fisheries and small-scale or artisanal operators, pressure must be brought to bear on two fronts. First, pressure should be applied in international forums to ensure that the fisheries and aquaculture which supply consumers in developed countries do not jeopardise access to aquatic resources for poor rural households in low-income countries (Kent, 1994). The possible role of the Marine Stewardship Council in enhancing ethical trade in aquatic products should be investigated in this

**The possible role of the Marine Stewardship Council in enhancing ethical trade in aquatic products should be investigated**

regard. Second, both public and private fisheries sectors in less-developed countries should be supported in applying the International Code of Conduct for Responsible Fisheries (FAO, 1995).

## Criteria for involvement in the aquatic resources area

### Data indicators

Data which indicates the relative importance of aquatic resources in rural livelihoods are rarely available. However, the following types of information may be available for certain sections of the population:

- nutritional data showing the contribution of fish to rural diets
- fish catch statistics (although these are often biased towards more commercial fisheries), and
- fish supply data (published periodically by the FAO based on national data).

Analysis of trends in these figures can provide some indication of actual and potential risks to the supply of aquatic resources, though important regional and seasonal variations are often masked. Shifts in the price of fish and the types and sizes of fish available in markets can also indicate changes in fishing pressure and resource access. Where access to aquatic resources is regulated and fees charged for resource use rights, the changing value of access rights can provide a good, quantitative indicator of levels of competition for the resource.

### Alternative indicators

Given the general paucity of adequate quantitative data on the role of fisheries in rural livelihoods, more qualitative indicators become particularly important. Analysis of the processes and trends underway in aquatic resource use – changes in fishing techniques, the organisation of harvesting and post-harvest activities, the status and numbers of 'professional' fishers – can provide important indicators of how the role of aquatic resources in rural livelihoods might be changing.

The occurrence of conflicts between aquatic resource users over access to and control of resources is probably one of the clearest indicators of the need for intervention. Not all such conflicts are amenable to resolution, and careful assessment of the attitudes of stakeholders and their commitment to finding solutions will be a prerequisite for effective intervention. The complexities of many aquatic resource user conflicts may be seen as a deterrent to donor involvement but many such conflicts occur precisely because of the lack of local institutions which are in a position to play the role of catalyst in seeking mechanisms for conflict resolution. Resources which are large and have complex patterns of use are more likely to generate conflict but are also more likely to play an important role in rural livelihoods; involvement can therefore be justified, despite the apparent complexity.

## Key References

Campbell, J. and Townsley, P. (1996) *Participatory and Integrated Policy: A Framework for Small-Scale Fisheries*. Exeter: IMM.

Harrison, E., Stewart, J.A., Stirrap, R.J. and Muir, J. (1994) *Fish Farming in Africa — What's the Catch?* London: Overseas Development Administration.

Kent, G. (1994) *Nutrition Rights in Fisheries*. A Study prepared for Greenpeace International.

Le Sann, A. (compiled by) (1998) *A Livelihood from Fisheries*. London: ITDG Publications.

## Other references

Campbell, J. (1996) *Participatory and Integrated Policy: A Field Guide for Policy Formulation in Small-Scale Fisheries*. Exeter: IMM.

FAO (1996) *Fish and Fishery Products. World Apparent Consumption Statistics Based on Food Balance Sheets (1961–1993)*. FAO Fisheries Circular No. 821 Revision 3. Rome: FAO.

FAO (1995) *Code of Conduct for Responsible Fisheries*. Rome: FAO.

FAO/RAPA. (1994) *Socio-Economic Issues in Coastal Fisheries Management*. Proceedings of the IPFC Symposium. Bangkok: FAO.

FAP 6 (1992) *The People of Shanir Haor*. Monograph prepared by FAP 6 Social Anthropology Team. Dhaka: FAP 6.

FAP 17 (1994) *Final Report: Supporting Volume No. 14. The Kai Project and Dekker Haor*. Dhaka: FAP 17.

IFAD (1992) *The State of World Rural Poverty: An Inquiry into its Causes and Consequences*. Rome: IFAD.

Stride, R.K. (1993) *Review of the Artisan Fishery in Maranhao State, Brazil*. ODA/FINE/LABOHIDRO Federal University of Maranhao, Sao Luis, Maranhao.

## Endnotes

1 The term 'common pool resources' is used here rather than common property resources as it has no tenure implications. There is considerable variation in the type of tenure regime to which aquatic resources are subject and also between the official tenurial status and the actual access arrangements recognised by resource users.

2 CAGES (Cage Aquaculture for Greater Economic Security) is a DFID-funded project implemented by CARE Bangladesh in partnership with local NGOs. It is concerned with providing poor rural households with improved options for income generation and food supply by promoting the cage culture of fish in waterbodies in Bangladesh where the poor are able to obtain secure access. IPM (Integrated Pest Management) is also being implemented in Bangladesh through CARE and local NGOs as part of the INTERFISH project and has provided small farmers with a wider range of options for pest management, resulting in lower costs and improved yields. The integration of fish culture into rice farming systems has proved to be an important part of this strategy.

# 11 Forestry and Sustainable Rural Livelihoods

## J.E.M. Arnold

## Forest outputs and rural livelihoods

The term 'forests' is used in this chapter to include all resources that can produce forest products. These can comprise woodland, scrub land, bush fallow and farm bush, and trees on farms, as well as forests. Such resources can be held under state, common property or private forms of ownership or governance, and their use often reflects overlapping combinations of tenure and rights (for fuller reviews of the material summarised in this section see: Townson, 1995; Falconer, 1990; Beer and Mcdermott, 1989).

The contributions that outputs from forest and tree resources can make to livelihood outcomes can be summarised as follows.

- *Increased income* – large numbers of people generate a portion of their income from forest/tree products; for some such activities can become a major and expanding income source.

- *Increased well-being* – forests are ever more widely the source of subsistence goods and materials, supplementing inputs from farming activities.

- *Reduced vulnerability* – forest and tree stocks provide a biomass reserve upon which people can fall back for subsistence and income in times of crop failure, unemployment and other kinds of hardship, or to meet exceptional needs.

- *More sustainable use of the NR base* – trees and woodland in agricultural landscapes can help protect crops and soil, and can contribute to maintaining site productivity.

The main features of forest output/livelihood relationships – and the ways in which they are impacted by change – are outlined in Table 1. This demonstrates that the extent to which these contributions to rural livelihoods materialise in practice varies greatly from situation to situation, among households in a particular situation and over time.

## Table 1: Forest outputs and rural livelihoods

| Livelihood elements | Characteristics | Impacts of change |
|---|---|---|
| Subsistence goods | Supplement/complement inputs of fuel, food, medicinal plant products, etc., from the farm system; often important in filling seasonal and other food gaps; forest foods enhance palatability of staple diets, and provided vitamins and proteins. | Can become more important where farm output and/or non-farm income declines.<br><br>Likely to decline in importance as incomes rise and supplies come increasingly from purchased inputs; or as increasing labour shortages/costs militate against gathering activities, or divert subsistence supplies to income-generating outlets. |
| Farm inputs | On-farm trees provide shade, windbreaks and contour vegetation; trees/forests also provide low-cost soil nutrient recycling and mulch.<br><br>Arboreal fodder and forage, fibre baskets for storing agricultural products, wooden ploughs and other farm implements, etc. | Trees can become increasingly important as a low-capital means of combating declining site productivity, and a low-labour means of keeping land in productive use (e.g. home gardens).<br><br>Increased capital availability and access to purchased products likely to lead to substitution by other materials (e.g. by pasture crops, fertiliser and plastic packaging). |
| Income | Many products characterised by easy access to the resource and low capital and skill entry thresholds; mainly low-return activities, producing for local markets, engaged in part-time by rural households, often to fill particular income gaps or needs (though they can be major sources of employment and income for forest-dwelling populations); overwhelmingly very small, usually household-based, enterprises (with heavy involvement of women, as entrepreneurs as well as employees).<br><br>Some forest products provide the basis for more full-time and higher-return activities; usually associated with higher skill and capital entry thresholds, and urban as well as rural markets.<br><br>Some low-input gathering activities involve raw materials for industrial processes and external markets. | With increasing commercialisation of rural use patterns some low-input, low-return activities can grow; however, others are inferior goods and decline, some are displaced by factory made alternatives, and others become unprofitable and are abandoned as labour costs rise.<br><br>Higher-return activities serving growing demand are more likely to prosper, particularly those serving urban as well as rural markets; as this happens an increasing proportion of the processing and trading activity is likely to become centred in small rural centres and urban locations.<br><br>Gathered industrial raw materials tend to be displaced by domesticated supplies or synthetic substitutes. |
| Reduced vulnerability | Can be important in diversifying the farm household economy – e.g. providing counter-seasonal sources of food, fodder and income.<br><br>Also important in providing a reserve that can be used for subsistence and income generation in times of hardship (crop failure, drought, shortage of wage employment, etc.); or to meet special needs (school fees, weddings, etc.). | The 'buffer' role of forests and trees can continue to be important well into the growth process.<br><br>Likely to decline in importance as government relief programmes become more effective, or as new agricultural crops or access to remittance incomes make it less necessary to fall back on forest resources. |

People living in forest environments and practising hunting, gathering and shifting cultivation are likely to draw heavily on that forest and its outputs. Elsewhere, the importance of forest products is usually more in the way they fill gaps and complement other sources of subsistence inputs and income than in their absolute magnitude or share of overall household inputs.

Ease of entry and proximity to widely dispersed rural markets enable very large numbers of people to generate some income from forest products. Forest products can therefore be very important to the poor, including poor women, in situations in which they are unable to obtain income or sufficient income from agriculture or wage employment, and where few other options exist. In such cases forest-related activities are likely to be labour-intensive and household-based (e.g. collecting/ gathering and mat making).

Typically low-return and often tedious and arduous, these activities are likely to be abandoned once more rewarding and congenial alternatives become available. Alternatively, rising incomes may lead to displacement of the product by purchased alternatives. In situations where per capita incomes are rising and growth is demand-driven, the pattern of forest product activities is likely to shift towards more productive and remunerative activities such as vending, trading and production to meet growing and diversifying rural and urban demands. Under these circumstances, the production and sale of forest products increasingly shifts from being a part-time activity undertaken by very large numbers of people to becoming a more specialised year-round occupation for a few. Skill and capital requirements are higher, which means that many of those previously engaged in the simpler forest product activities are excluded.

A distinction can therefore be drawn between the contribution that access to forest resources makes to reducing vulnerability and increasing well-being and the contribution that it makes to increasing the incomes of rural households.

These relationships can be further influenced by issues related to access to the resource. Problems of overuse are frequently aggravated by measures that alienate the resource to the state or result in *de facto* privatisation by the wealthier and more powerful users or by outsiders. Increasing demands on labour reduce effective access to more distant resources. As a consequence, many users are progressively restricted in their choice to resources available in bush fallow and farm bush on their own lands, and to resources they can generate themselves by growing trees on their farms. However, where fallow cycles are declining, bush fallow/farm bush is also likely to be diminishing as a resource. Moreover, the shift from forest to farm is only possible for those who have access to land, and sufficient resources to work the land. Many poor farmers still need to look to off-farm resources to help supplement what they can produce on-farm. Common pool forest resources and local management

**The shift from forest to farm is only possible for those who have access to land**

and control regimes that enable rural people to use these resources in an ordered manner – therefore continue to be of vital importance.

## Potentials and constraints

The scenarios outlined below reflect frequently occurring types of forest-related situations that can be important to rural livelihoods. For each scenario, policy and technical issues and constraints (which may require policy or project interventions to remove or reduce) are identified. Particular categories of people are associated with each scenario; the categories are not mutually exclusive. Many situations will include households from more than one category of involvement with forest product activities. Also, there is much movement between categories as developments in the surrounding economic and social environment enable some to take advantage of new forest product opportunities (which may then reduce or eliminate the opportunities available to others). Where several types of activity co-exist in a particular location, more than one kind of intervention may be needed.

### Scenario 1: Forests continue to be central to livelihood systems

#### Context
In this scenario, users are principally hunter-gatherer/shifting cultivation populations, who manage and use their forest habitat as a common pool resource. Traditional, labour-intensive livelihood practices are often difficult to sustain in the face of seasonal migration to wage employment, or when agricultural options improve with better access to markets. Moreover, they often provide only limited opportunities for livelihood improvement. When the system does change it is therefore likely to become closer to the fifth of the categories outlined here (i.e. needing to shift away from many existing forest-based activities).

Possible options while the focus is forest-based can include:

- expansion of market outlets for gathered forest products
- transformation of the forests into agroforests containing commercial species as expanding rural infrastructure improves access to markets (e.g. durian in Kalimantan, acai palm in the Amazon delta), and
- employment in forest industries (however, the boom-and-bust cycles of much of the timber harvesting industry may mean that such employment is not sustainable).

#### Policy and technical issues
Where communal practices and systems of forest management and control continue to function viably, policies are needed that recognise these local rights and provide the holders with legal and regulatory support in

protecting them (e.g. against forest industry, agencies of the state, encroachment by other population groups). This may require harmonisation of related policies (such as those dealing with land settlement where this encourages clearance in forest areas, as has often been the case in Latin America – see Southgate and Runge, 1990).

Considerable attention has been paid in recent years to expanding trade in a number of the forest products which originate from such livelihood systems (e.g. extractive reserve programmes in Brazil). However, these product trades have often proved to be susceptible to unanticipated changes in market requirements, to domination by intermediaries and to shifts to domesticated or synthetic sources of supply. As a consequence, they have not been sustainable. They can therefore expose rural households to high levels of risk, particularly where the trade has encouraged people to move away from more diversified and less risky agriculture-based livelihoods (Browder, 1992).

## Scenario 2: Products from forests play an important supplementary and/or safety net role

### Context

Users tend to be agriculturalists who still draw on forest/woodland for inputs that cannot be produced on-farm, or that can be more efficiently supplied from off-farm resources. There are likely to be multiple user groups with overlapping claims on the resource. Internal differentiation of asset endowments among households can also lead to competing claims on the land as well as on the tree resource. The poor within such communities are likely to find it more difficult than others to benefit from the opportunities that increasing commercialisation of forest products present. They can often be in danger of losing access to a resource because it passes into the control of wealthier or more powerful elements who are better able to exploit new market opportunities and engage in higher-return activities or who seek to privatise the land and put it to non-forest uses.

### Policy and technical issues

In many situations the greatest need may be for a policy and legal framework that legitimises participation by poor user groups in co-management of the resource and provides mechanisms to operationalise this. Where local capabilities to control and manage have become eroded or broken down, external assistance is likely to be needed to strengthen and monitor resource sharing and management mechanisms. Project interventions should pay attention to rebuilding social capital and minimising sources of conflict, to equity considerations between different stakeholder groups (and within them – e.g. by gender) and to minimising the transaction costs to user groups. Assisting with sustainable management of the forest is also important (Arnold, 1998).

The potential for continued forest product use systems based on resources that are held in flexible overlapping combinations of private, state, common property and open access tenure regimes is likely to be influenced by current policies promoting land titling (especially in Africa). Unless such titling is carried out in ways that protect the rights of present users, many of these rights could be threatened with extinction. The insecurity that such change, or the threat of change, induces is also likely to favour short-term activities (such as destructive harvesting and slash-and-burn agriculture) that assure more certain, though lower, returns than might be obtained from woodland conservation and management.

Because they are unable effectively to monitor what happens in forest areas, many governments have set in place forest and environmental policies and regulations designed to limit rather than encourage production and sale of forest products. These can include restrictions on private harvesting and trading of wood products and requirements to sell other forest products to state marketing boards (as is found in parts of India). Unless such constraints to their access to the benefits are removed, there can be little incentive for people to involve themselves in forest management (Dewees and Scherr, 1996).

## Scenario 3: Forest product activity opportunities are increasingly based on agroforest sources

### Context

In this scenario, the potential for increased tree growing on farms reflects: a decline in supplies from forest sources; increasing demand for tree products; a recognition of the protective and other risk-reducing values of trees in agricultural areas; and changes in factor availability and allocation. Because trees require lower inputs of labour to establish and maintain than most other crops, tree crops are often adopted as a response to increasing shortages of farm labour (consequently an improvement in the functioning of labour and other factor markets could reverse the trend). In other situations trees are favoured by poor farmers as a low-cost means of enhancing site productivity (e.g. through home gardens, shade, shelterbelts). Sometimes such resources can be created from a forest rather than a planted tree starting point (e.g. rubber and fruit gardens in Indonesia (Michon and de Foresta, 1995)).

Most farm-level tree management is primarily to meet household needs, with production for sale developing incrementally from this base. Production of tree products such as pulpwood that compete with industrial and state producers is usually confined to areas where entrepreneurial agriculture dominates and to farmers who do not rely on the land for food and/or who have other sources of income. It is therefore likely to be of only limited relevance to small and poor farmers, though linkages with user industries through out-grower and contract schemes have enabled some such participation (e.g. in South Africa, the Philippines (Arnold, 1997)).

### Policy and technical issues

The potential for tree growing can be constrained by tenure conditions, which may need to be clarified or modified. Tree growing may be inhibited by tenurial rights that enable, or appear to enable, the state to expropriate land that has trees on it. More widely, it is affected by insecurity of tenure, and hence by the threat or possibility of tenurial change. Sharecropping and some other forms of tenancy can also prevent or discourage tree growing (Fortmann, 1984).

Increased income from tree growing is more likely to be achieved by providing producers with better access to markets than by the subsidies for tree planting which have been the main form of intervention in the past. Priority often needs to be given to changing the policies and practices that create these restrictions and that depress market prices for their forest/tree products. In addition to the factors noted in the previous section, these commonly include lack of market information, poorly functioning trading systems for small producers, fuelwood prices that are depressed by subsidies to alternative fuels and competition from subsidised supplies from state forests and plantations. There is a danger that, by hindering farmer access to tree product markets, governments may inadvertently be interfering with the shift from a subsistence to a market economy (Dewees and Scherr, 1996).

Technical support to small farmers can often most usefully take the form of expanding the menu of *appropriate* species and technology options from which these farmers can choose. Care must be taken over which species are provided; too many past farm forestry support projects have only provided industrial forestry species and in so doing have mainly benefited the larger farmers/landowners able to take advantage of this crop option (as happened in parts of northern India (Saxena, 1994)). Few projects have provided flexible options appropriate to the incremental, niche approach to tree growing adopted by most poor farmers, though there have been some notable exceptions (e.g. the CARE-supported agroforestry project in western Kenya (Scherr, 1994)).

> **By hindering farmer access to tree product markets, governments may inadvertently be interfering with the shift from a subsistence to a market economy**

## Scenario 4: Opportunities exist to expand artisanal and small enterprise forest product activities

### Context

Small enterprise surveys consistently show that forest product activities rank among the three largest sources of employment in rural manufacturing and trading (Fisseha, 1987). Producers and prospective producers may require improved access to credit, skills, marketing services, etc. Different potential target groups have different needs and opportunities in this respect. New entrants driven by supply side forces – that is people searching for activities which can sustain their livelihoods – face different issues to those who are responding to market opportunities. Similarly, those in the process of

161

establishing commercial forest product activity face different problems and constraints to those seeking to expand existing operations.

### Policy and technical issues

There may be a need for intervention in order to ensure a policy environment that does not discriminate against informal sector activities generally (tax concessions, subsidised credit, licensing regulations, etc.). This may also apply to specific policies in the forest sector (e.g. the Indonesian ban on rattan exports to encourage industrial-scale manufacture of items that had previously been produced mainly by small enterprises).

Many of the support services needed are generic to the small enterprise sector. Requirements specific to forest product activities may include assistance in dealing with marketing and raw material problems (including help in addressing the constraints on market access discussed above). It is important that the focus on trades that are sustainable and growing and in which small enterprises are likely to remain competitive is maintained. Domestic markets for some non-timber forest products are likely to provide larger and more stable avenues for development than the industrial and niche export markets that have tended to attract the attention of intervention programmes. Similarly, intervention should avoid encouraging product expansion that will lead to depletion of the raw material resource (as happened, for example, with baskets in Botswana (Terry, 1984)).

## Scenario 5: People need to move out of declining forest product activities

The concentration of the poorer sections of those who generate income from forest products in low-return activities that can offer no more than marginal, unsustainable livelihoods presents particular issues. Providing support to such activities once higher return or less arduous alternatives emerge could impede the emergence of better livelihood systems for the participants. That being the case, it may be more fruitful to help people move into more rewarding fields of endeavour rather than seeking to raise their productivity in their current line of work. The alternatives may be other forest product activities, but could equally well be activities not associated with forests or trees. In either case, care needs to be taken to ensure that future growth prospects are indeed better in the alternative product lines to which people are being encouraged to move.

However, in the shorter term, there may be no alternative to these minimal-return forest product activities for many. Interventions should therefore focus on how to support them. There will often be a need to distinguish between those situations in which action is needed to enable the poor to continue to alleviate their situation through access to forest

**Forests should some-
times be managed to
support growth and
sometimes to provide a
safety net**

products and those in which forest product activities can contribute to greater wealth. In other words, forests should sometimes be managed to support growth and sometimes to provide a safety net.

## Criteria for policy and projects

Inputs from forest and tree sources are typically small, yet integral, parts of rural household systems. This implies that the present and likely future importance of forest products must be looked at in the context of household systems as a whole – patterns of and trends in subsistence use, sources and allocation of household income, household availability and allocation of labour and land, etc. Such information is best obtained through surveys and studies of these broader parameters.

Criteria for involvement in the forest area which relate to patterns of and trends in forest product sourcing, use and trade, and to factors triggering change in these, will need to be obtained through more specific studies. Recent work has shown that quite a lot of relevant information can be obtained from existing sources or from quite broad-based enquiries. For example:

- *National household living standards surveys*: The survey in Ghana supported by the World Bank and DFID contains information on household purchases of six major forest products, allowing estimation of patterns and levels of purchased use and elasticities of demand for each product (Townson, 1995).

- *National or regional surveys of small enterprise/non-farm employment activity*: The surveys in six African countries carried out by the USAID-funded GEMINI programme collected information on production for sale of and trading in five principal forest products. This enabled estimates to be made of the importance of each type of product, in terms of both absolute market size and employment opportunities. Rates of growth (or decline) were also measured and an analysis was made of some of the main household factors causing change (Arnold *et al.*, 1994).

Studies that cover both household consumption and sourcing of forest products (such as those that DFID has supported in Ghana and Sierra Leone) can provide information on the relative importance of forest, fallow/farm bush, and managed trees on farms – and of how (and why) these patterns of supply are changing (Falconer, 1994; Davies and Richards, 1991).

Such surveys and studies have enabled considerable progress to be made in understanding the relationships between forest resources and products and rural livelihoods at a national or regional level. They would need to be supplemented by more situation specific studies in order to assess and monitor project-level situations. However, the information they yield can provide a useful framework for designing and targeting these more detailed assessments.

Where the source of forest products is a forest resource, rather than tree stocks on farm or other individually controlled land, there are additional institutional issues to be considered when assessing possible poverty-related interventions. These can be more difficult to analyse, but they are of particular importance where there is shared access to the resource and where access, particularly for poorer members of the user group, depends on there being an effective control and management system in place.

It is becoming increasingly clear that many local bodies to which forest management responsibilities are being devolved under co-management programmes are unrepresentative, not accountable to their constituents or lack the authority and capacity to exercise control. In these cases transfer of control is likely to give powers over the resource to particular individuals or groups of individuals within the community, effectively limiting or excluding access by the poor (Hobley, 1996; Ribot, 1997).

This often reflects the erosion of the social capital that historically enabled many communities to control use of local common pool resources. The question then arises as to whether the necessary communal leadership and capacity can be recreated or whether it would be more effective for an external body to exercise a direct role in management. Where the latter seems to be appropriate, there will be a continuing need to work with forest departments and interested NGOs, but with a greater emphasis on developing institutional arrangements that are designed to deliver equitable access to forest resources. It should be recognised that a single community-level institution may not always be an appropriate framework within which to plan, negotiate, manage and monitor systems of use involving so many, often disparate, groups with an interest in and claims on local forest and tree resources. Other approaches that reflect and involve the interplay of several institutional forms and pressures within a community may be more appropriate (Leach *et al.*, 1997).

As a final, related, point, where people's links to local forest resources are changing over time in the ways outlined in this chapter, it can be important not to put in place or encourage institutional arrangements which are likely to be inconsistent with these changes. For instance, does devolution of responsibility for forest management to local communities make sense in those situations in which the role of forest products is likely to decline? What would happen to control and management of forests if the former users' interest in forest products and their time available for forest management and protection declines after responsibility has been effectively transferred from the state to them? These questions appear to reinforce the argument for continuing involvement of the state even in situations where devolution of responsibility for forest management is appropriate in the short to medium term. In the longer term this can facilitate further institutional change, should that be necessary.

## Key references

Arnold, J.E.M. and Dewees, P.A. (eds) (1995) *Tree Management in Farmer Strategies: Responses to Agricultural Intensification.* Oxford: Oxford University Press. (Also published as *Farms, Trees and Farmers: Responses to Agricultural Intensification* (1997) London: Earthscan Publications.)

Hobley, M. (1996) *Participatory Forestry Management in South Asia: The Process of Change in India and Nepal.* Rural Development Forestry Study Guide. London: Overseas Development Institute.

Leach, M., Mearns, R. and Scoones, I. (eds) (1997) 'Challenges to Community-Based Sustainable Development: Consensus or Conflict?', *IDS Bulletin* 28(4) .

Ruiz Pérez, M. and Arnold, J.E.M. (eds). (1996) *Current Issues in Non-Timber Forest Products Research.* Bogor: CIFOR and ODA.

## Other references

Arnold, J.E.M. (1998) *Managing Forests as Common Property.* Forestry Paper 136. Rome: FAO.

Arnold, J.E.M. (1997) *Trees as Out-Grower Crops for Forest Industries: Experience from the Philippines and South Asia.* Rural Development Forestry Network Paper 22a. London: Overseas Development Institute.

Arnold, J.E.M., Liedholm, C., Mead, D., and Townson, I.M. (1994) *Structure and Growth of Small Enterprises Using Forest Products in Southern and Eastern Africa.* O.F.I Occasional Paper No. 47. Oxford: Oxford Forestry Institute. **and** *Growth and Equity Through Microenterprise Investments and Institutions, Bethesda.* GEMINI Working Paper No. 48.

Beer, J. de and Mcdermott, M. (1989) *The Economic Value of Non-Timber Forest Products in Southeast Asia.* Amsterdam: Netherlands Committee for IUCN.

Browder, J.O. (1992) 'The Limits of Extractivism: Tropical Forest Strategies Beyond Extractive Reserves', *Bioscience* 42(3) pp 174–82.

Davies, A.G. and Richards, P. (1991) *Rain Forest in Mende Life: Resources and Subsistence Strategies in Rural Communities Around the Gola North Forest Reserve (Sierra Leone).* A report to ESCOR, UK: Overseas Development Administration.

Dewees, P.A. and Scherr, S.A. (1996) 'Policies and Markets for Non-Timber Tree Products', EPTD Discussion Paper 16. Washington D.C.: International Food Policy Research Institute.

Falconer, J. (1994) *Non-Timber Forest Products in Southern Ghana: Main Report.* Republic of Ghana Forestry Department and Overseas Development Administration. Chatham: Natural Resources Institute.

Falconer, J. (1990) *The Major Significance of 'Minor' Forest Products: The Local Use and Value of Forests in the West African Humid Forest Zone.* Community Forestry Note 6. Rome: FAO.

Fisseha, Y. (1987) 'Basic Features of Rural Small-Scale Forest-Based Processing Enterprises in Developing Countries', in *Small-Scale Forest Based Processing Enterprises.* Forestry Paper 79. Rome: FAO.

Fortmann, L. (1984) 'The Tree Tenure Factor in Agroforestry with Particular Reference to Africa', *Agroforestry Systems* 2, 231–48.

Michon, G. and de Foresta, H. (1995) 'The Indonesian Agro-Forest Model: Forest Resource Management and Biodiversity Conservation', in Halladay, P. and Gilmour, D.A. (eds) *Conserving Biodiversity Outside Protected Areas: The Role of Traditional Agro-ecosystems.* Gland: The IUCN Conservation Programme, IUCN.

Ribot, J. (1997) *Participation without Representation: Chiefs, Councils and Forestry Law in the West African Sahel.* Voluntary Paper prepared for the XI World Forestry Congress, Antalya, Turkey, 13–22 October 1997.

Saxena, N.C. (1994) *India's Eucalyptus Craze: The God that Failed.* New Delhi: Sage Publications.

Scherr, S.A. (1994) 'Tree Growing to Meet Household Needs: Farmer Strategies in Western Kenya', in Arnold, J.E.M. and Dewees, P.A. (eds) *Tree Management in Farmer Strategies: Responses to Agricultural Intensification.* Oxford: Oxford University Press.

Southgate, D. and Runge, C.F. (1990) *The Institutional Origins of Deforestation in Latin America.* Paper prepared for the Conference on Economic Catalysts to Ecological Change, February 1990, University of Florida Center for Latin American Studies.

Terry, M.E. (1984) *Botswanacraft and Hambukushu Basketry: The Effects of a Major Marketing Operation on a Group of African People, Their Traditional Craft, and the Natural Resources.* Report to the Botswanacraft Marketing Company, Estha, Botswana.

Townson, I.M. (1995) *Forest Products and Household Incomes: A Review and Annotated Bibliography.* Tropical Forestry Paper 31. Oxford: CIFOR and Oxford Forestry Institute.

Townson, I.M. (1995) *Patterns of Non-Timber Forest Products Enterprise Activity in the Forest Zone of Southern Ghana: Main Report.* Report to the ODA Forestry Research Programme, Oxford Forestry Institute, Oxford.

# 12 Land Tenure and Sustainable Rural Livelihoods
## *Julian Quan*

### Introduction: land tenure and livelihoods

Secure rights of access to land are the basis of smallholder agrarian livelihoods. Land also provides an important component of more diverse livelihood strategies for those who rely at least in part on off-farm employment and income. For the rural poor generally, land is the basis of subsistence, farm incomes and a source of employment for family and community labour. Communities' rights of access to natural resources other than land – pasture, tree products, water and aquatic resources – are also essential to landless rural people and those reliant on non-farm livelihoods, who are frequently among the poorest.

Secure access to land and natural resources can strengthen the resilience of livelihoods, helping to protect against stresses and shocks induced by climate, price instability or unemployment (for instance, by allowing households to maintain subsistence production of drought-resistant crops, or to lease, loan or borrow against land holdings). For those who migrate to urban areas, land held within extended families remains an important asset and source of security.

Land tenure institutions (whether modern and formalised in law or customary, governed by kinship and tradition) determine rights to land and other forms of natural capital. The degree of security of these rights has a fundamental bearing on the options, planning horizons and investment decisions of land and resource users, both large and small. Secure land and resource rights facilitate long-term planning, investment and the adoption of sustainable production methods. Tenure institutions and the rights to land they determine are thus central factors in determining the livelihood strategies of the rural poor

The institutions which allocate land and natural resources at local level are also central to matters of rural governance; they help set the framework within which people's basic needs are met, the use of natural capital is regulated and disputes among claimants are resolved. Because claims to land and natural resources frequently compete and conflict, as may the sets of rights and sources of legitimacy which underpin them, clarity of tenure rules and transparency in land rights management are important for good governance.

Access to land can also influence prospects for economic growth and the extent to which this will benefit the poor. Equitable patterns of secure land access can promote income generation, accumulation, investment and employment within rural communities, and there is evidence that egalitarian land distribution may promote higher levels of agrarian growth than where land ownership is concentrated in the hands of the few.

Depending on the role of land in livelihood strategies and the adequacy of existing patterns of land access and tenure systems in promoting sustainable livelihoods, intervention to promote land access, tenure security and clarity of tenure rules may be important for rural societies as a whole or for particular groups of the poor. In considering interventions to promote land rights for the poor, it is necessary to distinguish between the redistribution of land for the benefit of the landless, normally referred to as land reform, and tenure reform which involves the strengthening or clarification of land rights, notably in respect of the security they provide, by changing the terms and institutions of land tenure.

## Gender and land

Secure land tenure is of particular importance for rural women because of their widespread role as family food producers. However, both customary and formal tenure systems discriminate against women (though customary systems may be more favourable to women as formal systems often confer exclusive rights on males). Gender differences in land access and security are almost universal across the developing world and gender issues are therefore critical in the development of pro-poor tenure systems.

## Tenure and the commons

Tenure arrangements over common pool resources (CPRs) – forests, rangelands, wetlands and aquatic resources – merit consideration because of the value of these resources to rural people, especially in times of stress. CPRs are of particular importance to the poor, those without access to arable land, women (for whom they provide sources of fuelwood and wild produce) and specific, often marginalised groups, such as forest dwellers and pastoralists who may have no other access to natural capital.

Globally, CPRs are under pressure. The pressure arises not only because of the growing demands of increasing rural populations, the expansion of agriculture and the growth of towns, but because CPRs are often misunderstood in policy terms. Unaware of the customary tenure regimes under which they are held and managed by rural people, states frequently allocate common resources for other uses (e.g. granting concessions to private users). This can result in confusion, insecurity and resource conflict, often leading to excessive short-term exploitation and the degeneration of common tenure regimes into open-access situations.

## The variability of tenure issues and their importance

The importance of land tenure must be seen in a dynamic context of economic, demographic and agrarian change. The history of agrarian societies and land ownership, including the political agendas of governments and other stakeholders, must be taken into account. In some cases existing tenure arrangements and the distribution of land assets may not present significant problems; in others political considerations and the entrenched powers of land owners, often closely linked with governing groups, may limit the scope for intervention.

In *sub-Saharan Africa*, land distribution tends to be relatively equitable and many rural areas remain dominated by customary tenure systems. However, under modern law, African governments have generally vested ultimate rights for large land areas in the state, while also allocating freehold or leasehold rights to private land users. Land policy is characterised by dualism, a continuing tension between the two systems (most marked in southern Africa, where 'communal' or customary lands are territorially separated from commercial estates) and a widely held belief that customary systems hold back development and must be reformed. This is despite ample empirical evidence that, while they may break down under pressure, customary systems are often robust and capable of evolution to accommodate population growth and market development, providing secure, individual, and sometimes exclusive, transferable rights. However the individualisation of land tenure, with the active encouragement of private investors, creates opportunities for land concentration by national and local elites and foreign interests. Many African governments are currently struggling to put in place coherent land policies which meet the needs of both national economic development and the livelihoods of their rural populations.

**Customary systems are often robust and capable of evolution to accommodate population growth and market development**

In most countries of *Latin America*, land distribution is highly unequal. Widespread land reforms throughout the twentieth century have not in general achieved equitable outcomes, although they have served to modernise agrarian economies. Exploitative tenancy is now a diminishing problem, but absolute landlessness and tenure insecurity remain common. Neo-liberal economic reforms since the 1980s have provided stronger protection for private property, thereby supporting structural inequalities and renewing land concentration. Land issues can be highly political. In Brazil a lack of opportunities for land access has led to land invasions and widespread forest encroachment. World Bank-supported programmes of market-based land reform in Brazil and Colombia show some promise but may yield few benefits for the very poor. A resurgence of interest in the resource rights of indigenous people has led in many countries to the passage of laws which provide for recognition of traditional lands. Thus far, implementation has been weak and continuing conflicts make indigenous land rights a focus for donor intervention.

*Asia* has also seen a wide variety of modernising agrarian reforms, most successful in Taiwan and South Korea. While equity has generally improved, exploitative tenancy and debt bondage (linked to social divisions of caste) are continuing features, notably in Pakistan, some Indian states and Nepal. Landlord avoidance of land ceilings and taxes is widespread. Landlessness and land fragmentation are particularly problematic in high population density areas throughout south and south-east Asia, and political upheavals in post-communist countries such as Vietnam and Cambodia have created complex circumstances in which land rights are unclear and unspecified. The issue of the lack of land rights for indigenous and tribal peoples has also been problematic. Only in the Philippines has this been addressed through legal reforms. In south Asia joint management of forests and other CPRs is beginning to provide more secure rights for the poor while assisting in sustainable resource management.

Forms of tenure and the importance of intervention for the poor can also vary within countries, according to the types and intensity of land use and the patterns of land ownership which have arisen historically. Table 1 attempts to summarise the range of forms of tenure and issues which arise. Note, however, that the key issues for land users relate to the nature of the rights they enjoy regardless of the system of tenure. In principle, both private and public ownership under modern law and customary systems can provide secure, transferable rights for individuals and groups, though frequently they do not.

## Global changes and impacts on land tenure

Changes in policy conditions and the development context impact on both tenure systems and land policies and on the significance of land as a source of livelihoods. The main drivers of change are global economic development, internally and externally led policy change, demographic growth and political and military conflicts in developing countries. Table 2 summarises the tenure effects and poverty implications of these and other changes.

Economic liberalisation improves the climate for investment and economic growth, but can also stimulate land claims by national and

## Table 1: Types of tenure regimes and tenure issues in different settings

| Type of area | Forms of tenure | Tenure issues |
|---|---|---|
| Urban areas | Private land titles<br>Public or collective customary land ownership with individual occupancy rights | ○ Demarcation of plots<br>○ Security of tenancies |
| Peri-urban and rural high potential/high density | Private or customary, with individualised rights of tenure | ○ Land rights management and dispute resolution; land markets likely to be active, with conflicts between different land uses and disputes amongst claimants |
| Commercial estates | Private or public ownership | ○ Land distribution and equity<br>○ Tenant security and labour issues |
| Land development schemes, e.g. irrigation | Public or private, with individual user rights | ○ Tenancy and labour issues where private<br>○ Access to irrigable plots<br>○ Exclusion of traditional water users<br>○ Dispute resolution |
| Medium–low density arable | Customary or private smallholdings | ○ Legal incorporation of customary land holding<br>○ Survey and registration generally not needed except where competing claims arise |
| Discrete CPRs (village pasture and woodlands, etc.) | Customary or public/ de facto open access | ○ Institutional and legal frameworks for local CPR management<br>○ Customary access to public land<br>○ Usufruct rights and exclusion issues affecting non-land-holding groups |
| Extensive CPRs (rangelands, forest belts, wetland systems, aquatic resources) | Customary or public/ de facto open access, or with competing customary/ private/public rights | ○ Collaborative or joint management<br>○ Recognition of customary rights<br>○ Legal and planning frameworks for multiple use<br>○ Dispute resolution<br>○ Stakeholder participation |

foreign private investors who wish to secure private title or accumulate land holdings. Liberalisation may involve the privatisation of customary or public lands and the allocation of individual land rights through titling programmes which can undermine the land security of the poor, especially women and secondary right holders. Trends towards economic and cultural globalisation also extend the reach of the transnational private sector in developing countries and encourage convergence of tenure systems towards a western model of exclusive, transferable private rights.

## Table 2: Global changes and their effects

| Sources of change | Tenure effects | Poverty impacts ( + or – ) | Land and policy implications |
|---|---|---|---|
| **ECONOMIC LIBERALISATION** | | | |
| Market development | ○ Increased land values<br>○ Greater land insecurity | + New income opportunities<br>– Risk of loss of land rights, especially for women and non-landowners | ○ Need for land market regulation |
| Withdrawal of the state | ○ Diminished state capacity for land administration | – State land administration fails to respond to poor | ○ Role for civil society in land administration |
| Land and resource privatisation | ○ Creation of new sets of rights<br>○ Competition between customary and private users | – Loss of customary land rights and access to CPRs | ○ Need to resolve contradictions of dualistic land policies |
| **DEMOCRATISATION** | | | |
| Decentralisation of government | ○ No direct land tenure effects | + Increased responsiveness in local land administration (yet to be widely realised) | ○ Empowerment of village groups and customary institutions as land holders and as parties in decentralised government |
| Increased transparency/ participation | ○ Greater clarity of land use decisions and tenure rules<br>○ Greater scope for community-based natural resource management | + Greater security over land and natural resources | |
| **POPULATION GROWTH** | ○ Land saturation, pressure, competition<br>○ Fragmentation and inheritance problems | – Scarcity and degradation of natural capital, increase in disputes | ○ Creation of off-farm incomes<br>○ Land distribution<br>○ Farm technology improvement<br>○ Conflict resolution |
| **URBANISATION** | ○ Rising land values<br>○ Individualisation of rights | – May undermine security of customary rights | ○ Land market regulation<br>○ Improved settlement and land use planning |
| **GLOBALISATION** | ○ Convergence with western tenure models<br>○ Greater private access to technology | – Undermining of customary rights, increased land competion | ○ Pro-poor land policies and regulation of land markets |
| **POLITICAL AND MILITARY CONFLICT** | ○ Breakdown of tenure systems<br>○ Changes in land occupation | – Land insecurity, enforced displacement and loss of land rights | ○ Restoration of governance and tenure institutions<br>○ Land rights management in conflict resolution context |

**Democratisation, decentralisation and good governance can enhance the scope for locally responsive land and resource rights management**

Policy movements towards democratisation, decentralisation and good governance can enhance the scope for locally responsive land and resource rights management which meets the needs of the poor. The growing acceptance by governments of community-based natural resource management, for instance, can provide new livelihood opportunities for the poor and improve environmental sustainability. The rolling back of the state, however, reduces the public sector's capacity to administer land resources and requires the development of policy frameworks in which civil society and the market can both play a role in the allocation and management of land rights.

Endogenous contextual changes also have important impacts on land-based livelihoods. Population growth increases land pressure, leading to intensification of land use and the fragmentation of land holdings. Resulting changes in farming systems may prove unsustainable, in the absence of suitable technological innovations. Migration and population displacement resulting from conflict and climatic shocks also lead to increasing pressures on land and local resource management systems. The development of towns and urban markets increases the value of peri-urban land and enhances both farm and non-farm business opportunities for smallholders and private investors. (In customary tenure systems, these processes can all stimulate evolution towards more individualised, transferable rights.) On the other hand, the expansion of urban employment and the informal sector can also increase livelihood opportunities for the poor, helping to reduce rural land pressure. The balance between rural and urban development and between on- and off-farm opportunities has a great bearing on the sustainability of farming systems and the demand for land, with implications for the importance of land tenure as an entry point for poverty elimination.

Political and military conflicts cause changes in the structure of land occupation as a result of population displacement and land seizures. They may also involve the collapse of local and national governance. In post-conflict situations the issue arises of how tenure systems can be re-established. Because conflict may have roots in inter-group competition over land and resources, the development of new institutions which can resolve land disputes and tenure claims in transparent and equitable ways is particularly important.

## Trade-offs and synergies

In most rural communities, secure access to land and natural resources is a necessary, but not sufficient, condition for livelihood sustainability (although there will always be some who do not directly depend on the land for their livelihoods). It is therefore particularly important to examine the trade-offs and synergies between land tenure interventions and related areas of rural development. Trade-offs are important because tenure issues may not be a constraint; other interventions on behalf of the poor (such as improving agrarian services, technologies and markets, or efforts to improve off-farm livelihoods) may be more beneficial. Conversely, investment in other areas may in some circumstances fail to reduce poverty or have limited results, if issues of land access and security for the poor or the functioning of tenure institutions are not addressed. Synergy is important because tenure or land reforms will generally have very limited results unless accompanied by action on other fronts. The balance of emphasis will depend upon the context, and can only be determined by systematic analysis of asset endowments and livelihood constraints.

Specific areas for intervention which may complement or be traded off against work on land tenure include involvement in:

- agrarian services (including extension, input supply and market and other infrastructure)
- technology for sustainable intensification of agriculture (especially in circumstances of land pressure)
- access to water (especially for rainfed systems in semi-arid areas)
- access to affordable credit, without highly restrictive or punitive conditions
- CPR utilisation and community-based management
- mechanisms for stakeholder participation in regional land use planning (especially in contexts of multiple demands on CPRs and arable land and in peri-urban areas)
- non-farm employment and livelihoods
- literacy, education and training for rural people and farmers.

There are also important synergies with the development of enabling policies and institutions which can support the implementation of pro-poor rural development measures and set a framework within which the poor can secure land and resource access. Key objectives here include the promotion of competitive and accessible markets for farm and other natural resource-based produce and the promotion of good governance (including the development of decentralised, locally responsive government institutions).

## DFID priorities

In general terms improving land access and security of tenure for the poor is beneficial to rural livelihoods and their sustainability. Improvements in the availability of land and other types of natural capital for the poor can be pursued in two ways:

(i)  directly, through projects within individual country programmes, and

(ii)  indirectly, through the development of knowledge about pro-poor land policies and tenure institutions – in this context DFID can also strive to promote debate and consensus among national stakeholders (rural people, governments, donors and the development community) about land issues.

The framework presented in Chapter 1 of this book highlights two broad approaches to promoting sustainable rural livelihoods (which DFID can undertake either directly or promote more widely through multilateral partnerships). First, donors can focus on strengthening, restoring and developing the capital asset base of the poor. Access to land and natural resources is mediated by both formal and informal institutions as well as by social and economic relations. Promoting people's access to and participation in the institutions which grant and regulate land and resource rights is therefore particularly important. This can take the form of engagement with and support to indigenous social networks and forms of governance, community-based organisations, village and district assemblies and formally constituted bodies for land administration and conflict resolution. Effectively this is strengthening the social capital of the poor, the benefits of which will extend beyond the area of land. Developing human capital, through education and literacy skills training, is important in promoting participation by the poor and in achieving local capacity for decentralised, bottom-up development. Since monetised transactions in land are increasingly prevalent, developing poor people's access to financial capital through income generation, credit schemes and land grants is also relevant.

Second, actions can be taken to develop enabling land policies, including: pro-poor land legislation; responsive, transparent, decentralised institutions for land administration; regional land use planning and resource conflict resolution mechanisms; and complementary sectoral policies and programmes for agricultural investment and natural resource management.

A first step in either case is to undertake country-specific (or area-specific) diagnosis of the importance of land and resource tenure as an entry point for promoting sustainable rural livelihoods. Contextual issues for assessment include the nature and structure of the agrarian sector, the balance between rural and urban sectors in the economy and the balance between NR-based rural livelihoods and non-NR-based employment and incomes for the poor. Where poverty and vulnerability are not linked to landlessness, tenure insecurity and land pressure, work on land tenure is unlikely to be a priority. However, it is also important to guard against and mitigate the adverse impacts on poor people's access to land, resulting from, for example, civil and military conflicts, population growth, spontaneous migrations and macro or sector policy change.

**Where poverty and vulnerability are not linked to landlessness, tenure insecurity and land pressure, work on land tenure is unlikely to be a priority**

Possible actions can also be considered under DFID's recently adopted Poverty Aim Markers (enabling, inclusive and focused actions against poverty). Table 3 sets out possible interventions with comments on their likely impacts and country examples.

### Table 3: Land tenure and DFID's Poverty Aim Markers

| Types of action | Land tenure interventions | Impacts on SRLs and related issues to address | Country examples |
|---|---|---|---|
| **Enabling actions** | Support stakeholder participation in land policy process | + but governments may resist | Uganda |
| | Decentralised institutions for land management and conflict resolution | +, – or 0 depending on responsiveness to poor | Senegal |
| | Legislative reform to strengthen security, access and clarify tenure rules | + but must integrate needs of poor | Uganda 1998 Land Law |
| | Legislative reform to strengthen women's land rights | + but may face cultural barriers | Zimbabwe 1997 Inheritance Law |
| | NR sector policies for co-management of CPRs | + where resource rights of poor are strengthened | some Indian states |
| **Inclusive actions – national programmes** | Land redistribution and resettlement | + but may affect (+ or –) prospects for growth; complementary measures needed | Zimbabwe Phase 1 resettlement South Africa |
| | Individual land titling | + for beneficiaries, often – for others | Kenya |
| | Registration of community land rights, including secondary rights | + but not widely tested; may be complex | Côte d'Ivoire South Africa |
| | Tenancy reform | + | Philippines |
| | Market-based programmes for land access | + but may not reach poor | Brazil, Colombia |
| | NR sector programmes for CPR management | + provided poor represented in design and implementation | Zimbabwe, Namibia |
| **Focused actions** | Popular education, information and advocacy on land rights | + but may be controversial | Mozambique NGOs |
| | Village land and CPR management projects | + provided poor gain share of benefits locally | West Africa, India, Brazil, Bolivia |
| | Building farmers', women's and community organisations | + strong synergy with other aspects of rural development | *Gestion de terroir* in west Africa, NGO work in east Africa |

*Enabling actions* support policy, legislative or institutional reform to safeguard land rights for the poor and to promote transparency and accountability in land administration. This category might include specific initiatives to promote debate and consensus on land tenure at national or regional levels and to encourage the development of pro–poor land policies (e.g. DFID's role in relation to proposed land reforms in Uganda, and in west Africa, through the Anglo–francophone initiative). Such actions have strong synergy with efforts to promote good governance and the responsiveness to poverty of policy and institutions.

*Inclusive actions* or sectoral programmes of tenure reform, land distribution and the development of systems of land rights management can support land access and security for the poor on a national scale. However, these types of action are seldom a priority, except in circumstances of accelerated political and economic change and where there is a strong basis in popular demand. Successful donor involvement in land or tenure reform requires strong partnerships with government and sustained political will at the national level. Such programmes are also relatively costly.

*Focused actions* promote land access and resource security by concentrating on the capital assets of particular groups of poor people. This can be done through specific development projects or advocacy and education work in partnership with both governments and NGOs. This approach can combine land tenure activities with action on other fronts to address the perceived priorities of the poor (such as popular education and the strengthening of social capital through the development of farmer and community-based organisations).

## Costs of land tenure interventions

National programmes of land reform and resettlement tend to be very costly (e.g. to finance land acquisition, provision of infrastructure, the creation of national capacity in land survey and cadastre and new institutions for land administration). Where there is a need for such programmes, they are probably best tackled in partnership with other donors on the basis of strong consensus about needs. By contrast, the costs of enabling and focused actions are much lower. The primary requirements are for technical assistance and the development of human and intellectual capital at various levels through education, skills training and research. The strong synergy between enabling policies and grass roots development means that these types of action can have important multiplier effects and are likely to prove more cost-effective and less risky than large national land reform programmes.

Cost-effectiveness can be jeopardised by misguided donor action, which often transfers the cost onto the poor themselves. For instance:

- Kenya's long-running programme of individual land registration undermined established customary rights, particularly for women and various groups of poor.

- The first phase of resettlement in Zimbabwe failed to provide for sufficient tenure security, targeted agrarian services, off-farm employment, grazing and woodland commons and social infrastructure.

- Tanzania's earlier land bill was drafted with donor assistance, without consideration of the underlying policy's effects on the poor.

- World Bank technical assistance to promote active land privatisation (e.g. in Malawi and Tanzania) was based on macro-economic considerations without adequate assessment of existing tenure systems, stakeholder consultation or coordination with other donors.

**National programmes of land reform and resettlement tend to be very costly ... they are probably best tackled in partnership with other donors on the basis of strong consensus about needs**

## *Developing partnerships*

Partnerships with national governments should be approached with care since land reform at national level can be highly politicised and controversial. Where donors concur with national policy objectives and understand their impacts, they can support land or tenure reforms; they should not attempt to drive them. DFID can, however, seek to develop national partnerships by: supporting land policy processes from an early stage; assisting government to consult with stakeholders; providing training and information about land policy options, their impacts and the comparable experiences of other countries; and facilitating participation by the poor in public land policy debate.

Effective partnerships among donors are likely to achieve more far-reaching results than actions by a single donor. The DFID agenda advocates pro-poor land policies. Other donors, notably the World Bank and USAID, have concentrated on promoting economic efficiency in land allocation. However, the UK's practical experience and intellectual capital in the area of land tenure reform is relatively weak, as is that of many individual donors. Policy dialogue, joint programmes for research and learning and, in cases of national-scale land reform, coordinated donor programmes are the main avenues for developing donor partnerships.

## When to intervene

It is appropriate to consider criteria for identifying land and resource tenure problems which may generate demands for donor intervention.

- Analysis of land/population ratios and diagnosis of the sustainability of farming systems provide an indication of whether or not improved land access is necessary for sustainable livelihoods.

- Levels of land concentration indicate structural inequalities in land distribution (e.g. Gini coefficients measure the distribution of assets within economies and can be calculated for land holding, where data is available).

- Incidence of land disputes and inheritance problems within and between rural communities are indicators of problems with tenure systems and land administration which may require reform. Recurrent competition in land claims between rural communities, local elites and the private sector indicate land policy failure and the need for clarity in tenure rules (e.g. resolution of the contradictions of dualistic policies incorporating overlapping formal and customary tenure regimes).

- Incidence of landlessness among women indicates the need for protection of women's land access and security.

In land-inequitable societies, analysis of the relative performance of the smallholder and estates sectors in terms of output, revenue and employment may indicate the importance of land redistribution in strategies for pro-poor economic growth. Vested political interests in the status quo are, however, likely to limit opportunities for intervention. Unless new land can be supplied or inequitable land distribution can be altered, the creation of off-farm livelihoods and improved technologies for intensification will often be areas of higher priority for action.

There are two principal difficulties with criteria such as these. First, it is difficult and costly to move beyond aggregate national pictures to capture relevant information on local circumstances. Second, in order to demonstrate the relative importance of land tenure vis-à-vis other sub-sectoral issues (such as agrarian services, water and non-farm livelihoods), simultaneous, integrated assessment of priorities and opportunities in those areas is required. Both of these difficulties underline the need for country and locally specific analysis incorporating well-chosen qualitative and quantitative case studies of the nature and context of poverty, and how to address it. The approaches taken by Participatory Poverty Assessments indicate a way forward, although these assessments have generally not focused on land and related issues.

Land access and resource security problems may also point to possible opportunities for action, though the appropriateness of these will depend on national political circumstances. The existence of programmes of legislative and policy change affecting land tenure or demands for change within civil society are criteria which indicate clear scope for donor involvement. Against this background, openness in government and a collaborative attitude to civil society and NGOs would suggest that donor support for pro-poor land tenure will be welcomed. Government programmes of decentralisation and interest in sub-sectoral institutional and policy reform (in areas such as forests and wildlife) may also indicate the scope for donor support to locally responsive land administration and community-based land and natural resource tenure arrangements.

## Conclusions

While it will seldom be appropriate to focus exclusively on land and resource tenure issues, these should always be considered within project and programme design. In general, donor priorities are likely to lie in enabling and focused actions against poverty: measures which promote good governance through policies and institutions or which target specific groups of poor people to help them extend their asset base. If the emphasis is laid on strengthening participation in local organisations and the responsiveness and accountability of local government, there is scope for strong spill-over benefits in other areas.

**Table 4: Approaches to sustainable livelihoods and poverty reduction through land tenure interventions**

| Main approaches | | Interventions | Partnerships |
|---|---|---|---|
| Strengthening capital assets | FOCUSED | ○ Land rights education and advocacy<br>○ Building CBOs<br>○ Community-based natural resource management projects<br>○ Local land reforms | ○ Bilateral agencies, NGOs (ethical production and trade)<br>○ Responses to local demands in civil society<br>○ Not only land-focused; private sector |
| Developing enabling policies and institutions | INCLUSIVE | ○ Land distribution/agrarian reform programmes<br>○ Comprehensive land rights management programmes<br>○ Sub-sector programmes for CPR management<br>○ Institutional support to land administration | ○ Multi-donor programmes<br>○ National demands at policy level<br>○ Land-focused with cross-sectoral linkages<br>○ Role for private sector cooperation |
| | ENABLING | ○ Participation in land policy debate<br>○ Pro-poor land legislation<br>○ Progressive inheritance law<br>○ Participatory bodies for land administration and conflict resolution<br>○ Strengthening indigenous resource rights | ○ Bilateral and multilateral<br>○ Response to demands in state and civil society in partner countries<br>○ Engagement of private sector in debate and consensus |

Inclusive actions or sector programmes of tenure reform, land rights management or, occasionally, land redistribution may be appropriate in a few cases, where land rights and tenure institutions stand in need of comprehensive adjustment as a result of accelerated political or economic change. Actions of this type can be very costly and are likely to require multi–donor programmes and strong partnerships with government.

Table 4 summarises the range of land tenure–related interventions open to donors. The table relates the DFID's Poverty Aim Marker categories to the principal approaches identified in the sustainable rural livelihoods framework (namely, strengthening the capital assets of the poor and developing enabling policies and institutions) and draws out implications for the partnerships which will be crucial in determining whether donors will succeed in this area.

# 13 Water/Irrigation and Sustainable Rural Livelihoods

*John Soussan*

## The nature and uses of water resources

We live in a rapidly changing world, in which the lives and livelihoods of all, but especially of the poor, are diverse and dynamic. For the world's poor, their relationship with their resource base is the key to their survival and prospects. These points apply to most people–resource relationships, but are of particular pertinence in any discussion of water resources and irrigation. These resources are fundamental to life and are the basis of many livelihoods.

Water resources come in different forms and have multiple uses. Water is present in surface stocks (lakes, ponds) and flows (rivers), as groundwater in aquifers or as soil moisture. All can be used directly in livelihood activities and all are important to the viability of ecosystems on which livelihoods depend. Water resources also move and vary over both space and time, with the variability operating at different temporal and spatial scales. The movement of water, flowing over the surface and through aquifers, means that water resource issues can never be purely local. These multiple sources and multiple uses of water resources mean that there are likely to be various stakeholders with competing interests, especially since water use often involves externalities whereby secondary costs or benefits do not accrue to the water user him/herself.

The multiple nature of water resources and their uses is reflected in a move away from traditional sector approaches to what has become known as integrated water resources management (IWRM). The interrelationships between these uses and the societal context of their use are represented in Figure 1.

The relationships presented in Figure 1 provide a structure through which we can understand the diversity of water resource/use combinations that characterise the livelihoods of the poor. If the goal is to enhance the assets available to the poor, from a water resources perspective we need to understand:

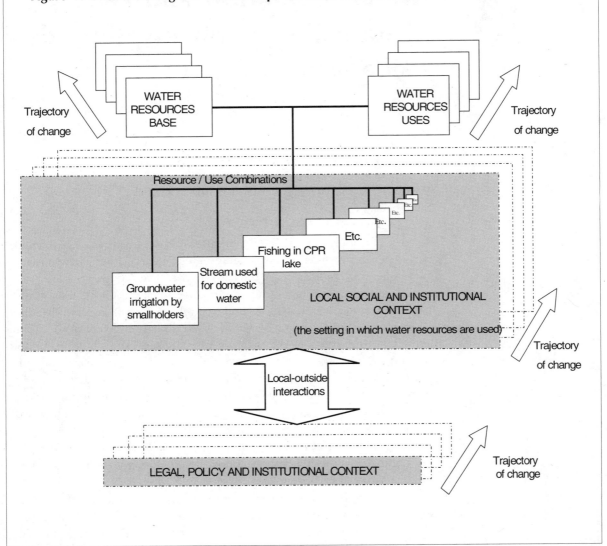

Figure 1: Understanding the relationships between water resources and users

- the potential resource base, including both the quantity and quality of water resources available within the area with which we are concerned

- the existing and potential pattern of use of these resources, including which groups are using which particular water resources and the contribution that these resources are making to their livelihoods

- the legal, policy and institutional context within which resource use takes place and access is granted

- the local social and institutional context of water resources use, including the processes through which decisions are reached and the links between local-level and external institutions involved in water resources management, and

- the trajectories of change of all of these factors (for water resources use, in common with much of rural life, changes constantly and often rapidly) – a central principle of a sustainable rural livelihoods (SRL) approach should be that positive directions of change are facilitated and enhanced while negative ones are mitigated.

## Water and rural livelihoods

Good management of and secure rights to water resources are crucial to livelihoods and particularly to people's capacity to cope with variability. Different individuals, households and social groups will have varying levels of interest in agricultural production, livestock, the management of common property resources, non-agrarian production, domestic water uses and so on. Specific combinations of water use will determine the form of people's stake in these resources. Structure can be provided to the necessary analysis through consideration of specific forms of livelihood/water resource relationships, notably:

- water and food security

- water and household maintenance

- water-based livelihoods and livelihood diversification, and

- water and ecosystems maintenance.

### *Water and food security*

Food security is one determining feature of livelihoods. Sustaining and improving yields (whether of subsistence or cash crops) is key to the viability of many rural livelihood systems, and water resources play a critical role in this process, for the yields of all crops are dependent on sufficient supplies of water. Access to and the management of water are one of the keys to sustainable agriculture and, conversely, variability in water supply lies behind much of the uncertainty that characterises the fragile livelihoods of many poor rural people.

In many developing countries irrigation is the most effective means of reducing this variability and extending the cropping period. However, there are concerns over the sustainability and equity of water allocation and use for irrigation. Irrigated land produces about 40% of the world's food and yields in irrigated areas are on average 2.2 times higher than those in non-irrigated croplands. Irrigation is particularly important for the production of staple food grains, especially in countries such as China, Egypt and Pakistan. Large-scale irrigation developments often exhibit poor performance, but it is now asserted by many that the success and sustainability of irrigation systems is related more to the degree of participatory management than to the scale of the irrigation scheme *per se*. Poor understanding and management of water resources in the past has led to over-extraction from rivers or aquifers. The lack of management and poor drainage have led to farmland becoming saline, and there has been insufficient attention to maintenance. Irrigation development has also led to inequalities, with development favouring the owners of better-quality land, to the detriment of lower-income groups such as the land poor, landless and pastoralists.

**It is now asserted ... that the success and sustainability of irrigation systems is related more to the degree of participatory management than to the scale of the irrigation scheme**

Small-scale, low cost 'irrigation', including the development of flooded lands, swamps and spate irrigation, can be very significant for the rural poor. Such schemes can be locally managed and are likely to be more efficient and less vulnerable to the operation and maintenance problems which have characterised government-run schemes (Box 1). Irrigation is thus generally well suited to a poverty-focused programme. However, the development of local water markets can prove to be highly inegalitarian and subject to capture by local elites: rights over and access to water resources are crucial.

---

### Box 1: Small-scale irrigation in an agro-pastoral area

In the Baringo-Bogoria basin of the Kenyan Rift Valley, the Il Chamus people have traditionally supplemented livestock rearing with small gravity irrigation schemes. Long canals lead from weirs on seasonal or perennial rivers to the fields. Most households have rights to land on more than one branch canal and can shift between plots according to fertility and the abandonment and rehabilitation of whole canals. Irrigated agriculture is labour-intensive, especially at the end of the dry season; poorer households have difficulty in combining irrigation and herding and tend to opt for the latter, with a resulting long-term loss to their own food security and to the survival of their animals. Richer households can increase herd productivity through irrigated fodder production. A scheme was proposed which entailed fixed intakes and blocks of permanent fields nearer the rivers. This idea was dropped when it became clear that the community was afraid of the conflicts and inequity that might arise from reallocation of land. There were also concerns about the reduced scope for: using canal water for domestic purposes; shifting away from exhausted or weed-infested fields; and irrigating according to personal preference and labour availability. Instead only permanent intakes were provided, and neither canal length nor field patterns were changed. Other more thoroughgoing interventions in the same area, providing larger and entirely new schemes, appear to have been less successful.

*Source*: Bakker, 1991

Rainfed agriculture still produces most of the world's food and is the main source of livelihood for the majority of the rural poor. In rainfed areas, as in many irrigated areas, the starting point for building sustainable rural livelihoods is to improve on-farm water management. There may also be considerable scope for enhancing water harvesting and conservation which also helps to retain nutrients and reduce erosion.

Homestead plots and gardens are often a vital source of nutrition, providing variety and security. These plots are, in many areas, tended by women, who grow fruits, vegetables and keep small livestock to supplement the staple diet and/or trade in local markets. The plots are intensively cultivated and depend upon adequate water supplies that may have to be carried long distances.

In arid and semi-arid areas, pastoral production is often the basis for livelihoods. These are typically dependent on common property resources and are often nomadic or semi-nomadic. In these regions, water availability has often been considered the limiting factor to stock sizes. However, water may not be the only limiting factor and outsiders should be cautious about interfering with complex and sophisticated pastoral systems.

The poor also depend for food on both plants and animals gathered from the wild (typically from common property resources), especially in times of real hardship. The availability of wild foods is often closely linked to water resources. This is most obvious for fish and other aquatic animals, but is also true of terrestrial animals and plants whose range and abundance are tied to the availability of water.

## Water, health and household maintenance

**The availability of adequate water for use in and around the homestead is a fundamental need for all**

The availability of adequate water (both quantity and quality) for use in and around the homestead is a fundamental need for all. Water is used directly in the household, for drinking, cooking, bathing, washing clothes, cleaning the house and utensils, etc. as well as for homestead cultivation and other income-generating activities. Poor quality or availability affects the health, productivity and workload of the poor, and especially of women who assume the primary burden for the provision of water and its many domestic uses.

Water-based health problems severely affect the poor. The morbidity threats of direct water-borne and water-related diseases (including cholera, diarrhoeal diseases, schistosomiasis, malaria and others) are differential, affecting the poor disproportionately and, among the poor, children most severely. The mitigation of these health threats is fundamental to the establishment of sustainable rural livelihoods, for good health is directly valued and affects productivity, the planning of family sizes and perceptions of risk and security.

The issue of access to adequate and safe water for domestic use is consequently central to a SRL strategy. This means more than simply the provision of supplies of water close to the point of need, though this is essential. The overall social context of water use needs to be understood before conclusions are drawn (see Box 2).

## Water-based livelihoods and livelihood diversification

In many areas there are distinctive minorities whose main source of livelihood is based on the exploitation of water resources (groups such as professional fisherfolk, boatmen and others). There are also often artisanal groups who use water in their production (groups such as potters, weavers or tanners). Their use of the water can significantly affect its quality and, consequently, availability for other uses. For example, preserving fish habitats and movements may not be compatible with water use for irrigation or land drainage for cultivation. Similarly, water used to rinse dyed cloths or tanned hides can be unusable for domestic or irrigation purposes. There are no simple answers to such mixes of incompatible uses, but a sustainable rural livelihoods approach must take into account the needs of both majority and minority interests.

Water also provides a means for the diversification of livelihoods. This can take several forms. Many households gather a range of products from common property resources. These products (including fish, other aquatic animals, aquatic plants and materials such as sand and gravel) are fundamental to the viability of their livelihoods. They can be used to meet subsistence needs and/or to provide secondary income sources. In certain locations there is also the potential for water power to be directly harnessed to contribute to livelihood diversification (e.g. for milling, husking and oil extraction, or for rural electrification).

---

### Box 2: Domestic water in Bangladesh

Most households in rural Bangladesh now have access to hand pumps which supply water for drinking and cooking. The quality of the water is generally adequate. This does not mean, however, that there are no longer any domestic water problems. A recent survey of domestic water patterns in one village* has shown that, whilst nearly everyone has access to a hand pump, only 30% of households actually own their own pump. The remaining 70% use the hand pumps of others. Use is generally confined to water for drinking and cooking; other domestic water uses, and in particular bathing and cleaning clothes and utensils, are still undertaken in the open ponds and channels which run through the area. These water bodies have extremely high levels of microbial infections and other pollutants and the risks of infection are still great. Focus group discussions suggested that the incidence of water-borne diseases is as high as it was before hand pumps became prevalent. The issue is more than a simple matter of better awareness, for social custom would limit bathing at the hand pumps (especially for women) and the informal use rights would be likely to disappear if these far more intensive uses were practised at the hand pumps.

*Part of a DFID-funded research project being executed by the University of Leeds and the Bangladesh Centre for Advanced Studies

---

## *Water and ecosystems maintenance*

The central role of water availability in defining the character and health of ecosystems may be adequately understood, but the critical role of these ecosystems in the sustainability of the natural and hydrological cycle is less so; ecosystems are users and, critically, suppliers of water. There has been growing awareness of the need to actively manage ecosystems (including many wetland and aquatic ecosystems such as swamps, mangroves, rivers and lakes and coral reefs). Threats to such ecosystems often reflect a combination of: unsustainable exploitation of their assets; the conversion of the lands to other uses (farmland, shrimp farms, etc.); the impacts of pollution; and the modification of the hydrological system upstream. This not only undermines the integrity of these unique ecosystems (a matter of importance in itself), but also affects the long-term sustainability of the livelihoods which depend upon their maintenance. The links between poverty eradication and environmental maintenance are not well understood, but what is clear is that the achievement of sustainable rural livelihoods will be jeopardised by the degradation of the ecosystems upon which the poor depend. Their maintenance is consequently more than just an environmental issue: it is closely linked to concerns about poverty and its eradication.

## Scarcities, conflicts and responses to stress: defining the challenge

In the analysis of people–water resources relationships, the dominant paradigm has been one of scarcity, an assumption that a lack of water as a physical entity is the underlying factor behind water resources problems. This simple – but misleading – analysis leads to an equally simple solution: increase supplies (typically through the introduction of more 'efficient' technologies) and problems will disappear. If scarcity is viewed differently, not as a lack of water itself, but rather as the limited availability of or access to the many different services water resources provide, then things look different. For many, the critical issues are: the quality of the water resources; the consequences of competition between incompatible uses; or the social, economic or institutional barriers which limit access to resources. It is these things, rather than the absolute availability of water in the system, which affect their livelihoods.

Scarcity (and who suffers from scarcity) is consequently socially defined, reflecting the structure of rights and entitlements of different sections of the community. Scarcity is not a simple, one-dimensional concept – it is multi-faceted, dynamic and finds expressions across the range of uses of water resources. Where scarcity exists, it often leads to conflicts: conflicts between different users for the same purpose or between different types of use. Four issues derive from this; these issues are at the core of water livelihoods challenges.

(i) The understanding of these conflicts and the institutional processes through which they are expressed and can be mitigated is crucial to actions to address the needs of the poor through interventions in water livelihoods relationships.

(ii) These issues can be neither understood nor addressed at a purely local level. They are found at all scales, ranging from disputes between neighbours to international tensions over rivers such as the Nile and the Ganges. Whatever their scale, they can be mitigated or exacerbated by the legal, political and institutional processes through which they are expressed.

(iii) The nature of scarcity and the conflict which it generates is inherently dynamic, reflecting patterns of change to the resource base, the needs for and uses of these resources and the social, economic and institutional context at local and wider levels which condition these patterns of exploitation.

(iv) Where such stresses exist, people are not passive victims, but respond to scarcity and stress in a variety of ways (see Box 3). These responses can fundamentally change the nature of water resources/livelihoods relationships and are central to defining indicators of and strategies to mediate water-based stress.

Box 3 provides a basis for identifying the nature of water resources livelihoods challenges, with the responses being potential indicators that could help inform choices about action. Where scarcity exists, it is essential that the best use of the resources is made. However, the multiple uses of water make comparisons difficult. Reliance on economic valuation usually biases calculations in favour of marketable goods. Harder to measure, but of central importance, is the efficiency in resource terms (that is, the intensity) of the resource use. Support should be provided to the development of both better valuation methods (e.g. contingent valuation) and measures of water resources use intensity if robust indicators of water resources scarcity and potential are to be developed.

## Setting the priorities

In the preceding sections a necessarily brief analysis of the relationship between water resources management and sustainable rural livelihoods has been presented. The diversity of local needs and water resource uses and the framework of laws, policies and institutions through which rights and access to water resources are mediated have been stressed. Based on this analysis, the priorities for DFID support and action in the field of water resources (including irrigation) should be:

---

**Box 3: Responses to water resources stress**

Responses to water resource stresses are, of course, localised and dependent upon the type of resource, the nature of its use, patterns of access to and rights over the resource, the alternatives available and the institutional context through which decisions are made and rights and entitlements enforced. The list presented here is by no means definitive, or even partially complete, but is rather an attempt to provoke thought on how to understand these issues. One of the advantages of such an analysis of response to stress is that it reflects the dynamics of these processes and in particular the needs and priorities of the communities concerned. It is also often much easier to identify such responses, rather than measuring many other indicators of water resource use relationships. The responses consequently make good indicators that both reflect the specifics of local circumstances and form a basis for planning interventions.

- Scarcity is often expressed in **increased time** to collect the water, catch the fish or whatever other management actions are involved. This is an early response, which can increase gradually or can arise suddenly.
- Scarcity can also lead to decisions to **invest money** in new infrastructure (pumps, canals, storage facilities, etc.); this means that money is being channelled away from other livelihood needs.
- People can **switch to alternative sources** of water when the preferred one becomes scarce. This can lead to greater costs and/or inferior resource quality.
- More **efficient use** of the resource may emerge, through better conservation and/or conversion to less resource-intensive patterns of activity.
- Scarcity and increased difficulties in obtaining water resources can lead to **longer storage**, with added costs and potential decline in quality (especially for domestic water).
- Emerging scarcity can lead to **changes in access rights**, changes which will reflect local power structures with the risk of capture by elites and alienation of the poor.
- Greater scarcity can also lead to **changes in property relations**, in particular the commodification and/or privatisation of formerly common property resources.
- Scarcity and changes in access rights can lead to **greater conflict**, as groups seek to defend perceived rights in the face of greater demand and declining resources.
- They can also result in **livelihood changes**, as the scarcity of critical resources makes existing livelihoods untenable.
- Scarcity of water resources can lead to the **loss or disposal of other assets**, such as the abandonment of land or the death or sale of livestock.
- A classic reflection of scarcity is the **over-exploitation of resources**, resulting in their degradation (for example, lowering water tables or declining fish stocks).

---

- directly to support rural livelihoods through actions to enhance the sustainable productivity of water resources management, and

- to build institutional capacity that empowers the poor, with an emphasis on securing rights of access to and mitigating conflicts over water resources.

These two arenas of action will provide a structure through which policies and programmes concerned with water resources can be integrated into a broader sustainable rural livelihoods approach without losing a focus on the specific challenges these resources present.

## *Enhancing the sustainable productivity of water resources*

Improvements in the management of water resources must form part of a broader programme of assistance. In this, a balance between technical, economic and social interventions is needed and complementarity between these activities and the policy and institutional reforms is essential. There are long traditions of support by DFID and other agencies in fields such as irrigated agriculture and water supply and sanitation provision. These traditions should not be abandoned, but should be built upon and augmented, where appropriate, by additional spheres of activity.

- The clearest example of this is the need for continuing support to improve the functioning of irrigation systems. The case for major new schemes is doubtful. However, there are millions living in and reliant upon existing schemes, most of which are far from optimal in their efficiency. A mix of institutional support and technical intervention is crucial if the best use is to be made of 'sunk' capital. For example, the improved management of large command areas in Asia could significantly increase the level and sustainability of the livelihoods of the poorest tail end farmers.

**There is a strong case for support to farmer-managed irrigation**

- There is a strong case for support to farmer-managed irrigation. This is particularly true where such schemes would reach small, marginal farmers whose productivity is limited by uncertain water supplies. In developing such schemes, the right balance of private sector and local organisational involvement is essential to ensure access rights for the poor.

- A central area of support should be to on-farm water management, whether in irrigated or rainfed areas. There is a vast array of techniques for improved water harvesting, water retention, soil and nutrient conservation and so on, many of which are derived from traditional practices. Their potential is as yet not fully realised, but any programme in this area would need to be able to capture locally specific needs and opportunities.

- There is scope for the improved management of common resources (such as wetlands, rivers and lakes) that have intrinsic value and are important sources of foods and other materials. These are susceptible to rapid degradation and many are affected by uncertain property rights in rapidly changing rural economies. Actions to support collective management and resolve uncertainties over rights and entitlements will be critical to a livelihoods approach in many areas.

To these four spheres of action can be added actions to improve domestic water and sanitation provision. The form these will take will vary greatly. In some areas it is a question of ensuring adequate supply, while in others quality issues are the main challenge. In all cases, ensuring rights of access and links with health care and hygiene education programmes will be of central importance as will be the incorporation of gender considerations. In such programmes, the totality of homestead water usage should be considered, including homestead cultivation, livestock, washing and, where found, homestead-based artisanal production. Assisting those who rely on water-based livelihoods (such as fishing, water transport and traditional artisanal production) to adjust to change is crucial. It is often distinct, minority groups, with very weak asset bases (many rely on common property resources) who practice these livelihoods. The demand for their products (e.g. potters or boatmen) or the resource base on which they depend (especially for fisherfolk) are often in decline and their weak asset base and social position limit the scope for retaining control over the resource base or identifying alternative livelihood options. Actions to support their traditional livelihoods, where viable, should be a priority. Otherwise, support to diversification/substitution should be provided.

The role of water resources in livelihood diversification has been noted. Options for diversification can be threatened by changes to property rights and the degradation of resources, especially common property resources. The impact of reduced availability of products from these resources differentially affects the poor, who have the weakest asset bases and who are most reliant on such resources.

## Building institutional capacity

A prerequisite to enhancing the contribution of water resources to sustainable livelihoods is an institutional context which helps to create conditions whereby the rural poor can gain access to the resources on a sustainable basis. This a complex and long-term process, the specifics of which will vary. The process should address all levels, local to national, of the institutional structures concerned. Development assistance has for too long focused on the project level only, often setting objectives for projects that cannot be achieved within a project structure. The need for assistance to policy reform is now recognised, but the links between policy and livelihoods are still not well understood (see Figure 2).

More action-oriented research is needed to understand these linkages. In particular:

- There is a need to enshrine in law the rights and entitlements of the poor concerning their access to water resources at different times and in different places. Such legal changes are complex and difficult to achieve but essential.

- This should be supported by integrated water resources policies which reconcile the needs of different users and establish priorities for action.

- Linked to this should be a process of institutional reform designed to enhance subsidiarity, efficiency and inter-agency cooperation (both between state agencies and between the state and civil society).

- Finally, the implications of related policies in fields such as agriculture, fisheries, environment, infrastructure development, settlement planning and macro-economics (taxes, subsidies, import restrictions and so on) must be understood and articulated.

**Figure 2: Internationally accepted water policy principles, poverty and rural livelihoods**

| Policy Principle* | Poverty Implications | Links to Rural Livelihoods |
|---|---|---|
| Water as an economic good | Although water always has value, its relative value to the poor can be far greater than is reflected in its costs and the principle of the user bearing costs can be both hard and expensive to enforce. | The different values of water resources uses to different stakeholders can be hard to compare in economic terms and may not reflect the worth of non-marketed goods and services. |
| Integrated, holistic approach | Traditional, technical approaches tend to exclude the needs and involvement of the poor. | Interventions must consider all water resources and the interests of all stakeholders. |
| Desirability of decentralisation | Centralised bureaucracies have particularly excluded the poor, both formally and in their informal operations. | An institutional structure which does not replace centralisation with local elite domination is needed. |
| Stakeholder participation (especially women) | Traditional power structures are dominated by elites, males and outsiders. | Subsidiarity is needed which represents all stakeholders and gives real power to the devolved institutions. |
| Private sector participation | The dominating role of the state in areas such as water supply and irrigation is both excluding and inefficient. | The role of the private sector is crucial, but must not exclude the poor: markets are not the only answer. |
| Demand-management rather than supply augmentation | Top-down, technical approaches have not under-stood the needs and interests of the poor and are expensive and inefficient. | The goal should be to improve the choices open to those in need, starting with improving existing resource uses before adding new ones. |
| Polluter pays | The ability to externalise tends to benefit the 'haves', with the poor paying the price in degraded resources and ill health. | The goal must be both to increase benefits and to maintain the resources, with rights balanced by responsibilities. |

* Based on Carter (1998), p. 123

Action at the policy/national level should be balanced by support to the development of an institutional context at the local level that provides the channels through which the participation and representation of the poor can be guaranteed. Many water resources are common property and have multiple, competing uses. They can be the source of conflicts and because of this the key will be to ensure that local institutions governing their use represent the needs and interests of all. Conventional approaches of forming 'user groups' have consistently failed; a more effective approach would be to build upon existing local structures, formal and informal, and to integrate water management issues into the wider fabric of local–level social and economic relationships.

Links between the local and national levels are crucial. Multi-agency subsidiarity should be advocated, linking into the processes of decentralisation and democratisation found in many countries. A key challenge is to define which is the appropriate tier of authority for different functions, and to ensure that adequate skills and resources are available at the lower tiers of authority. Some, such as cross-border river sharing negotiations, are the natural function of central government. Others, such as the management of small rivers, aquifers or ponds, are essentially local in character. Still others lie somewhere in between and need institutions which operate at or have authority at these intermediate levels. The natural unit for planning is the river basin or catchment at the local level, but the hydrological logic of this cuts across administrative boundaries for management functions.

> **A key challenge is to define which is the appropriate tier of authority for different functions, and to ensure that adequate skills and resources are available at the lower tiers of authority**

Support to awareness raising, research and human resources development is vital for creating an awareness of the relationships between water resources and the livelihoods of the poor and for enhancing the human resource base at all levels from the community to central agencies. In these activities, strong partnerships with local agencies are needed, as is continued support to research and a better synergy between research and the DFID bilateral programme.

It is useful to lay down some guidelines that stimulate thinking when defining specific projects and programmes. A preliminary set of such guidelines is presented here in the form of questions. These questions should be considered in all stages, from initial conceptualisation through planning and design to implementation and monitoring. They should be used to guide the dialogues with all stakeholders in reaching a consensus on what should be done, where and when. Both the guidelines and the process in which they will be used must be actively reviewed and developed.

The questions are:

- Will the actions provide the best balance between the different needs of all water resources users, including those upstream and downstream?

- Will the actions remove distortions and perverse incentives that lead to wastage of water and provide incentives for transfer of water to higher-level uses?

- Will the actions improve access to and control over water resources for specified target stakeholders?

- Will the actions minimise the effects of the variable and uncertain character of water resources?

- Will the actions support sustainable management, whereby maximum benefits for all are reaped without jeopardising the quality and sustainability of the resources?

- Are the institutions involved accessible, transparent, legitimate, accountable and representative of all stakeholder interests?

- Do the actors have the knowledge, human and physical resources to make wise and effective choices in managing the resources and allocating benefits?

- Does effective subsidiarity, where decisions (and the authority and material means to make the decisions meaningful) are devolved to the lowest appropriate level (which does not necessarily mean the local level), exist?

- Does the wider policy, legal, economic, political and institutional environment support or militate against the objectives behind the actions?

It is hoped that the above questions, and the analysis presented throughout this report, will provide the basis for the integration of water resources issues into a sustainable rural livelihoods approach and will help DFID personnel to define the process through which this will be achieved.

## Key references

Allan, J.A. (1996) 'Policy Responses to the Closure of Water Resources: Regional and Global Issues', in Howsam, P. and Carter, R. (eds) (1996) *Water Policy*. London: Chapman Hall.

Briscoe, J. (1997) 'Managing Water as an Economic Good: Rules for Reformers,' in Kay, M., Franks, T. and Smith, L. (eds) (1997) *Water: Economics, Management and Demand* London: Chapman Hall.

Ministry of Foreign Affairs (1998) *Water for the Future: Integrated Water Resources Management*. The Hague: Ministry of Foreign Affairs.

Stockholm Environment Institute (1997) *Comprehensive Assessment of the Freshwater Resources of the World*. Stockholm: SEI.

## References

Bailey, R. (ed.) (1996) *Water and Environmental Management in Developing Countries* London: CIWEM/ODA.

Bakker, S. (1990) *Adapt the Pastoralists to the Scheme or the Scheme to the Pastoralists*. Paper 2C, Contribution to the International Workshop 'Design for Sustainable Farmer-Managed Irrigation Schemes in Sub-Saharan Africa', February 1990

Bergkamp, G. *et al.* (1998) *Maintaining the Functioning of Freshwater Ecosystems: The Key to Sustainable Management of Water Resources*. IUCN paper prepared for the UN Commission on Sustainable Development. Gland: IUCN.

Calow, R.C. *et al.* (1997) 'Groundwater Management in Drought-Prone Areas of Africa', *Water Resources Development* 13(2) 241–61.

Carter, R. (1992) 'Small-Scale Irrigation in Sub-Saharan Africa: A Balanced View', in ODA (1992) *Priorities for Water Resources Allocation and Management.* London: Overseas Development Administration.

Carter, R. (1998) 'Prospects for Sustainable Water Management Policy in Sub-Saharan Africa', in Vajpeyi, D.K. (ed.) (1998) *Water Resources Management: A Comparative Perspective.* Praeger Publishers.

FAO (1994) *Water Policies and Agriculture.* Rome: Food and Agriculture Organisation.

FAO (1996) *Food Production: the Critical Role of Water.* Rome: Food and Agriculture Organisation.

Inter-American Development (1997) *Integrated Water Resources Management Strategy Paper.* Washington D.C.: I-ADB.

Meinzen-Dick, R., Reidinger, R. and Manzardo, A. (1995) *Participation in Irrigation.* Washington D.C.: World Bank.

Ministry of Foreign Affairs. (1998) *Sustainable Irrigated Agriculture.* The Hague: Ministry of Foreign Affairs.

ODA (1992) *Priorities for Water Resources Allocation and Management.* London: Overseas Development Administration.

Raskin, P., Hansen, E. and Margolis, R. (1995) *Water and Sustainability: A Global Outlook.* Stockholm: Stockholm Environment Institute.

Seckler, D. (1996) *The New Era of Water Resources Management: From 'Dry' to 'Wet Water Savings.* Colombo: IIMI.

Wood, G. and Palmer-Jones, R. (1990) *The Water Sellers: A Cooperative Venture by the Rural Poor.* West Hartford: Kumarian Press.

WWF/IUCN (1998) *Focus on Freshwater: Recommendations to the CSD.* Gland: WWF/IUCN.

# 14

# Additional Contributions
# to NRAC
*Compiled by Diana Carney*

The 1998 DFID Natural Resource Advisers' Conference was intended to provoke discussion and thought about how to operationalise the sustainable rural livelihoods approach, in order to achieve poverty eradication. In addition to the main papers which are contained in this volume, several shorter – but no less important – papers were presented. Contributions were invited from various other sections of DFID. Speakers from outside the organisation (from UNDP and the Institute of Development Studies) added their thoughts as to the challenges and potential of the SRL approach. This chapter summarises these shorter papers and talks.

## Contributions from within DFID

All the speakers welcomed the opportunities for working together which are inherent in the SRL approach. However, all also pointed out the challenges that these create and pointed to practical issues which must be addressed if the full potential of the approach is to be realised.

### Environment (presented by Chris West, Environmental Adviser)

Concern for the environment and sustainability is one of the cornerstones of the SRL approach. The approach offers an opportunity to 'mainstream' the environment. As a starting point, the paper looked at the extent to which this has been the case in natural resources (NR) projects to date. The following table draws out some aggregate answers from NR projects with a value of over £500,000 funded since 1994. It was drawn up using the database of NR projects (NARSIS) and through recall of those involved.

The fact that consistently across the regions only about 30% of projects show systematic and documented consideration of environmental issues in

## Table 1: Natural resource projects and the environment

| | Latin America and the Caribbean | West and North Africa | East Africa |
|---|---|---|---|
| Number of NR projects | 22 | 10 | 11 |
| Environmental issues investigated during project design | 27% | 30% | 27% |
| Environmental OVIs included in Logical Framework* | 18% | 20% | 18% |
| Environmental activities funded as part of project | 50% | 40% | 45% |
| Environmental risk monitored during implementation | 54% | 40% | 36% |

\* An OVI is an objective verifiable indicator within the logframe planning system.

their design suggests that (untested) assumptions are being made about the environment in quite a large number of NR projects.[1] The lack of environmental OVIs included in project logframes suggests that, though we recognise the importance of the environment to poverty eradication (hence the larger number of projects with environmental activities), we are not actually reflecting this in our project monitoring systems. Another reason for the discontinuity between environmental activities and environmental OVIs might be that a number of the environmental activities are effectively 'add ons', not originally scheduled in the project. The suggestion is not that 100% of NR projects should include environmental activities, but certainly that there should be more consistency in the design and monitoring of those that do.

The table shows, therefore, that there is some way to go before environment can be considered to be truly 'mainstreamed' so that both environmental opportunities (for added value) and risks are identified during project design. Environmental screening notes are required for all projects but more training is required so that the full value of these is realised. Unless we take a more active and systematic approach to 'mainstreaming' the environment, there is a danger that little progress will be made.

The question of trade-offs was also raised. Trade-offs between different livelihood outcomes are implicit in the SRL framework. There is a need, however, to delve further into this area and to think about how decisions about trade-offs are made. Natural capital cannot and should not be protected against any type of change and at any cost. But how do we decide which trade-offs are acceptable? What level of change to the natural capital base would give rise to unsustainable practices that would actually prevent us

**Unless we take a more active and systematic approach to 'mainstreaming' the environment, there is a danger that little progress will be made**

from achieving our poverty eradication targets? Environmental appraisal, though sometimes crude, can help us get started on making decisions in this and related areas.

Finally the issue of national strategies for sustainable development (nssds) was raised. The White Paper includes a commitment to support the development and implementation of such strategies in order to reverse trends in environmental losses by 2015. It was stressed that these strategies are not necessarily national – many are effective at a regional or a local level. Second, they are not strategies in the sense of being documents presented, but are rather approaches and ways of achieving policy changes either at a particular level of government or in an area or sector. They are, though, highly compatible with the SRL approach in the sense that both emphasise the need to think strategically about development and to include a wide range of stakeholders in the process. Just as the SRL approach should not be perceived as being led by the NR Division, so nssds should not be considered to be the territory of the environmentalists alone. We should all be working together on these issues to secure the full value of the holistic analysis.

## Enterprise Development (presented by David Wright, Head of the Enterprise Development Group – EDG)

**The SRL approach explicitly recognises the role of the private sector, both as a player in development, but also as a potential partner**

The EDG welcomes the fact that the SRL approach explicitly recognises the role of the private sector, both as a player in development, but also as a potential partner. It has amassed considerable expertise in working with the private sector and recognises the opportunity for working with NR Advisers in providing support to the private sector in rural areas. Indeed, discussions are already underway between the two departments in a number of countries, including Uganda, Tanzania and Zimbabwe. Perhaps if resources of various sections of DFID are concentrated in a particular geographical area, very positive results might be forthcoming which would provide an important example to others elsewhere.

Another strong point of the SRL framework, in the eyes of EDG, is the recognition it gives to the importance of access to financial services. This is an area in which there have been many successes, but to which DFID has perhaps not paid adequate attention in the past (though 40% of EDG's current portfolio is in financial services). One suggestion was that NR Advisers might benefit from attending training courses on the delivery of financial services to poor people, to build up their confidence and awareness in this area. Awareness should also be raised within DFID of the activities of CGAP, the World Bank-supported Consultative Group to Assist the Poorest, which is concentrating specifically on micro-finance and standard setting in this area.

Related to the provision of financial services is the question of market access (both domestic and export), something which EDG feels might require added emphasis in the new SRL approach. Although it is a clear objective of the approach, the feeling from the Enterprise Development Group was that its importance is such that it should be considered as an objective on its own, to make sure that it is given adequate weight and support. Likewise, it must be assured that adequate emphasis is given in rural areas to off-farm (e.g. agro-processing) and non-farm (non-NR-based) activities and that natural resource-based activities do not become the default due to lack of familiarity with other options.

## *Social Development (presented by Andy Norton, Social Development Adviser)*

There is much common ground between the Social Development Division (manifested most fully in the support this division has given to Participatory Poverty Assessments) and NRPAD's interpretation of the sustainable rural livelihoods concept. In particular both share:

- a multidimensional view of well-being, poverty and deprivation

- an emphasis on vulnerability and on the dynamic nature of poverty which highlights the importance of assets, and

- a belief that poor people's priorities and realities should be the starting point which leads naturally to a cross-sectoral, integrated and locally determined approach to planning (because households and communities do not themselves plan by sector).

SDD also welcomes the emphasis in the SRL framework on poor people's capacities and assets and on the broad interpretation of these. Human capital, for example, is too often seen as an outcome of the top-down delivery of health and education services. It is important that the detailed and sophisticated nature of local peoples' knowledge is recognised as well (as it is in the framework).

The SRL approach presents a clear opportunity for the different departments of DFID to work together and to share their expertise in particular areas. As 'cross-cutting' Advisers, Social Development Advisers can assist by helping to make links with other sectors. SDD also has particular experience with the type of social analysis which must underpin (and precede) the proposed livelihoods analysis. It is important that we do not assume homogeneity in rural populations; groups must be deaggregated according to class, caste, ethnic origin, gender, etc. Decisions will need to be made about which 'fault lines' are relevant in any particular case. There is scope for links to be made here with Participatory Poverty Assessments in which categories are determined by the people themselves.

**It is important that we do not assume homogeneity in rural populations; groups must be deaggregated according to class, caste, ethnic origin, gender**

The concept of social capital should be treated with some caution. As it stands it is no more than a rough and ready metaphor for the idea that social networks can have helpful outcomes in terms of meeting objectives. But the nature of the objective varies from governance to growth and social cohesion. Social capital can also have problematic outcomes; people organise to exclude others and oppress as well as to achieve solidarity/development. In addition, social capital is, on the whole, a conservative concept unless informed by a thorough analysis of power relations. Working to support social capital can thus entrench the status quo (which is frequently antithetical to the interests of the poorest).

Though attractive as a concept, the SRL framework has some way to go before it represents a practical tool for assessment. Equally, while it tends to bring different disciplines together, we should not underestimate the institutional challenges of operationalising this approach within both DFID and partner organisations (particularly governments). On the DFID side the approach represents a challenge to the professions and will require a change in values so that development is based on local realities and capacities. On the partner side there are clear implications for DFID's work on governance and rights. The approach places a premium on providing support to locally responsive planning systems.

## Engineering (presented by Peter Roberts, Deputy to the Chief Engineering Adviser)

Engineering Division (ED) saw the publication of the White Paper on International Development as an opportunity to reassess and to adopt a more user-oriented approach in its work. As other divisions, ED has a role to play in a number of different areas, notably:

- helping to meet basic needs (through the provision of clean water, sanitation, affordable and safe shelter, clean energy and by providing access to food markets)

- contributing to human development (through providing better facilities for basic education and health and better access to those facilities, also through improving the scope for social contact between individuals and communities, reducing people's sense of isolation, and

- opening up increased opportunities for people to escape from poverty (through the provision of transport and processing facilities, irrigation for on-farm activities and better transport of inputs and outputs).

ED welcomes the discussions which have been held around the sustainable rural livelihoods approach, which opens up opportunities for it to contribute, particularly in the provision of basic infrastructure and in spanning the divide between rural and urban livelihoods.

Improvements in water supply and transport are usually high among the priorities of poor people (this has been borne out by the many poverty assessments which have been carried out in Africa and elsewhere over recent years). Since water supply is considered elsewhere (see Chapter 13), the focus in the paper was on transport services. Physical access and transport services are crucial if rural people are to improve their health and education opportunities as well as increase their economic and income-earning opportunities (and reduce the burden of drudgery, particularly for women).

As with other rural services, the low level and dispersed nature of demand make it very difficult to establish a reasonable level of service in a cost-effective manner. However, the problems in this regard appear to be less severe if an asset-based approach is adopted in preference to considering individual needs for transport. Such an approach highlights the skills and resources which are (or realistically could be) available locally to meet livelihood needs. It stresses the importance of matching design with resources and of seeking multiple uses (of both skills and equipment) to reduce costs (for example, using small tractors for numerous uses on- as well as off-farm). Opportunities for exploiting such multiple uses are frequently overlooked, often as a result of a single-sector project intervention.

Not only does the inter-sectoral, asset-based perspective which is encouraged by the livelihoods approach show how apparently different demands may be met more effectively, the improved viability which results also offers opportunities for enterprise development and the emergence of local private sector capacity. The more broadly based such emerging enterprises are, the better will be their chances of finding a sufficiently active market and of evolving into a competitive small-scale industry.

There is a need for a strengthened (but simple and demand-led) approach to planning rural interventions. This should result in donor support which reflects local priorities and which ensures that local-level activities are coordinated with adjacent and 'higher-level' planning units. The enabling environment must include appropriate regulation and legislation as well as the capacity for strategic planning. Where relevant, urban/rural linkages should be strengthened through the development of physical infrastructure and improved communication systems.

## *Health and Population (presented by Ceri Thompson, Health and Human Development Specialist)*

DFID's Health and Population Division (HPD) has a role to play in meeting all three objectives laid down in the White Paper, as Figure 1 shows.

HPD has not traditionally worked very closely with NRD, despite the numerous linkages between the areas of activity of the two sections of DFID. Very briefly, a few of these are as follows.

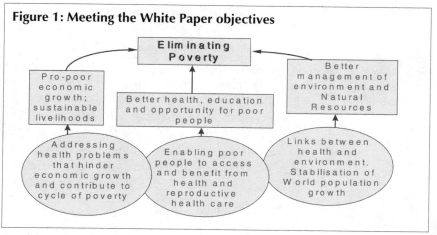

**Figure 1: Meeting the White Paper objectives**

### At the macro level

- reducing global population growth will relieve pressure on scarce resources, particularly natural assets
- food shortages cause malnutrition and poverty.

### At programme level

Agricultural and livestock projects have important human health implications.

- Changes to the type, quantity or location of crops grown may result in an increase or decrease of a disease vector – such as the mosquito – and lead to changes in the health status of nearby communities (e.g. the incidence of malaria has risen among resettled communities in south east Asia which have established farm plots within the forest reserve where the disease is rife).

- Livestock carry diseases (such as cryptosporidium and Rift Valley Fever) which can affect human health. The same challenges are often inherent in efforts to control the spread of disease among both humans and animals. During the Rift Valley Fever epidemic in Kenya the Government of Kenya emergency task-force team brought together epidemiologists, doctors and veterinarians to address the problems which threatened both disease and starvation.

### At household level

- People suffering from diseases such as malaria are unable to go out and tend to their assets. Equally, people without assets are vulnerable to malnutrition and disease and are less likely to be able to afford essential treatments and health services.

**Different sections of DFID lack knowledge about each other's work and therefore about options for collaboration**

What, then, are the constraints to greater collaboration between the disciplines? Clearly, different sections of DFID lack knowledge about each other's work and therefore about options for collaboration. It is very time-consuming to absorb information about other sectors' portfolios.

Even if we do advocate greater cross-sectoral working, how much information from other sectors can an individual realistically absorb? Do we have the human resources to devote to developing better relationships with our colleagues in other areas (the development of sector-wide approaches with partner governments have shown us how much investment this can take). Or is it more a question of structures within the organisation which fail to encourage cross-sectoral working? The thematic groups which meet to discuss certain issues, such as Sustainable Rural Livelihoods, are one way of getting round this problem, but perhaps they are not in themselves adequate. Does the dialogue need to be backed up by some sort of targets (and associated funds with which to achieve them)?

**Possible ways forward**

At an organisational level we may need to review our priorities if we are to embrace the notion of cross-sectoral working. For example, over the past three years HPD has invested a lot of time and energy in learning how to improve its dissemination about health issues and best practice. Perhaps, though, we should compromise a little, reduce the time spent on this activity in order to spend more time learning about the work of other colleagues. It is hoped that the management information system under development in DFID should help us access useful information in this regard.

At a project level we should perhaps endeavour to build upon each other's partnerships, working in the field with the same groups to achieve multiple benefits. One way to achieve this might be to appoint 'Link Advisers' who have a specific mandate to bridge the gaps between sectors. For this we may need new advisers with different skills who see themselves more as facilitators rather than as 'technical quality control'. In the shorter term a more manageable option might be to commission an 'audit' of the DFID portfolio to identify best practice in developing linkages between sectors. This could result in the development of, for example, natural resources 'tool-kits' for health staff (and *vice versa*) which would help point up possible entry points for cross-sectoral activities. Such an audit would also reveal whether any projects already incorporate indicators from other sectors in their design (and could help encourage the spread of such practice where relevant).

In conclusion, then, we certainly need to work more closely with other professional disciplines if we are to maximise our effectiveness. The causes of poverty are multi-dimensional and reinforcing; if a household has limited assets, limited educational opportunities *and* limited access to health services we cannot expect to improve the overall poverty level by focusing on only one of these fronts at a time.

# Contributions from other organisations

Two other organisations were asked to present short papers at NRAC '98. Both have made significant contributions to the development of the conceptual thinking behind the sustainable livelihoods approach. UNDP also has experience in implementing the approach while IDS is conducting a research programme in this area and has experience of analysing livelihoods in a number of countries.

## *United Nations Development Programme (presented by Naresh Singh, Senior Adviser on Poverty and Sustainable Livelihoods in UNDP's Social Development and Poverty Elimination Division)*

UNDP has adopted the sustainable livelihoods approach which it views as a means of achieving poverty eradication within a sustainable human development context. It applies the approach – to which there is a commitment in Chapter 3 of Agenda 21 – in both rural and urban settings and views it as being equally as applicable in developed countries as in developing countries. Indeed, unless we increase the sustainability of livelihoods in affluent countries, it is unlikely that we shall be able to achieve sustainable livelihoods for those who currently live in poverty.

UNDP operates with a programme approach. This means that there must be in place a national development framework, in the country in which it is working, to which it can commit its support. If no such framework or policy statement exists, UNDP will first work with the government in question to develop one. This will be done using the sustainable livelihoods approach: for sustainable livelihoods is an *approach*, a way of thinking about development. Projects can be informed by the approach but it makes no sense to talk about sustainable livelihoods projects, in and of themselves. The difficulties of attaining this approach when constrained to work with today's institutions and structures should not be underestimated. However, the potential rewards are high. The approach is fundamentally empowering, rather than being welfarist in its orientation.

The 'sustainability' side of sustainable livelihoods is of great importance to UNDP. This word has a number of connotations and denotes a range of qualities, including:

- the capacity to cope with shock and stresses (whether 'natural' or the product of human action, such as precipitous devaluation of currencies)
- economic efficiency in production (economic growth is seen as a means to achieve human development rather than an end in itself – it must therefore be of a particular quality)

- social equity (the promotion of the livelihoods of one group should not compromise the options for another group)
- environmental soundness or ecological integrity, and
- the ability to continue once outside support has been withdrawn.

For a livelihood to be sustainable it must exhibit all these qualities.

UNDP's entry points for sustainable livelihoods are the adaptive strategies of people, rather than any particular sector (natural resources or otherwise). UNDP also operates a multi-step process when planning its activities. The following is the sequence.

(i)   *Assessment of assets and strengths:* The development of an understanding about what it is that people do right, and in what way they can be assisted to do it better.

(ii)  *Policy analysis:* The development of an understanding of which policies support local livelihood strategies and which disrupt them. This analysis runs from the micro to the macro and crosses sectoral boundaries. UNDP has begun to develop tools in this area which it is happy to share with DFID and others.

(iii) *Analysis of technology and investment opportunities:* What type of inputs in these areas would help improve productivity and make better use of existing strengths? How can science and technology be put to the service of the poor? (Discussions are being opened with the International Agricultural Research Centres on this matter.)

UNDP is working to develop appropriate indicators for its work; indicators not only of performance but of inputs, outputs, impact and process. All the time it is learning, for sustainable livelihoods is a participatory learning approach. There are no experts; everyone must learn and continue to develop skills.

The approach has been more readily accepted in field offices where people recognise that it reflects the reality of those living in poverty than it has been in UNDP headquarters. However, even when this type of holistic thinking has been initiated, there always remains a temptation to revert to a more simple, fragmented and piecemeal approach. The countries in which UNDP has moved farthest in implementation are: South Africa, Malawi, Swaziland, Yemen and Egypt. UNDP is keen to work with other organisations, including DFID, both to develop tools and on the implementation side.

## *Institute of Development Studies (Presented by Ian Scoones, Sustainable Livelihoods Programme)*

IDS is currently managing a DFID-ESCOR (Economic and Social Committee on Overseas Research) funded Sustainable Livelihoods Programme. This programme, which started in 1997, has entailed both the development of a framework for the analysis of sustainable livelihoods

(Scoones, 1998) (which was the basis of the framework presented in Chapter 1 of this book) and the analysis of livelihoods in various countries in Africa, and to a lesser extent Asia. [2]

During its work IDS has identified some of the key challenges of livelihoods analysis. It has tried to understand livelihood sequences, and particularly the combinations of assets and strategies which secure sustainable livelihoods for people. All the time the programme has been struggling to understand the complexity inherent in livelihoods and it continues in its efforts to develop appropriate methodologies for such analysis, including specific tools. The challenge is to ensure that these methodologies are cost-effective and yet sufficiently sophisticated to be able to capture reality, including the multiple functions of formal and informal institutions.

IDS has laid a particular emphasis on analysing institutional/organisational influences on access to livelihood resources and the composition of the portfolio of livelihood strategies (whether agricultural intensification, livelihood diversification or migration). This area of analysis has been neglected in previous more economic attempts to describe and understand livelihoods. Yet these institutions and organisations are the 'gateways' to sustainable livelihoods and an understanding of them is therefore key to designing interventions which improve sustainable livelihood outcomes.

An institutional approach also sheds light on the social processes which underlie livelihood sustainability. Achieving sustainable livelihoods is not a deterministic affair; contestations, negotiations and trade-offs are evident at every turn. An insight into social relationships, their institutional forms (both formal and informal) and the power dynamics embedded in these is therefore vital. Interventions in support of sustainable livelihoods must be attuned to such complexity if suitable institutional entry points are to be found.

IDS has identified a number of important questions and issues relating to livelihood capital assets or resources. These are as follows.

**Institutions and organisations are the 'gateways' to sustainable livelihoods**

- *Sequencing:* What is the starting point for successfully establishing a particular livelihood strategy? Is one type of resource a prerequisite for gaining access to other resources?

- *Substitution:* Can one type of capital be substituted for others? Or are different capitals needed in combination for the pursuit of particular livelihood strategies?

- *Clustering:* If you have access to one type of capital, do you usually have access to others? Or is there a clustering of particular combinations of livelihood resources associated with particular groups of people or a particular livelihood strategy?

- *Access:* Different people clearly have different access to different livelihood resources. This is dependent on institutional arrangements, organisational issues, power and politics. A socially differentiated view to analysing livelihoods is therefore critical.

- *Trade-offs:* In pursuing a particular portfolio of livelihood strategies, what are the trade-offs faced by different people with different access to different types of livelihood resource? Depending upon who you are, differential access to different types of capital may have positive or negative implications in terms of the success or otherwise of your quest for a sustainable livelihood.

- *Trends:* What are the trends in terms of the availability of different types of livelihood resource? How are different capital assets being depleted and accumulated and by whom? What are the trends in terms of access? What new livelihood resources are being created through environmental, economic and social change?

All these questions and issues should be investigated and – where relevant – taken into consideration when conducting livelihood analysis.

Finally there is the issue of indicators, a difficult question for everyone. IDS had no fixed answers in this area but did stress the process of negotiation between local and external indicators, those derived from the groups with which we are working and those which relate to our own objectives and concerns.

## Conclusion

Much thought has been put into developing the ideas behind the sustainable livelihoods approach. Increasing efforts are now being put into designing tools and methodologies which will help us to operationalise the approach. The different sections of DFID as well as the external organisations which contributed to NRAC '98 all demonstrated in their talks that they recognised the potential of the new approach. But all stressed that there would be challenges inherent in its operationalisation, both institutionally and in terms of skills, tools and costs. These issues were also raised in the various breakout groups into which participants at NRAC '98 gathered during the three days of the conference itself. The questions raised by these groups and the issues posed in this book now provide us with a basis for moving forward, for further work and, it is hoped, for significant achievements in the quest to eradicate poverty.

## Reference

Scoones, I. (1998) 'Sustainable Rural Livelihoods: A Framework for Analysis', *IDS Working Paper* 72. Brighton: IDS.

## Endnote

1 These figures are backed up by the findings of the Environmental Evaluation synthesis study currently underway which has found that about 27% of the sample of 'green' projects reviewed had not addressed environmental risk during design or implementation.

2 For further information on the IDS Sustainable Livelihoods Programme and its work in Bangladesh, Ethiopia, Mali and Zimbabwe, including details of the range of Working Papers produced to date, see the IDS website at – http://www.ids.ac.uk/ids/research/env/index.html or contact the Programme Assistant, University of Sussex, Falmer, Brighton, BN1 9RE.

# Biographical Information

**Stephen Akroyd** is an economist at Oxford Policy Management. He has had six years' experience in agricultural policy formulation. His recent work has been on issues relating to farmer service reform and support to developing the sector approach to public expenditure management.

**J.E.M. Arnold** is a consultant in forest economics and policy, presently working mainly with the Centre for International Forestry Research and the Overseas Development Institute. He was earlier at the Oxford Forestry Institute, and before that was Chief of the Forest Policy and Planning Service in FAO. His recent work has focused on management of forests as common property, trees in farmer management strategies, and forest products in rural household livelihoods.

**Diana Carney** is a Research Fellow in the Rural Policy and Environment Group of the Overseas Development Institute. She has acted as the Facilitator for DFID's Sustainable Rural Livelihoods Advisory Committee. Her other work has been on the role of government in rural areas and on agricultural technology policy.

**Alex Duncan** is an economist with Oxford Policy Management, and is Visiting Professor in Agricultural Development, Wye College, University of London. He works on policy, institutional and budget reform, primarily in eastern and southern Africa.

**Frank Ellis** is a Professor in the School of Development Studies, University of East Anglia, where he teaches and conducts research in the areas of agricultural economics, policy and rural development. His current research interests are in rural livelihoods, the diversity of rural household income sources and policy implications arising.

**Ian Goldman** has worked in institutional development and rural development in Europe, Africa and Mexico, working with local government, NGOs and provincial government. He is currently with DFID in South Africa, working with the Free State, Northern Cape and Lesotho governments.

**Izabella Koziell** has 10 years' professional experience in environment and development issues, in both project management and research collaboration. Her work interests include: biodiversity management (focus primarily on land and wildlife), government issues and institutional development. She has done many years fieldwork in both Tanzania and Ghana.

**Livestock in Development** is an independent research and consultancy group specialising in the development of policy, organisations and personnel in the veterinary, livestock and natural resources sectors. The group's skills and interest centre on people-centred approaches to sector development and, in particular, the institutional, economic and social analysis of change. The paper was jointly authored by Steve Ashley, Sarah Holden and Peter Bazeley, all of whom are Directors of Livestock in Development.

**Natural Resources and Ethical Trade Programme, NRI** was prepared by a multi-disciplinary team consisting of Mick Blowfield, Annabelle Malins, Bill Maynard and Valerie Nelson, members of NRET. The programme is currently working with the private sector, international development agencies, NGOs and developing country organisations to provide advice on the development of ethical trade initiatives.

**Natural Resources Research Department, DFID** manages DFID sectoral funds which support eleven natural resources research programmes, contracting the management of these programmes to institutions within the UK science base. The programmes aim to generate and disseminate new knowledge relevant to the management of agriculture, fisheries and forestry. NRRD also manages DFID investment in the strategic research programmes implemented by the International Agricultural Research Centres of the Consultative Group on International Agricultural Research.

**Julian Quan** is a senior member of the Social Development Group at the Natural Resources Institute, University of Greenwich. He specialises in social issues in land and natural resources policy and environmental management, focusing on sub-Saharan Africa and Brazil. He is currently seconded to DFID as a land tenure advisor.

**John Soussan** has worked in Leeds University since 1994. Before that he was based in Sri Lanka for three years and, prior to that, taught in the Geography Department at Reading University. He has worked extensively on different aspects of people–resource relationships (especially water, forestry and energy) in South and South-East Asia and Africa.

**Cecilia Tacoli** coordinates an international research programme on 'Rural–Urban Interactions, Livelihood Strategies and Socio-Economic Change' at the International Institute of Environment and Development. The programme is conducted in collaboration with a number of institutions in Africa, Asia and Latin America.

**Philip Townsley** has an MA in Rural Social Development from Reading. He has worked for 10 years for fishing and coastal communities in Asia, Africa and the Pacific. His particular areas of expertise are PRA and community-based resource management. He works as an independent consultant and is based in Italy.